THE SOLICITORS OFFICE PROCEDURES MANUAL

VICKY LING AND MATTHEW MOORE

Published by Professional Compliance Publishing Ltd

Copyright © 2015 Professional Compliance Publishing Ltd

The moral rights of the authors have been asserted.

Professional Compliance Publishing Ltd

2 Crown Lane

Sutton Coldfield

West Midlands

B74 4SU

ISBN 978-0-9933833-0-4

British Library Cataloguing in Publication Data.
A catalogue record for this book is available from the British Library.

Typeset in Calibri by Troubador Publishing Ltd

Printed and bound in the UK by TJ International, Padstow, Cornwall

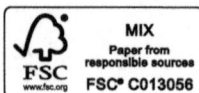

FOREWORD

THE SOLICITORS OFFICE PROCEDURES MANUAL SECOND EDITION

Since this publication first appeared in 2012 numerous practices have used it to create a manual, or to update or replace their existing versions. Projects to develop or update manuals tend to arise when a practice decides to apply for formal accreditation to an external standard such as Lexcel, or when the SRA enquires about the compliance systems that are in place, but the Office Manual should be seen as being first and foremost about the smooth and efficient running of the practice. The Manual should be seen as the definitive source of information on "how we do things around here", and so the first port of call if anyone is unsure of what is expected of them. Properly used in this manner the Office Manual will be a real asset to the practice, as opposed to being simply yet another management burden.

Sole practitioners should note that we created a separate sole practice version of the publication in 2013 and this has also been updated in like manner to a second edition. The most significant changes to this edition are those that were needed to address the revised requirements of Lexcel 6 which took effect in all assessments to that standard from the 1st May 2015. We have also provided an additional guidance table on the Law Society's Core Practice Management Standards which are of increasing significance in relation to various of the Society's accreditation schemes. Apart from this there have been various changes of responsible bodies – the Legal Aid Agency for the Legal Services Commission, the National Crime Agency for the Serious Organised Crime Agency etc. One of the most problematic changes has been the application of the Consumer Contracts Regulations 2013 in place of various earlier and simpler provisions on this topic, including the Distance Selling Regulations.

The first edition of this book was accompanied by a CD of the main precedents which purchasers were able to use to develop their own materials. This had the rather obvious limitation that the materials supplied might have been out of date before they were fully implemented, so in order now to access the materials from the book for editing it will be necessary to become a subscriber to the linked business of Infolegal Ltd. Once registered subscribers will receive updating alerts as to all of the contents of the Manual as they become necessary for as long as they remain subscribers, and in this way the Manual can move beyond being a one-off purchase and become instead a core element of a general compliance support service for law firms. Purchasers of the book are entitled to a discount on the Infolegal subscription price – see www.solicitors-opm.co.uk for details.

With similar considerations in mind we decided to remove the former appendix on the model provisions for retainer letters and terms of business documentation from this edition. Here the use of out of date materials could have serious implications for any given practice, so the equivalent advice will now to be found in one of the many factsheets on the Infolegal website, also available to subscribers. This will again mean that we can keep our advice on these critical compliance issues fully up to date at all times.

Please bear in mind that there are two optional formats for section 2 (Policies and Structures) – the more commonly used traditional manual format and also a more ambitious, but also more forward-looking, intranet model. So as not to confuse firms that are outside the legal aid sector the additional contents that are required for compliance with the various demands of the Legal Aid Agency are provided by way of supplementary advice in section 7. Whereas we placed the various compliance checklists for the provisions addressed by this publication at the start of the first edition they now appear at the end. Other than this the structure and format of the book remain much as before.

Thanks are due to Duncan Finlyson of Infolegal for his guidance on the issues which need to be covered within an IT policy and to Jennifer Parker of Troubador Publishing for her patience with the many challenges which a publication of this type presents.

Finally, whatever your particular circumstances or requirements we hope, as ever, that this publication and its accompanying support services will provide you with a cost-effective and highly practicable source of guidance and template materials for the better management of your practice.

Vicky Ling
Vicky@pqsonline.co.uk

Matthew Moore
mattmoore@infolegal.co.uk

ABOUT THE AUTHORS

Vicky Ling B.Sc., M.Phil, CQP.

Vicky Ling has provided specialist consultancy for organisations delivering advice and legal services for 20 years. Clients have included national organisations such as Citizens Advice, Law Centres Network, Resolution and the Law Society of England and Wales, as well as hundreds of individual firms of solicitors and not-for-profit agencies.

Vicky's expertise includes legal aid contract tenders, helping firms which are experiencing problems with the Legal Aid Agency, SQM and Contract compliance. She has also been involved in research on the developing legal market and has helped organisations update and modernise service delivery.

Vicky is a Chartered Quality Professional and has been an accredited Lexcel consultant since the start of the scheme.

Vicky writes extensively on legal aid practice management and has a monthly column in Legal Action magazine. Her most recent book (with Fiona Westwood) is the 'Complaints Handling Toolkit' published by the Law Society.

vicky@vling.demon.co.uk

Matthew Moore LL.B, MCIPD, C.Dip AF, Solicitor

Matt is a director of Infolegal Ltd, which provides a range of support and advisory services to the legal profession, and is also a consultant solicitor with the regulatory specialists Jayne Willetts & Co.. He was the authorised trainer for the Law Society in its Lexcel scheme from 1999 to 2007, writing during this time four editions of the widely used "Lexcel Office Procedures Manual" (his last version having appeared in 2007). His first publication was "The Law and Procedure of Meetings" (Sweet & Maxwell: 1979) and he has been responsible for numerous other titles since. Other than this manual (which is also available in a specialist sole practice version) his other current publication is "Money Laundering Compliance for Solicitors" (with Diane Price – also published by Professional Compliance Publishing).

After a first career teaching law at a number of colleges in Essex and Devon he was admitted as a solicitor in 1984 and worked for a while in high street practice in Coventry. He was subsequently appointed Co-ordinator, and then Marketing Director, of the then M5 Group (later NRM5) – an association of a number of leading commercial firms. He now has over 25 years' experience of law firm management and compliance consultancy and training for a range of firms from sole practitioners to the largest international commercial practices.

mattmoore@infolegal.co.uk

www.solicitors-opm.co.uk

HOW TO USE THIS BOOK

This book has been prepared on the basis that most firms will want to use it as a checklist for updates that need to be made to their existing manuals, or as a template for a new version. We recognise that most firms will therefore wish to continue to use a traditional format manual even if it is not printed in hard copy and is instead uploaded onto the firm's computer system or intranet.

With some imagination, however, the information contained in the manual can be presented in a much more modern and user-friendly format. In the earliest days of office manuals there really was no alternative to producing long documents for users to read or consult, but the office manual becomes a much more practicable tool if people can search electronically for particular contents. The use of hyperlinks can also take the user directly to external sources, such as legislation or Law Society practice notes, or internal sources such as policies and guidance notes that exist elsewhere on the Firm's information system. We hope that we will have enabled you to adopt this format if it is of interest to you by setting out section 2 – 'Policies and Structures' – in both traditional manual format at Part A and Intranet format at Part B.

The Intranet format of the manual will probably be more difficult for you to finalise, but the additional efforts are likely to be amply rewarded. People expect to be able to access information nowadays more directly and without working their way through lengthy documents. Under the Intranet format your starting point will be section 2: you will need to edit the text shown from pages 57–91 but then also edit in links to any external sources of information that might be helpful or other internal policies or forms that are already in place, or new materials taken from this publication. Under this format the other sections of this book simply become other attachments to this main Intranet Policies document. If you do decide to do so you will probably be best advised to adopt a simpler numbering sequence for all the other sections of the manual as each one will simply become a different linked part of the overall intranet programme.

For a fuller explanation and demonstration of how your documentation might look if you adopt this format please see the website for this publication – *www.solicitors-opm.co.uk.*

More basically, please remember that the suggestions made in this publication are precisely that. This publication suggests one way of addressing the issue under consideration, but it is by no means the only or the best way to do so. Where you have a policy, procedure or process that you feel works well you would be best advised to retain it and work it into your revised manual. Where compliance is assessed, as under the various quality management standards that we have listed above, some originality of contents is likely to count in your favour with most assessors. Your best advice is therefore to use this publication as a precedent and not a draft.

Finally, references to the Code of Conduct are P for principles (e.g. P1), O for outcomes (e.g. O(1.2)) and IB for indicative behaviours (e.g. IB(1.3)).

RESOURCES

Infolegal

The various template materials contained in this book, including the appendices and compliance tables, are available for download from the linked business of Infolegal Ltd, a specialist law firm compliance and risk management consultancy and training company. In addition to being able to download the book's contents Infolegal subscribers receive a monthly e-newsletter on all recent developments of note and are also able to access an extensive range of guidance notes and single topic factsheets. A number of computer-based compliance training modules can be accessed by subscriber firms, not just explaining some of the more complex regulatory issues facing legal practices but also enabling users to satisfy various of the training requirements in the Lexcel standard and, in the case of money laundering awareness, the law of the land.

Infolegal also provides consultancy support services and in-house training on most of the issues covered in this publication, especially in relation to Lexcel, COLP and COFA obligations and Combating Money Laundering and Terrorist Financing. The company is particularly involved in new business start-ups and the related application processes to the SRA.

For more details please see www.infolegal.co.uk, or contact co-author of this title and Infolegal director Matthew Moore, at mattmoore@infolegal.co.uk.

Legal Aid Handbook 2015-16

Published by the Legal Action Group www.lag.org.uk edited by Vicky Ling and Simon Pugh with Anthony Edwards. It provides a clear outline of the legal framework governing legal aid, explaining what is in scope post the Legal Aid Sentencing and Punishment of Offenders Act 2012. There is step by step guidance on conducting cases, getting paid, advocacy, financial and contract management, performance monitoring and quality standards plus an overview of policy developments. There are specialist chapters on

Crime, Family, Housing, Immigration, Mental Health and Immigration. It is the only single volume guide to the entire legal aid scheme and is equally valuable to caseworkers and managing partners.

The book is supported by a blog at www.legalaidhandbook.com which is regularly updated with news and alerts from a wide range of sources, including latest legal aid caselaw. You can also follow @legalaidhbk on Twitter.

The Law Consultancy Network
The Law Consultancy Network comprises a team of highly experienced law firm management consultants – Andrew Otterburn, Richard Burcher, Vicky Ling, Caroline Murphy and Colin FitzPatrick. They provide a range of management consultancy services to assist the development and success of their clients – law firms and barristers' chambers.

They have advised several hundred law firms on a wide range of issues, together with Government and the professional bodies.

LCN believes in:
- Helping clients make the most of market challenges and opportunities
- Providing practical, high quality support. The consultants' in-depth knowledge of the legal sector, together with their collective experience enables LCN members to provide effective, appropriate advice
- Developing close working relationships with our clients, who are often assisted over continuing periods of time
- Providing value for money

Services include:
- Practice review; retreat facilitation; strategy and management structures
- Mergers and acquisitions
- Law firm pricing
- Lexcel
- Performance management
- Law firm profitability and financial management
- Leadership development and business coaching
- Law firm management skills training
- Partnership issues
- Legal Aid Agency contract bidding, compliance and appeals

CONTENTS

Template Manual

Appendix policies to the intranet format

D: Staff handbook forms

E: Technology

SECTION 1

WELCOME TO [NAME OF FIRM]

Introductory note not included in the precedent materials which follow

This first chapter is intended as an introduction not just to the firm and so should be particularly helpful for staff induction processes. The main regulatory requirements addressed here are those relating to structures and management responsibilities as required by Lexcel and other quality management standards along with, to a lesser degree, the SRA Code of Conduct (referred to in the Manual as 'the Code of Conduct').

One of the main changes of note since the first edition of this book is that relating to business planning. Lexcel v6 has merged the separate requirements for business, marketing and services plans into a more general 'strategic plan' at para 1.2. Earlier versions of the Lexcel standard have gone down much this route before in relation to business and marketing plans, but it remained possible to present different, but linked, plans then and so it may well be now. So far as the business plan element is concerned the main requirement remains the identification of objectives for the current or future 12 months which, as ever, should be SMART (specific, measured, achievable, realistic and timed). There are new obligations to identify within the process the resources required to meet the objectives and also then to subject them to a 'documented risk evaluation'. The guidance at appendix 1A reflects the new preference in Lexcel for a more integrated approach to business planning and the greater emphasis on risk planning that is also now required within the process. The need for a business continuity plan continues to be a separate requirement within Lexcel at section 1.3, however, and guidance on its compilation appears at Appendix 2.

The SRA did express doubts as the value of formal COLP and COFA appointments in the smallest of practices in announcements in late 2014, but have since said that the requirements will remain but the nomination process for such practices will instead be simplified.

Another change within Lexcel v6 is that whereas there was previously a list of the main policies, plans and procedures which required the designation of the person responsible and a formal review process, the equivalent requirement now to be found at 3.6 is for a register of all plans, policies and procedures. This has required a revision of the table at Appendix 3 to add to the areas covered by the headings to address all sections of the Lexcel standard and therefore all procedures covered within them.

Precedent materials

1   Introduction to the firm

1.1   *[Name of firm]* was founded in *[year or era]* and is *[provide general description, e.g. 'a traditional high street practice catering for all the usual legal requirements of the local community'. Edit in more about the background to the firm and, ideally, what it is that you are committed to achieving as a practice]*.

1.2   Some office basics

Office hours

1.2.1   The firm's normal office hours are *[insert]*, with *[insert]* for lunch. The normal lunchtime break is to be taken *[insert]* but this might be varied to ensure cover or where work commitments require. Fee earners and senior staff are expected to work such hours as are necessary to enable them to deal with their commitments or to attend meetings. This is, however, subject to the Working Time Regulations 1998 which impose a maximum of 48 hours' work per week when taken as an average and the *[partners/directors]* are committed to ensuring that staff are able to comply with the Regulations. If you have any concerns that you are approaching or exceeding the stated maximum please contact *[name or title]*.

Dress code

[There is variety between firms on issues of dress code with some being very

much more relaxed or informal than others. Please insert wording that is suitable for your firm – a more conventional firm is described here.]

1.2.2 As a professional organisation most of our clients will expect people in the office to be smart in their appearance, regardless of their role within the firm. For this reason please be sure to dress in a manner that is consistent with the image we wish to convey. Some main rules are:

- Fee earners should usually wear a suit or other similar smart equivalent and men should usually wear a tie;
- Secretaries and administrators may wear smart jeans, but no rips or tears (designer or otherwise!);
- Tops should not display prominent logos and midriffs should be covered; and
- There are no strict rules in relation to body piercings and tattoos, but the [*partners/directors*] reserve the right to ask staff to remove or cover up any body jewellery or tattoos which in their opinion detracts from the image we wish to project as a professional firm. The [*partners/directors*] reserve the right to send staff home if, in their opinion, the style of dress is not acceptable to a professional office. Staff will be expected to make up any lost time should this be deemed to be necessary.

1.3   Structure and management

1.3.1 The firm is structured as a [*partnership/limited liability partnership/limited liability company*] providing legal services, and is registered with the Law Society of England and Wales. As such we are authorised and regulated by the Solicitors Regulation Authority (the 'SRA') which is the independent regulatory arm of the Law Society.

1.3.2 The [*partners/directors*] are as follows: [*Specify*].

1.3.3 [*Although the firm is registered as a company the directors have elected still to be referred to as 'partners' in line with accepted usage in law firms and so to avoid client confusion.*] The [*partners/directors*] are collectively responsible for the management of the firm and, in particular keeping the strategic plan of the firm, including its approach to marketing and the range of services provided. There are constraints in relation to the marketing and publicity activities of law firms as set out in the SRA Code of Conduct and as found in the outcomes of chapter 8, including that all publicity must be 'accurate and not misleading'. There is also a ban against unsolicited approaches to private clients at O(8.3) [*See Appendix 1 for a note on the preparation of the strategic plan*].

1.3.4   Our responsibilities to our clients are not suspended in the event that we experience problems such as a computer system failure, or we cannot get into our buildings as a result of fire, flood or some other major disruption to our usual operations. For this reason we have adopted a business continuity plan which is detailed at Appendix 2. Part of our planning is the need to be able to contact all personnel if necessary outside normal office hours, for example, to request that you make your way to temporary offices or, indeed, stand down for the day. In order that we can do so it is essential that you notify us of any change to your personal details, especially if you move or change your mobile or landline numbers. You should do so by contacting [*name or title*].

Management structure

1.3.5   [*Partners'/Directors'*] meetings occur [*explain*].

1.3.6   The other meetings that occur on a formal basis within the firm are [*set out here details of departmental, office or other meetings such as a staff consultative group, etc.*]

1.3.7   [*Provide profile of the management structure and responsibilities: e.g. The Senior Partner is .... As the chair of the practice (s)he has responsibility for its public profile. The Managing Partner is .... (S)he has responsibility for the overall business performance of the firm and, in particular: (specify)*

- *Risk management and the firm's quality management programme;*
- *Business planning and marketing; and*
- *Business continuity.*

The Practice Manager is .... In this role (s)he has responsibility for ... (specify)].

1.3.8   The more significant managerial roles and holders include:

Strategic planning	
Business continuity planning	
Client care policy	
Complaints handling	
Conflicts of interests	
Equality and diversity	
Financial management	
Human resources (personnel management)	
Health and safety	
Information and communications technology	
Library and research facilities	
Marketing	
Mortgage fraud avoidance	
Money Laundering Reporting Officer	
Office facilities (including outsourcing)	
Risk management	
Quality programme	
SRA applications and renewals	
Training	
Legal Aid Contract Liaison	

A more detailed list of the management responsibilities is to be found at [*see Appendix 3 and perhaps include as an appendix to this section in your manual?*]. The person named as having responsibility for SRA applications and renewals above is to be aware of the firm's responsibilities under chapter 10 of the Code of Conduct and, in particular:

• Ensuring that the SRA has all relevant information so as to enable it to decide if persons requiring approval are fit and proper for their role (O(10.5));

- Complying promptly with requests for information or responding to other written notices from the SRA (O(10.8-10.9)); and
- Conducting any enquiry required by the SRA promptly and effectively (O(10.11)).

It is the responsibility of all of the personnel named or identified above to monitor the policies and plans for which they are responsible, at least annually.

COLP and COFA

1.3.9   In addition to the above list of responsibilities there are two key roles within the practice in relation to our compliance obligations with the SRA: COLP ('Compliance Officer for Legal Practice') and COFA ('Compliance Officer for Finance and Administration'). The need for these two roles arose from revisions to the rulebook for solicitors – the SRA Handbook – in 2011. It is the responsibility of the COLP to:

- Ensure that suitable compliance arrangements are in place for all aspects of our operations other than compliance with the SRA Accounts Rules;
- Monitor for compliance with the SRA requirements, especially those contained in the SRA Code of Conduct ('the Code');
- Maintain records of non-compliance; and
- Report to the SRA all 'material breaches' of the same.

1.3.10   The COFA has the like responsibilities in relation to compliance with the SRA Accounts Rules.

1.3.11   The effective operation of both roles is a key requirement of the SRA. In order that we may discharge these responsibilities it is the duty of all personnel to report any instance of non-compliance with the professional duties that are set out in this manual to the COLP or COFA, depending on the nature of the breach, without delay.

1.3.12   You should note that the COLP is [*name*] and the COFA is [*name*]. [*Include here any details of deputies, more probably in larger firms.*] It is their responsibility in particular to ensure compliance with the requirements of the SRA Handbook.

1.4 Supervisors

1.4.1 The work of the firm is divided into a number of specialist departments as follows. The overall supervisor for each area is also shown:

Department	Supervisor
Crime	
Family law	
Conveyancing	
Personal injury	
Wills and probate	
[Others – amend this column as necessary]	

1.4.2 For the duties of the supervisors (or their deputies in their absence) see 3.1.

1.4.3 The main headings of work that we do and do not undertake are set out in a schedule to the services plan. [*The services plan might form part of the manual or be separate from it – see Appendix A1 for a template of the more commonplace areas of work in most firms.*]

1.5 Quality standards

1.5.1 The firm [*holds/is pursuing an application to be awarded*] the 'Lexcel' standard of the Law Society. This award is independently assessed and will confirm that we have the required management policies and processes in place, and that we are consistently following them. [*The firm has long held a similar award from the Legal Aid Agency in relation to the legal aid work that is administered through that organisation.*]

1.5.2 [*In addition,*] [*T/t*]he firm [*has been awarded/has applied for/intends to apply for*] certification to the Conveyancing Quality Scheme and/or the Wills and

Inheritance Quality Scheme ('WIQS) of the Law Society, which is/are an optional programme(s) that certify/ies that the work of our Conveyancing/Wills and Probate department[s] is/are run along 'best practice' lines as seen by the Law Society as our professional body.

1.5.3   Quality standards all have their place in the profile of the modern law firm, but are no substitute for the need for us all to be focused on doing our best for the clients of the firm in everything that we do. Please remember that we are part of an increasingly competitive market for providing legal services and the quality of experience that the client has with everyone in the practice will determine if they return here in the future and recommend us to others. For more details of our client care policy see Section 2.4.

1.6   Office manuals

1.6.1   This introductory document forms the first element of our compliance materials, which are collectively called 'the Office Manual'. These are intended to ensure that everyone is made aware of the right way of doing things and should always be your first point of contact if you are unsure of what is expected of you. Failing this, however, please ask.

1.6.2   The Office Manual consists of:

1.   This introductory guide;
2.   'Best practice' manual, setting out details of the main policies and processes of the firm [and links to these full materials (if you adopt the intranet format)];
3.   Case management manual, setting out how the core fee earning process of the firm is to be conducted;
4.   Accounts manual, detailing how client money and the firm's own 'office' monies must be administered;
5.   Office facilities and information technology manual, with guidance on how the office functions and will support your work in the firm; and
6.   Staff handbook, detailing how you might expect to be dealt with as an employee of the firm, including your rights and responsibilities.

The person responsible for all procedures contained in each of the sections of the Office Manual, unless otherwise stated here or in the table at [Appendix 3] is as follows. It is the responsibility of the persons listed there or within the table below for any other contents to keep the plans, policies and procedures for which they are responsible up to date and conduct a review of them at least annually.

Section	Person responsible
1. Introduction	
2. Structures and policies	
3. Case management	
4. Accounts	
5 Office facilities and IT	
6 Staff manual	

1.6.3   Suggestions for improvements, updates or corrections are always appreciated and should be addressed to the appropriate [*partner/director/manager*] responsible for that [*plan, policy, procedure or part of the intranet/Manual/section*]. If you are unsure as to the appropriate point of contact or what is required of you please consult [*name or title*]. The authoritative version of the firm's Office Manual is always that on the [*intranet/?drive*] and you are asked not to store copies of this guide or the following documents for future reference in case those copies become out of date. It is important to ensure that all revisions of the Office Manual comply with the requirements of the SRA Handbook and any other quality standards that the firm is accredited or committed to. [*Alternatively you will need to show how paper copies of the manual are kept up to date if you are relying on hard copy manuals, e.g. 'The current version of the manual is version X. You may be required to update certain pages from time to time if changes are required. The full log showing the correct and up to date contents is maintained by [name or title] who also maintains the authoritative version.*]

1.6.4   The Office Manual will be reviewed at least annually and this process is the responsibility of [*name or title*]. Only (s)he has the authority to make any changes to the Manual and will keep a record of changes and the dates on which they have been authorised and effected.

1.6.5   [*Name or title*] is responsible for ensuring that a review of all of the contents of the Manual, along with all related plans and policies, does occur as required (at least annually) and that records of this having been done are maintained.

1.7   Annual Quality Review

1.7.1   It is important that we learn from our experiences and continue to strive to improve our services where we are able to do so. We do so in part through the Annual Quality Review which is the responsibility of [*name or title*]. This involves analysis of:

- Claims made or circumstances reported to our insurers;
- Complaints received and the outcomes of our complaints management process;
- File reviews;
- Matters reported to COLP or COFA;
- Reports of material breaches reported to the SRA by either COLP or COFA;
- Situations where the firm has acted in a situation of apparent conflict of interests;
- Situations where remedial action has been taken; and
- Client surveys.

1.7.2   The report, which is prepared in [*(month) every year*] and contains recommendations for improvements where appropriate, is presented to [*the next (partners'/directors' meeting/annual strategy review meeting or other)*].

[See Appendix 4 for a template quality review plan.]

[You may wish to add here your version of Appendix 3 to show the longer list of responsibilities now required by section 3.6 of Lexcel v6.]

SECTION 2

POLICIES AND STANDARDS

PART A: MANUAL FORMAT

Explanatory text

2.1   **Introduction to the policies and standards section**

The aims of this section are to set out all the main policies of the firm and to highlight other key processes that are dealt with elsewhere. As with all parts of these template provisions it is important that you amend the materials as extensively as possible so as to reflect the actual systems and practices within your firm. The following drafting notes are intended to assist you to do so.

Part 1:   Main policies and processes

2.2   **The importance of compliance**

Although it would be unfortunate to set too negative and intimidating a tone it is important to make the point that compliance with the Manual as a whole cannot be seen to be optional.

2.3   **An introduction to the firm**

This section highlights the overlap with the preceding 'Welcome to the firm' section.

2.4   **Our objectives as a firm**

Although many lawyers are wary of broad policy statements it is a good idea to promote the values that you have as a practice, and the sort of culture that you aspire to develop or maintain. The sample policy wording provided here would address the need for a client care policy, now found in Lexcel v6.1. This provision does also require details of certain processes (but not all that relate to client care) on which see the Lexcel compliance table also provided with this publication. There is likely to be considerable overlap between the policy and the wording to be found at 2.10 of this section on risk management, the reality being that there is an orthodoxy of good management practice which should produce benefits in terms of: better client satisfaction; fewer errors, claims and complaints; and, it is to be hoped, better business performance and thus profitability.

It is advisable to link any commitment that the firm has to applying for or maintaining any quality accreditations so that it is made clear that such programmes are seen as the way in which to improve the operational effectiveness of the firm, rather than being peripheral 'badges' that do not impact on the mainstream activities of the firm.

2.5 Professional standards and conduct

It is a good idea to advise the whole firm that the SRA jurisdiction extends to all who work within the firm and not simply the solicitors, as was previously the case. In practice the risks of enforcement by disciplinary action against non-solicitors are unlikely, but they do depend on the nature of the breach. The greatest risk of action being taken against non-solicitors remains that an order is made against them that they should not be employed in a solicitors' firm in the future under section 43 of the Solicitors Act 1974 – usually as a result of some act of dishonesty on their part.

So far as solicitors are concerned, remember the duties that extend beyond your professional life as set out in outcome 11(1) of the Solicitors Regulation Authority ('SRA') Code of Conduct to the effect that you must not take unfair advantage of others in either your professional or personal life. Examples provided in the former, and much more detailed, 2007 Code of Conduct suggested that referring to your professional status in personal disputes could have offended the very similar previous provisions.

2.6 Equality and diversity

The issue of equality and diversity is one of the ten main principles that underpin the SRA Handbook, and thus the entire regulatory regime P.9 which requires practices to 'encourage' equality and diversity). It might therefore seem strange that the need for a policy dealing with the firm's approach to this topic is set out as a supposedly optional indicative behaviour (IB(2.1)) rather than a mandatory outcome. The better advice would be to ignore this distinction and to ensure that a suitable policy is adopted as set out in this section. If you are amending the draft, or if you opt to continue to use a policy that is already in place at your firm, be sure to bear in mind the guidance factors that are set out at IB(2.1) of the Code of Compliance as to the sorts of issues that need to be addressed.

There is often confusion as to the terms that are used in this area: avoiding illegal discrimination should be regarded as the minimum level of behaviour that should be expected within any organisation, whereas the concepts of equality and diversity are more aspirational in their nature. The issue of 'equality' is usually seen to refer to the former 'strands' of discrimination law, or the 'protected characteristics' as they are referred to in the Equality Act 2010, whereas 'diversity' is a broader concept that also includes issues that are outside the scope of the Act, such as social class.

Lexcel requires there to have been training on this issue – preferably awareness training and instruction in the firm's own policy (see 4.2.d).

When the Specialist Quality Mark ('SQM') was updated in 2009, the equality and diversity requirements were the elements of standard which were most revised. The SQM requires firms to comply with general legal requirements in particular ways, depending on the size of the firm. See Section 7: Legal Aid for more information.

2.7   Client confidentiality

In many firms, and perhaps in your existing manual if you are using this publication to review a manual that has been in place in your firm for some while, the issue of confidentiality is limited to the case management section. However, the issue is probably better dealt with here as the duty of client confidentiality is core to the firm as a whole and so needs to be understood by everyone in the firm, regardless of role or seniority. This section therefore highlights the duty of confidentiality that is now found at O(4.1) of the Code of Conduct, along with the linked duty of disclosure at O(4.2). Unlike the duty of confidentiality, the duty of disclosure is limited to the lawyers within the practice ('any individual who is advising a client') and is limited to those issues of which that person is aware. This would not permit the firm, however, to act for a client where there was a more basic conflict of interests, as is dealt with in the following section.

2.8   Conflicts of interests

The provisions dealing with conflicts of interests represented one of the more significant (and contentious) changes in the Code of Conduct 2011 compared to the previous Code, at least in relation to property conflicts.

There are two main issues to consider: the need for effective monitoring arrangements to ensure that potential conflicts are identified, and then the need to ensure that the firm does not act where a conflict does arise. The role of the Office Manual is more heavily weighted to the issue of conflict screening though some advice on the substantive rules on conflicts in chapter 3 of the Code of Conduct – is also provided.

The main reason for the increased emphasis on conflicts checking in the Code of Conduct was the SRA then gearing up to be able to regulate alternative business structures where there are often many more complexities of conflicts than tends to be the case in law firms. Outcome 3(1) therefore requires 'effective systems and controls' to be in place for checking for client conflict issues. In most firms this has long consisted of a check of the client database to uncover any current or prior dealings with the other parties involved, and as long as this is undertaken methodically this is likely to continue to be adequate.

For much the same reason there is also therefore more emphasis on 'own' conflicts, i.e. situations where the client's interests might be seen to clash with those of the firm, or someone within it. The sort of interests that could arise could be personal, financial or the holding of public offices such as school governorships. Outcome 3(2) requires the control systems for this type of conflict to be 'appropriate to the size and complexity of the firm'. This may necessitate – in larger firms in particular – an audit of external interests for all personnel within the firm, checks on new joiners and an obligation to notify and update any changes to any central records. This Manual has opted for a voluntary register of personal interests and an obligation to declare any such issues that come to light: in larger firms a mandatory register of personal interests might be required. As ever, you will need to ensure that the draft is amended so as to meet your particular compliance obligations.

On the more substantive issue of what amounts to a conflict of interests when an issue is identified, the main point to bear in mind is that a conflict can only be said to arise where the current instructions relate to the same or a related matter – see the definitions in the Glossary of the Handbook. This would mean that the fact that you have had (or even still have) dealings with an opponent does not prohibit you from acting on the new instructions, even if 'professional embarrassment' might actually lead you to conclude that it would not be appropriate to act, as a guidance note to the former 2007 Code acknowledged.

Perhaps the greatest concerns to emerge from the revised Code of Conduct in 2011, however, were those relating to the issue of conflicts in conveyancing transactions: where the same firm acts for seller and buyer, or acts for the lender as well as the borrower where a mortgage is obtained. On this point see appendix 7.

2.9 Environmental policy

This is an optional issue for firms to address and might form one element of the non-mandatory policy of 'community and social responsibility policy' to be found in Lexcel at section 1.4. Many larger firms have chosen to get involved in this issue either as a result of genuine concerns as to their impact on the environment or in response to contract tendering processes, or both. Those with an interest in this issue might wish to consult the Legal Sector Alliance – a link to its website is provided in the draft procedures.

Part 2: Risk management
2.10 Our approach to risk management

As highlighted above, there are likely to be links between the risk policy and the client care or quality policies. Within Lexcel the risk management policy must now include or refer to a compliance plan and risk register – see Appendix 5.

Within this template Manual the managerial responsibility for risk is dealt with in this section but the more detailed procedures by which risk is managed day to day are to be found in the Case Management Manual since they form part of the 'life of a file' process that that section is intended to track.

In most firms the Compliance Officer for Legal Practice ('COLP') is likely also to be the person responsible for risk, but this will not necessarily be the case and the roles of COLP and COFA (Compliance Officer for Finance and Administration) are therefore dealt with as a separate issue in the following section. If someone other than the COLP is in overall charge of risk it will be necessary to amend 2.11.2. Lexcel has now removed the classification of risk as being strategic, operational or environmental but we have retained these headings, not least as they remain part of the Law Society's Core Practice Management Standards for the time being. Note that Lexcel now requires a compliance plan and a risk register to form part of the overall risk management policy at 5.1, along with details of how risk management will be disseminated.

2.11   **COLP and COFA**

The roles of COLP and COFA have been covered in the preceding 'Welcome to the firm' but are explained again here and might well overlap with the reporting of claims in the following section.

2.12   **Potential claims against the firm**

There is an obligation on firms to report circumstances that could give rise to a claim against the firm as soon as they become aware of it under the minimum terms and conditions that regulate the dealings of the insurers and their law firm clients. It follows that a policy reminder to all personnel of the need to report problems as soon as possible is advisable.

2.13   **The SRA Accounts Rules**

The main purpose of this section is to highlight the importance of following the detailed procedures that ensure compliance with the SRA Accounts Rules to be found in Section 4 of this Manual. At policy level the opportunity has also been taken to highlight some of the more common errors made by fee earners where they are quite possibly acting without reference to the accounts department in relation to problems on files that impact on Accounts formalities.

2.14   **Data protection**

All law firms are very likely to be regarded as data handlers under the Data

Protection Act 1998 and, as such, must be registered with the Information Commissioner. The process of registration commits the firm to compliance with the data principles that are an implicit requirement under section 3.1 in Lexcel covering the need for an information management and security policy. Legal aid tender conditions also require firms to be registered. The processes and procedures that this will entail are set out in Section 5 of this Manual. With increased reports of 'cyber attacks' against firms whereby client accounts have been successfully hacked into by criminals this is bound to become a – perhaps the – major new management priority in years to come.

2.15 Whistle-blowing

The need for a whistle-blowing policy is dealt with an IB in the Code of Conduct (IB(10.10)) but is now also a requirement under Lexcel (at 4.9). So far as the SRA is concerned this provision is not mandatory as such, but larger firms in particular might be questioned as to why they have chosen not to follow this piece of 'guidance'. Since the reference appears in chapter 10 of the Code of Conduct, dealing with the relationship of the firm and the SRA as regulator, it seems reasonable to conclude that what is really intended is protection for any colleagues who report their concerns about malpractice to the SRA.

2.16 Health and safety

The main purpose of this section is again to highlight the policy required by law, and to direct your colleagues to the more detailed office procedures that will be found in Section 5 of the Manual.

Part 3: Financial crime

2.17 Money laundering and terrorist financing

The issue of money laundering may be more familiar within most practices now, but this does not necessarily mean that it is well understood by most law firm personnel. Money laundering is the process of converting criminal money, such as that earned from drug trafficking or robbery, into apparently legitimate funds or investments. The definition depends on the very wide definitions of 'criminal conduct' and 'criminal property' that are set out at s.340 of the Proceeds of Crime Act 2002, and so include the sorts of taxation irregularities that are commonly encountered in dealings with companies and certain private clients. There are similar offences in relation to terrorist financing and it is important that any compliance materials also address these related provisions.

Quite apart from the main statutory offences that arise under the main Acts, the Money Laundering Regulations 2007 ('MLR') impose certain obligations on all organisations that fall under their scope – the so-called 'regulated sector'. Most, but by no means all, law firms are within the regulated sector, especially those undertaking transactional work such as conveyancing. Since litigation does not generally fall within the MLR definitions, however, the obligations imposed by these provisions will not apply to all firms. A further complication is that many firms are, of course, mixed, in that some of their work is subject to the MLR and some not. This would mean that the clients of certain parts of the practice must be subject to the identity screening processes described as 'customer due diligence' in the MLR, but others need not be: in such instances most firms will prefer to apply the same disciplines to all clients across the board – the approach adopted in the draft policy and procedures that follow. This 'one size fits all' approach is by no means appropriate to all firms, however, and careful consideration needs to be given to how each firm should best address its particular regulatory obligations.

Lexcel requires firms to adopt an anti-money laundering policy at 5.13. A relatively short form policy and set of procedures has been provided. The issue of cash receipts has seen developments at many firms of late: many now take the view that £500 is lower than needed for compliance with their obligations, especially in relation to clients wishing to pay their bills in cash. Given the defence of 'adequate consideration' at s.329 POCA you may wish to authorise higher payments of cash than the norm where payment of the firm's fees is being offered.

2.18   The Bribery Act and accepting gifts from clients

The Bribery Act 2010 needs to be addressed by all businesses, law firms included. The Act created three main new offences:

- Offering or paying a bribe;
- Requesting or receiving a bribe; and
- Bribing a foreign official.

In addition, there is a corporate offence of failing to prevent bribery being undertaken on behalf of that organisation. Where such an instance arises the company will be liable unless it can show that it has adopted 'adequate procedures' to prevent bribery – thus the need for this issue to be addressed in any compliance manual, as also found in Lexcel at section 5.15. So far, so good, but whereas some firms have adopted policy manuals on this piece of legislation alone running to tens of pages others have elected much shorter versions. In this Manual we have adopted a lighter touch approach but, as ever when we touch upon possible issues of the criminal law in particular, it is for every user to consider the special factors within their firm that might cause them to add to or amend the draft provided, or to seek specialist advice.

The fact that the most fundamental obligation of a law firm, under Principle 1 of the SRA Handbook, is to uphold justice and the rule of law will mean that bribery – as, now, an illegal activity – will be seen to be prohibited in any event. It is unlikely, however, that so general a policy statement could be seen to amount to being 'adequate procedures' and more would be advisable, especially in relation to the giving and receiving of gifts. It is important also to highlight the link to money laundering: any client involved in activities that would offend the Act is involved in 'criminal conduct' which would result in them or another being in possession of 'criminal property', so it follows that a disclosure to the Money Laundering Reporting Officer ('MLRO') might be required and then, subject to the operation of privilege, to the National Crime Agency ('NCA').

2.19 Mortgage fraud

Mortgage – or property – fraud has become a 'should' item within Lexcel (5.10) but should be taken to be a 'must' by any firm that conducts conveyancing work. This might be addressed as a stand-alone policy as within this chapter or as part of your property department procedures.

Note that Lexcel requires a procedure for the checking the identity of other conveyancers not known to the firm. This should be undertaken against the relevant professional directory and further enquiries should be made if suspicions remain, bearing in mind that fraudsters have been able to infiltrate the SRA directory of firms (See *Davisons v Nationwide Building Society* [2012] EWCA 1626).

2.20 Financial Conduct Authority ('FCA')

Most firms will also be subject to the authority of the Financial Conduct Authority ('FCA') through the handling of 'regulated activities' under the Financial Services and Markets Act 2000 ('the Act') which established the FCA and provides wide-ranging powers set out to regulate the market by way of secondary legislation.

Solicitors are caught up in the provisions as a result of the 'general prohibition' at section 19 of the Act which provides that 'no person may carry on a regulated activity in the UK unless authorised or exempt'. Most law firms, however, unless they provide mainstream investment advice, fall under the wider category of 'exempt persons' under s.327 of the Act dealing with 'members of a profession'.

Most solicitors' firms carry out some 'regulated activities' – as they are now referred to – as a result of having to provide advice and make arrangements on the disposal of assets, such as redeeming investments in probate work or disposing of shares for commercial or family law clients.

There is also the related issue of insurance mediation, which arises wherever a firm advises on, arranges or assists in the performance of an insurance contract. Since this could include introducing a client to a broker, or even being involved in litigation featuring an insurance contract, it again follows that most firms are covered by these provisions.

Firms involved in all such activities need to ensure that they are permitted to do so by being registered with the SRA and then be aware of, and comply with, the SRA Financial Services (Scope) Rules 2001 and the SRA Financial Services (Conduct of Business) Rules 2001 ('COBR'), currently found in the section headed 'specialist services' in the SRA Handbook. There will need to be a Financial Compliance Officer. The easiest way to check your firm's status is on the 'exempt professional firm' ('EPF') register on the FCA website (www.fca.gov.uk).

For the most part compliance is simply an issue of ensuring that the necessary registration is maintained and that the issues are addressed in the firm's terms of business or engagement letters, but there are further obligations to provide contemporaneous 'demands and needs statements' in the case of insurance mediation which is explained further in Section 3: Case Management in this Manual. See also Appendix 22.

It remains to be seen if many more firms will be obliged to submit themselves to direct regulation by the FCA as well as the SRA as a result of the stricter regime on consumer credit licensing. There is an extension to the state of affairs prevailing at March 2015 until October 2015 and if there are further developments on this issue these will be notified to Infolegal subscribers who have purchased these materials by way of download. See also the Infolegal factsheet on this topic.

Part 4: Client service

2.21 Complaints

The main requirements of complaints handling are to be found at outcomes 1.9 to 1.11 of the Code of Conduct, and can be summarised as:

- You are required to inform clients in writing of their right to complain (O(1.9));
- Details must also be given to your clients – again 'in writing' – at the outset of the matter and at the conclusion of your complaints handling process of their right to complain to the Legal Ombudsman (O(1.10)); and
- You need to handle such complaints as you do receive 'promptly, fairly, openly and effectively' (O(1.11)).

The required elements of a complaints handling policy are to be found at IB(1.22) which includes the rule that you may not charge for your time in investigating a complaint, while IBs(1.23-24) deal respectively with the need to provide a copy of your written complaints handling procedure on request and to ensure that you provide the client with sufficient information about the handling of the complaint.

The draft policy and procedures below largely follow Law Society guidelines on this topic, in particular that they should be accessible to all and free of charge. You should question whether all clients can fairly access your process – people with certain disabilities might be unable to do so, for example, if you require all complaints to be notified to you in writing. See the 'guidance for lawyers' section on the Legal Ombudsman's website and the Law Society's Complaints Handling Toolkit 2014.

There are likely to be various stages to the complaints resolution process. The procedure adopted in this section envisages the fee earner handling the matter to be the first point of contact with a more formal stage following on from that. Remember that the Legal Ombudsman will expect you to have concluded your process within eight weeks and will generally only become involved thereafter. The involvement of the Ombudsman puts your firm at risk of a costs award against you under the Scheme rules, and an increasing number of firms take the view that it is likely to be in everyone's interests to acknowledge that the client is unhappy and do whatever they can to remedy this state of affairs without involving that office, even if they do not agree with the complaint that has been raised.

Complaints which have been subject to formal investigation by the firm have to be reported to the SRA annually. In this edition of the SOPM we have updated the internal complaints monitoring form so that it uses the same classification as the SRA, in order to make this easier to achieve.

2.22 Client feedback

There is a requirement in Lexcel (s.6.6) and the Specialist Quality Mark (G2.1) for some degree of ongoing or occasional client feedback monitoring. If you are accredited to Lexcel, it will be necessary for this to apply to all departments of the firm.

2.23 Legal aid

Legal aid continues to be an important source of funding for many firms, although a declining number, notwithstanding the often encountered view that the scheme no longer survives. The legal aid contract, Specialist Quality Mark and funding schemes impose particular requirements on practitioners which are irrelevant to those who do not do legal aid work. The approach we have taken throughout these template provisions is:

- Where a requirement can be explained in a few words, we do so in the main section relating to the topic;
- Where requirements are more detailed and complex, we refer you to the specific legal aid section.

In relation to policies, a number of general policies need some adaptation, which we have indicated as above.

The main 'legal aid only' policy is for referral and signposting. This is all that remains of the all embracing approach to a holistic 'access to justice' legal aid scheme envisaged under the Access to Justice Act 1999.

POLICIES AND STANDARDS

PART A: MANUAL FORMAT

2.1 Introduction

2.1.1 This section of the Manual is intended to summarise our approach to the work done within the firm and to set out details of the standards that we set for ourselves.

2.1.2 For more details of the responsibilities for updating the various policies that are set out in this part of the Manual see Section 1 'Welcome to [*firm's name*]' which also forms part of our induction training materials.

2.1.3 This section of the Manual is divided into four sections as follows:

Part 1: Main policies and processes

Part 2: Risk management

Part 3: Financial crime

Part 4: Client service

Part 1: Main policies and processes

2.2 The importance of compliance

2.2.1 We live and practise in an increasingly compliance-based professional and business culture. Failure to comply with the requirements of the relevant regulatory bodies and statutes governing the conduct of solicitors could lead to various unwelcome consequences for the firm, including:

- Negligence claims by clients and others;
- Disciplinary action by the Solicitors Regulation Authority (the 'SRA');
- Increased premiums for our professional indemnity insurance;

- Reputational harm; and
- Criminal liability for the firm or for its personnel.

2.2.2   It follows that compliance with the practice's policies and procedures is a requirement of all personnel and failure to do so may be regarded as a matter of serious misconduct, which may lead to disciplinary action including termination of employment.

2.2.3   The [partners/directors] are committed to keeping all of the policies and procedures that comprise the Office Manual under continual review to ensure that improvements are made where possible. We are also committed to the provision of appropriate training so that everyone is properly trained to meet all of their responsibilities. If you feel unsure of what is expected of you, or how to do any element of your job, please consult [a partner/your supervisor/your head of department/other].

2.3   An introduction to the firm

2.3.1   To see a brief history of the firm, and for details of our management structure, see 'Welcome to [firm's name]' which precedes this section of the Manual.

2.3.2   For details of the terms of your employment, including your entitlement to benefits, how we arrange training and our review processes, see Section 6: Staff Handbook.

2.4   Our objectives as a firm

2.4.1   We are committed to providing excellent service to our clients in terms of:

- Expertise – The firm is organised into specialist departments and it is important that all client work is undertaken within the appropriate department;
- Concern – Our clients should feel that we are fully committed to providing them with the best service possible, and that advising them is something that matters to each and every one of us; and
- Efficiency – One of the best ways to show concern is to be proactive on client matters and communicate in a manner that is timely, intelligible and helpful.

2.4.2   [*The firm provides a service to private paying and legally aided clients alike.*] As evidence of our commitment to providing a quality service to clients we [*have been awarded/are in the process of applying for recognition under*] the Law Society's Lexcel scheme – a quality management award that is subject to independent adjudication. [*The firm holds the 'SQM' as administered by the Legal Aid Agency and also has a contract for the provision of legal aid services.*]

2.5   Professional standards and conduct

2.5.1   [*Name of firm*] conducts itself in strict accordance with the SRA Handbook, which includes the Code of Conduct and also the SRA Accounts Rules. Please note that the rules of the SRA generally extend to all personnel working within the firm and not just the solicitors, as was previously the case. The SRA has indicated, however, that in relation to the steps it might take against non-solicitor members of staff 'the impact will vary depending on the nature of the work and the responsibility of the employee concerned'.

2.5.2   Whatever your precise duties, it is important that you adopt the highest professional standards and you do not compromise the integrity of the firm in any actions you take either within your work for the firm or in the manner in which you conduct yourself in your personal life. This includes a duty not to take unfair advantage from your position.

2.5.3   You are also required to notify [*name or title*] in the event that you are subject to any criminal enquiry other than regulatory offences such as parking violations.

2.5.4   It should be noted that there is a duty on all personnel to co-operate fully with any investigation about any claim for redress (O(10.6)).

2.6   Equality and diversity

2.6.1   The firm has adopted a policy dealing with equality and diversity, as required by chapter 2 of the Code of Conduct. This policy primarily addresses the 'protected characteristics' of the Equality Act 2010:

- Age;
- Disability;
- Gender reassignment;
- Marriage and civil partnership;

- Pregnancy and maternity;
- Race;
- Religion or belief;
- Sex; and
- Sexual orientation.

2.6.2 [*Name of firm*] is committed to avoiding discrimination on any of the above grounds in its dealings with clients and potential clients, other solicitors, barristers and third parties, and in relation to all current [*partners/directors*] and employees, as well as applicants for positions within the firm and all related recruitment activity, along with internal promotions and training opportunities. The [*partners/directors*] are also committed to promoting equality and diversity in all aspects of the firm's operations including client service.

2.6.3 In addition to the firm's obligations not to discriminate against, harass or victimise those with a disability the firm is also subject to a duty to make reasonable adjustments to prevent those employees, [*partners/directors*] and clients who are disabled from being at a disadvantage in comparison with those who are not.

2.6.4 Liability for acts of discrimination might extend beyond the individuals concerned to the owners of the firm. For that reason any breach is likely to be regarded as a serious disciplinary offence that might justify instant dismissal. Any internal complaint that a breach of this policy has occurred should be addressed to [*name or title*] without delay in accordance with our disciplinary process (see 6.21) and a complaint from outside the firm under the complaints process (2.21).

2.6.5 Training has been held on this topic and on this policy and will be repeated as necessary, to include the actual contents of this policy.

Disability considerations

2.6.6 Signing facilities will be provided by the firm at its own expense for clients who are in need of them. If a client has mobility problems [*state your arrangements here: do you have disabled access? If so, are you also able to offer toilet facilities? The primary obligation under the Equality Act is to make reasonable adjustments for disabled people, but limited to clients, colleagues and job applicants (i.e. not third parties such as counsel or opponents acting in person). If it is not reasonable for you to make the necessary adjustments to your offices to enable wheelchair access you should consider offering home visits within a reasonable radius of the office at no extra charge: to charge a disabled client who cannot access your offices more for your time in visiting them elsewhere could be seen to be direct discrimination against them on grounds of their disability. Much the same considerations apply to the issue of charging for signing interpretation.]*

Counsel and experts

2.6.7　If a client expresses a preference for an adviser that is based on any of the above grounds you should try to persuade them to modify their instructions. If they refuse to do so we may have to cease to act for them further.

Monitoring and review

2.6.8　This policy will be monitored periodically by the firm to judge its effectiveness and workforce diversity monitoring will be conducted as required by the SRA through a questionnaire-based exercise. The firm has appointed [*name or title*] to be responsible for the operation of the policy. The firm will aim to monitor the ethnic and gender composition of existing staff and applicants for jobs (including promotion) and the number of people with disabilities within these groups.

2.7 Client confidentiality

2.7.1　One of the most important duties owed by solicitors and their staff to clients is the duty to maintain the confidentiality of all information received in relation to client matters, whatever its source. It might be tempting to discuss client matters outside the firm, but to do so could lead to disciplinary action against the firm by the SRA and so is likely to be treated as a serious disciplinary offence.

2.7.2　There are very limited exceptions to the rule requiring us to safeguard client confidentiality, most obviously in relation to money laundering and terrorist financing, on which see Section 2.17 of this document.

2.7.3　As a result of the SRA's requirements in relation to conflicts of interests you are required to notify your [*head of department/supervisor/other*] if you have any personal knowledge of or any close connection to the client or others involved in any matter that you are working on (see 2.8).

2.7.4   You should not discuss a client's affairs outside the office except with the express consent of a [*partner/director*] (other than in the course of carrying out the client's instructions).

2.7.5   Other than in the normal course of business you should not name clients or inform or confirm to a third party that the firm acts for a person unless that client has expressly given consent for us to do so. Please note that this extends to enquiries from the police as to whether we are acting for a particular individual or concern – an increasing number of law firms report 'fishing expeditions' by the police along these lines. Our duty to co-operate with police enquiries is mostly limited to our money laundering policy – (see 2.17).

2.7.6   For similar reasons you must not answer any questions from the press or even confirm if we are acting for a particular client, let alone provide their address. Please refer any such enquiry to [*a partner/your supervisor/other*].

2.7.7   Please also exercise care in how you dispose of unwanted letters and documents (including drafts and unwanted photocopies). Any papers, etc. which identify a client must be disposed of confidentially. [*Explain how confidential waste should be disposed of if special arrangements are in place.*]

2.7.8   Should you become aware or suspect that a breach of confidentiality has occurred, you must report the details to [*name or title*] immediately. See also 3.11 of this Manual.

2.7.9   Please also be wary of conversations about client matters, both in the reception area and outside the firm (especially with mobile phone conversations in public places). Also be wary of carrying files that show information on the cover that would identity what we are doing and for whom (e.g. Mrs McGregor, 43 Acacia Avenue, Divorce). Do not leave files in unlocked cars, and in no circumstances in cars overnight.

2.8   Conflicts of interests

2.8.1   The firm will not act where there is a conflict of interests as defined by chapter 3 of the SRA Handbook, or where there is a significant risk that such a conflict might arise at a future date. The Code of Conduct distinguishes between 'own' conflicts, where the client's interests could be seen to conflict with the interests of the firm or anyone within it, and client conflicts.

2.8.2   You must declare to [*name or title*] any personal interest – family, commercial, financial or otherwise – that might lead the client to suspect that we have not acted in their proper interests. This would also extend to any public office appointments you hold, such as school governorships, where we are instructed to act against that institution.

2.8.3   Certain exceptions to the rule against acting where there is a conflict of interests exist in relation to client conflicts (but never 'own' conflicts). These are where:

- There is a substantially common interest between two or more clients;
- A retainer can be agreed with two or more clients to confine the firm's role to aspects of the instructions that are not, or are not likely to become, in dispute; or
- Acting for different parties with their informed and written consent where they are competing for the same asset and the conditions stipulated in the Code of Conduct are met.

Conflict searches

2.8.4   A conflict search must always be carried out before new instructions to act for a new client or on a new matter for an existing client are accepted. This is done by [*state how this is done in your firm*]. Remember that the quality of result is only as effective as the information provided, especially in relation to linked parties (such as directors of companies to be represented).

2.8.5   Where there is a question as to whether a conflict of interests does exist the issue must be referred to [*name or title*].

Property conflicts

2.8.6   There are restrictions in chapter 3 of the Code of Conduct as to the ability of law firms to act for seller and buyer in the same transaction, and also to act for both lender and borrower. The firm's policy on this is to be found [*include here or state where it can be found – see Appendix 7*].

Confidentiality and disclosures

2.8.7   In practice, most of the difficult issues to arise under conflicts are those where the conflict is not between clients but where we hold relevant information from another client or matter that is now relevant to the new instructions. Such conflicts of information are the domain of chapter 4 of the Code of Conduct. This provides that:

- There is an ongoing duty of confidentiality to clients and former clients that can only be waived in certain exceptional cases, or by client consent;
- There is a duty to disclose to all clients all relevant information on that matter of which the fee earner is aware; and
- Work must be declined where the duty of confidentiality to one existing or former client would be put at risk by accepting instructions from another (i.e. the duty of disclosure to the new client would compromise the duty of confidentiality owed to another client or former client).

Information barriers

2.8.8   Information barriers do not overcome conflicts of interests but can permit us to act, or to continue to act, where the problem is one of relevant information being held in one part of the practice and it is withheld from another. Key to understanding their operation is that the duty to disclose all relevant information to clients at O(4.2) of the Code of Conduct is stated to be a personal obligation and confined to lawyers – i.e. the duty is to disclose that which that lawyer is aware of rather than the firm and does not extend to administrators and secretaries. You cannot therefore be censured for not disclosing issues that others in the firm might be aware of but you are not.

2.8.9   At an informal level this might involve ensuring that a new member of staff with experience of working for an opponent at their previous firm will not be assigned to a relevant matter. The firm does not operate under the formal information barriers employed in the largest commercial firms [*If this is not the case refer on to your policy on this issue*].

2.8.10   Training is provided on the issue of conflicts for all relevant personnel. [*This is a Lexcel requirement – a training module on this topic is available via the Infolegal website.*]

2.9   Environmental policy

2.9.1   [*Name of firm*] is committed to acting responsibly in relation to environmental issues. The firm is working towards lessening its adverse impact on the environment through its business practices and through the services it offers.

2.9.2   [*Set out details here of any policy you have in place. For more information on this topic see www.legalsectoralliance.co.uk.*]

Part 2: Risk management
2.10   Our approach to risk management

2.10.1   Risk is a fact of life for all professional and commercial organisations. The risk of undesired or unwelcome developments can never be eliminated, but it can be properly managed so as to avoid, reduce or mitigate that risk so as to bring it within acceptable levels. We regularly review risk issues and communicate updates to the appropriate [*partners/directors*] and staff. Risk management is addressed as follows:

- *Strategic* – The risks implicit in business developments are considered in the business planning processes adopted by the [*partners/directors*]. [*State any processes whereby the business plan is shared with or communicated to staff if required.*]
- *Operational and regulatory* – Our client service standards, especially as set out in Section 3 of this Manual, address the established principles of risk management in law firms and our regulatory obligations as set out in the SRA Handbook and more generally.
- *Environmental* – We have all the same obligations as any other professional or commercial concern arising from our activities as employers and occupiers of premises. Our various obligations in

relation to the use of our office facilities are set out in Section 5: Office Facilities and IT.

2.10.2   The application of this policy will mean that sometimes we decline to act as a result of the risk profile of the instructions received or we may decide to do so under special 'high risk' controls.

2.10.3   As suggested by the SRA Authorisation Rules, and as required by Lexcel, we maintain a compliance plan and risk register as part of our overall risk management policy (*see appendices 5 and 6*).

2.11   Compliance Officer for Legal Practice ('COLP') and Compliance Officer for Finance and Administration ('COFA'): Reporting of non-compliances

2.11.1   It should be noted that the SRA Handbook introduced for all law firms an enhanced duty to report to the SRA any 'material' breach of the SRA rules, including the Accounts rules. There is also an obligation to keep records of other less serious breaches of the professional rules. Failure to make the necessary reports to the SRA will amount to a professional offence with potentially significant consequences for the firm and the personnel concerned.

2.11.2   The firm's COLP is [*name, and add details of deputy if relevant – more likely in larger firms*] and the COFA is [*ditto*]. Details of how they meet the obligations imposed on them by the SRA can be found in the firm's compliance plan (*see appendix 5*). As COLP [*name*] is also the person responsible for risk management and the risk policy as in 2.10. [*Adapt if this is not the case*]

2.11.3   Where you are unsure whether any problem that arises is relevant to the Code of Conduct or any other part of the SRA Handbook please consult with either of the above depending on the nature of the possible breach.

2.11.4   For other managerial and risk responsibilities see 1.3.

2.12   Potential claims against the firm

2.12.1   The firm sets great store by the quality of its work. Nonetheless, errors are bound to happen from time to time. Whatever the problem, delay in reporting it is likely to make things much worse and may therefore be treated as a serious disciplinary issue by the [*partners/directors*]. There are also professional obligations to point out certain circumstances to clients (when errors or omissions on our part could mean that they could bring a claim against us – see O(1.16) of the Code of Conduct). Any error made whilst acting for a client – to include failing to take certain steps when required – must therefore be reported to [*name or title*] as soon as possible.

2.12.2 The firm is committed to helping lawyers to resolve situations where errors have been made and will be supportive, providing that early notification is made.

2.13 SRA Accounts Rules

2.13.1 For the most part compliance with the SRA Accounts Rules ('SAR') is achieved by controls in place [*by the Accounts Manager/Cashier/other* or *within the Cashiers/Accounts team*] who [*has/have*] expertise in the obligations regarding how finances must be managed in a law firm. All others are required to follow the provisions of our Accounts Manual but, in addition, please note the following issues where fee earners could inadvertently cause the firm to breach its obligations to the regulator.

2.13.2 Rule 14 of the SRA Accounts Rules covers dealing with client accounts. Of particular relevance are:

- Rule 14(1): All client account receipts must be banked 'without delay' which is taken to mean on the same or next working day. Cheques are generally taken from the post when it is opened, but it is possible that the presence of a cheque might have been overlooked, or you may receive a cheque at a meeting with the client or by a hand delivery. It is essential that you forward or hand this cheque over to the [*Accounts Department/Other*] immediately upon receipt by you.

- Under Rule 14(3) we are obliged to clear all outstanding client balances 'promptly'. In particular, this means that unless there are clear and present underlying client instructions to explain why funds are in client account they must be returned to the client as soon as possible. This provision is closely linked to rule 14(5) which provides that law firms may not provide a banking facility to clients, in part because they are not legally permitted to do so under the Financial Services and Markets Act 2000 and in part because law firms could thereby become inadvertently involved in money laundering activities or aiding and abetting perverting the course of justice, as where funds are not being declared in divorce proceedings. It is essential, therefore, that you co-operate with the [*Accounts Department/Other*] in returning client funds when there is no adequate reason to justify the firm retaining them.

- Finally, rule 14(4) provides that if we are required to retain client monies at the end of a matter for some valid reason (e.g. in respect of possible warranty claims) the client must be informed of this in writing, along with an explanation for the retainer, and this correspondence must be updated at least annually.

2.13.3   On occasions we will be left with outstanding client balances where we cannot trace the client or perhaps are even unable to identify the client, as where an organisation has been taken over and it is unclear who the successor concern is. In these circumstances we are required to make reasonable attempts to contact the clients in order to account properly to them. Please note that to bill anything to the file in such circumstances – as for reviews or even the work undertaken in attempting to contact the client – will almost certainly be a breach of the SAR. Such actions have often triggered disciplinary action against firms and, in some cases involving larger amounts, strikings-off. Where all reasonable attempts to locate the client have failed we are now permitted (since November 2014) to pay sums of up to £500 to charity, but on the basis that if the client will be refunded in full if they are subsequently identified and located. The charity/ies we use for such purposes is/are [*Solicitors Benevolent Fund/Access to Justice Foundation/other*] which has undertaken to return any individual donation in these circumstances. If the figure involved is more than £500 specific SRA consent will be required before such a donation may be made.

2.13.4   Please also note that we are required to account to the client for any commission received by the firm in relation to their instructions (e.g. insurance commission), regardless of the amount concerned. Commissions payable to the firm in such circumstances are nonetheless deemed to be 'client money' under SAR rule 12(2.f) and must be dealt with as such.

2.13.5   Another important change is that we are required to have in place a policy on the payment of interest to clients and can no longer rely on the former provision entitling us to retain sums up to £20 without notice to the client. In accordance with suggestions made by the SRA we have adopted a policy – as set out in our terms of business document – that we will retain sums up to [£20] earned from general client account in this way but will account to the client for any figure above this sum or all interest earned if monies have been placed on special deposit.

2.14   Data protection

2.14.1   The firm's responsibilities under data protection legislation and the rules of conduct of the SRA are set out in our data protection policy (see 5.13). This policy deals with the responsibilities that we are subject to as data handlers and explains how we deal with data subject requests.

2.14.2   In addition, the firm is legally and professionally obliged to ensure that it sets out clear procedures on the use of information and data, including the content and format of e-mails and responsible use of the internet. We are also subject to certain contractual commitments in this regard in relation to our access to the Land Registry portal for conveyancing work.

2.14.3   Our policy contains an 'acceptable use policy' which all personnel are required to sign. This not only sets out your agreement to use the firm's IT facilities in accordance with its provisions but also indicates your consent to the monitoring of e-mails received and sent by you.

2.15   Whistle-blowing

2.15.1   The firm has a whistle-blowing policy as suggested by IB(10.10) of the Code of Conduct and now required by Lexcel. This can be found in the Staff Handbook (see 6.11).

2.15.2   Please bear in mind that the operation of such policies in a law firm is still subject to our duties of client confidentiality. If, for example, we are representing a local business that has been charged with pollution offences the legislation would not excuse any partner or staff member approaching the press to tell them that the client had admitted their guilt to us. The aim of the policy is to enable concerns about misconduct or poor service to be brought to the attention of the [partners/directors] without fear of recriminations against anyone acting in good faith in this regard.

2.16 Health and safety

2.16.1 The [partners/directors] are committed to complying with the Health and Safety at Work etc. Act 1974, as amended. This involves a commitment by the [partners/directors] to providing a safe place of work. Details of the firm's procedures under this policy are to be found in Section 5 of the Manual.

2.16.2 Your attention is drawn to your duty to take proper care of your working conditions and conducting yourself responsibly in relation to your colleagues and others.

Part 3: Financial crime
2.17 Money laundering and terrorist financing

Introduction

2.17.1 The firm must safeguard against becoming involved in the processing of illegal or improper gains for clients. As a professional practice the firm is particularly attractive to criminals wishing to convert gains to a respectable status. It is the policy of the firm not to assist them to do so. Breach of this policy could in any event be an unlawful act on the part of anyone concerned and could place the firm and/or its representatives at risk of criminal and/or civil proceedings.

2.17.2 We are obliged to establish the identity of our clients as a result of the Money Laundering Regulations 2007 and also to screen all work to ensure that:

- We know the identities of other related parties who might be involved (those with a beneficial interest);
- We extend these searches to anyone paying us more than £10,000 by way of an 'occasional transaction'; and
- We are satisfied that we are aware of the nature and purpose of the instructions and that the work will not put us at risk of involvement in illegal or unprofessional conduct.

2.17.3 The [partners/directors] have determined that all work conducted by the firm should be regarded as being covered by the Money Laundering Regulations with the consequential need to conduct identity checks in all areas of our practice. (*Or state if your practice is outside the scope of the MLR 2007 or any exceptions to certain areas of work in a mixed practice.*)

Client checking ('CDD')

2.17.4   Fee earners must ensure that we obtain evidence of identity for all clients as soon as possible after contact is first established between the firm and the potential client, often with the assistance of receptionists and secretaries. The Law Society guidelines make the distinction between 'identification' (being told or coming to know a client's identifying details) and 'verification' (obtaining some evidence which supports this claim of identity). In general 'customer due diligence' (as it is referred to in the Money Laundering Regulations 2007) requires both elements to be addressed. The evidence of identity check must be undertaken by completion of forms ML1 and ML2 (*Appendices 8 and 9*) which must appear on the matter file in question.

2.17.5   Further guidance is provided here on a number of options. Although these requirements may seem onerous you should bear in mind that these checks are a legal requirement which could be enforced against us if we are in breach, and that numerous firms have been penalised for falling victim to launderers and fraudsters. Where fraud is involved quite apart from the distress and inconvenience this will cause to our client this could lead to substantial increases in the firm's indemnity insurance costs: in some cases this has left firms unable to obtain cover at all (or at an affordable price) and has led to the consequential closure of some firms.

- Individual client met in person

    You should ask the client to bring the normal documentation as listed on form ML1 into the office for inspection and copying. Form ML1 must be signed and dated by the person checking the documents along with the Passport/Driving licence checking form (form ML2). When undertaking this process please refer any concerns to a partner/director (e.g. you do not think that the photo is a likeness of the client presenting it). Where we are acting for co-clients we must certify each of them – it is not permissible for one to bring in the documents on the other where the person checking has not met that other client.

- Individual client not met in person

    Please note that every attempt should be made to meet the client in person to verify the evidence provided, but where this is not possible the client should be asked to obtain certification through local solicitors or other professionals. Certification is permissible if received from:
    - o   Other solicitors in private practice;
    - o   Accountants in private practice;
    - o   Mortgage brokers or other agents if regulated by the FCA and well known to us; or
    - o   The Post Office's documentation checking service.

    Wherever distant certification is obtained from another professional the adviser must make a check of the validity of the referring firm or organisation in a current directory such as the SRA website and print off the relevant entry if possible and place this on the matter file. Where the referrer is not well known to us you must also phone the person who has provided the certification to check if they did indeed do so: be sure to use the number in the professional directory rather than the number on the notepaper in front of you as that notepaper might be false and therefore part of the 'bogus firm' scam. Where repeat usage is made of a particular referrer (e.g. a mortgage broker who introduces multiple matters to the firm) there is no need to have this copy on every matter file.

    Finally, we should also commission, with the client's agreement, an electronic search on the basis of copy documents and details provided.

- Companies

    In the case of commercial clients a companies search must be obtained at the outset of the first matter for that client, along with details of the identity of at least two directors or officers, if possible, unless the representatives are known to the firm and have had personal ID checks undertaken already. Further checks may be needed in the case of non-domiciled companies. It is, in any case, important to check that those who purport to represent an organisation are actually entitled to do so.

PEPs and Sanctions

2.17.6   An electronic search should also be conducted wherever there is a risk that the client or someone else involved in the matter is or could be a 'politically exposed person' ('PEP') or might be on the UN/UK Sanctions list. You should question any client with a foreign connection (including UK passport holders who have recently been based abroad) if they have held a high ranking position in a foreign government or international organisation and/or conduct an electronic search.

Much the same considerations apply to anyone that might, from their activities or profile, appear on one of the sanctions lists. To check this for yourself go to:

https://www.gov.uk/government/publications/financial-sanctions-consolidated-list-of-targets.

Third parties

2.17.7   It is becoming increasingly common for third parties to make payments to us, especially as more purchasers in conveyancing transactions obtain assistance from parents or other relatives. The approach of the firm is that the source of funds must always be known about in advance and where the sum is for a significant amount (again, a matter of judgement depending on the circumstances, but always where more than *£1000* is to be received) questions must be made as to how that money was acquired. If 'savings' then you do need to profile how this person might have acquired this sum, such as detailing their occupation. Where possible check the information with a Google search and file any useful information that you find and/or request six months of bank statements to look for regular salary payments or unusual and large receipts.

2.17.8   Where more than £?? is to be received directly by us you must conduct an identity check as if the party was a client, save that it is permissible to undertake an electronic search only if the client or third party prefers. Be sure to maintain any evidence collected on the matter file together with an attendance note detailing what checks you have made and why.

2.17.9   If the client or third party resists your questions you may be apologetic but should point out that the firm has no option but to comply with the duties that are placed upon it by law. If the required information is not forthcoming please consult [*a partner/director/supervisor*] and it may well be that we will have to cease to act.

Form ML1

2.17.10 In line with Law Society advice it is permissible for a partner/director to 'sign in' a client they know well in all cases other than where the CML Handbook applies (*but see 3.1.5 on this point in CML Handbook*). In all cases the 'lawyer certification' part of the form must be ticked by a fee earner (not a secretary) and signed.

Ongoing monitoring

2.17.11 In relation to regular, established clients the firm will compile a directory of standing checks of identities. Even then the current address should always be checked in relation to any future instructions.

2.17.12 For those more occasional clients that have instructed the firm before, the usual CDD process should be conducted if there is a gap of three years since the end of the client's last matter with us, save that it is open to a [*partner/director*] to verify that the client is well known to him/her. Where possible we should be sure to be relying on up to date documents – i.e. passports should be current if possible. The full CDD process should therefore be repeated if possible where a passport has expired and must also be conducted whenever there is any doubt as to the identity of the client or the matter itself.

Records

2.17.13 The firm is obliged to maintain records for at least five years of:

- What has been done for the client; and
- Any disclosures made (completed form reference or name).

Please bear this in mind when deciding a destroy date when archiving files. In addition the firm must maintain ID evidence for at least five years from the end of the 'business relationship' or the close of the 'occasional transaction'.

Cash receipts

2.17.14 The mere fact that a client pays in cash or wishes to do so is not in itself a cause for suspicion. Nonetheless, the larger the intended cash payment, the more likely it is that the client actions are suspect. Substantial amounts of cash might be criminal in origin or are often the result of failure to declare income to HM Revenue and Customs and, as tax evasion, would amount to criminal conduct under the anti-money laundering regime.

2.17.15 The approach to cash receipts is therefore as follows:

- In the absence of any complicating factors the firm will accept sums of up to £500/£1000 in cash (complicating factors could include, most obviously, doubts about the source of funds).
- Sums of over £500/£1000 should not be accepted and can only be accepted with the permission (to be noted on file) of the Money Laundering Reporting Officer ('MLRO') or, if (s)he is unavailable, another partner/director.

2.17.16 Where a significantly larger payment than you can accept is offered you must speak to [*name of MLRO*] and may have to complete a report form (ML4) in order that (s)he can consider if a disclosure should be made. Some judgement is needed here as the circumstances will vary from case to case, but it is envisaged that an offer of £?,000 or more of cash should always be reported by you to the MLRO.

Reporting to the National Crime Agency ('NCA')

2.17.17 A disclosure could be necessary for one of two reasons. First, the Proceeds of Crime Act 2002 (POCA 2002) s.330 imposes a duty to make a disclosure if, in the course of practice in the regulated sector, a person forms a suspicion (or should reasonably have done so) that money laundering is or could be occurring. The position is complicated by the fact that this is stated to be subject to legal professional privilege. The defence of privilege will mean that in most circumstances there is no need for the practice to make a report to the NCA on the basis of instructions received. This is not always the case, however, especially where third parties are involved, so please refer any concerns to [*name of MLRO*] in case a disclosure is required.

2.17.18 You are encouraged to have a discussion with [*name of MLRO*] at any time and you might then need to make a formal report by use of form ML4. Even if (s)he does not share your concerns it is your entitlement to send him/her a completed ML4 as in most cases this will be your defence to a charge that you have committed an offence under POCA (See appendix 11).

2.17.19 Secondly, it should be noted that a disclosure might also be necessary to gain a defence to a charge under the principal offences under POCA 2002, ss.327–329, most probably that of 'entering into an arrangement' whereby money laundering is facilitated under s.328. There are similar offences in relation to terrorist financing in the Terrorism Act 2000, ss.15–18. Where a suspicion arises the firm may, subject to the complex provisions relating to legal professional privilege, need to make a disclosure and gain permission to continue to act. The rules on this requirement differ according to work type, so again please contact [*name of MLRO*] if any concerns arise.

2.17.20 Do not store a completed ML4 report form on the matter file to which it relates. This would create a risk that the client might see the disclosure report, especially if the file is sent out of the office. Please make sure that any of your colleagues who might become involved in the work being done on the file are informed that the issue of a possible disclosure to NCA has arisen so that they may also proceed with caution.

Responsibilities

2.17.21 As Money Laundering Reporting Officer [*name of MLRO*]'s duties are to:

- Ensure that satisfactory internal procedures are maintained;
- Arrange for periodic training for all relevant personnel within the firm;
- Provide advice when consulted on possible reports and receive reports of suspicious circumstances;
- Report such circumstances, if appropriate, to the NCA on behalf of the firm;

- Direct colleagues as to what action to take and not take when suspicion arises and a disclosure is made; and
- Report annually to the partners on the operation of the anti-money laundering policy and procedures.

2.17.22 It is the duty of all personnel within the practice to:

- Attend training arranged within the firm if required to do so;
- Conduct identity checks and other due diligence enquiries unless the MLRO signifies that this is not necessary in the particular case in hand;
- Report without delay all circumstances which could give rise to suspicion that the firm is being involved in some element of the money laundering process for a client;
- Be wary of payment arrangements different from those anticipated or deposits of cash into client account;
- Follow the directions of the MLRO when a disclosure has been made, bearing in mind the personal risk to the adviser of 'tipping off' the client in question either expressly or by implication; and
- Maintain the utmost caution in maintaining confidentiality for the client and the firm when suspicious circumstances arise.

2.17.23 In certain circumstances fee earners/advisers may or must report to the client that a disclosure will be made. They might also sometimes have the option in exceptional circumstances of informing a client that a disclosure has been made concerning another party or even the client themself, notwithstanding the offences of 'tipping off' and 'disclosing an investigation' (POCA 2002, s.333) or, in relation to work outside the regulated sector, 'prejudicing an investigation' (POCA 2002, s.342). There are, of course, significant risks in doing so and in all such cases the advice of the MLRO must be sought and his/her instructions must be closely followed.

2.17.24 Property lawyers should note the source of funds form (ML3) and use it as part of our duty to obtain information on the funds to be used in any purchase.

Other resources

2.17.25 Helpful details on the obligations on all firms in relation to money laundering and terrorist financing can be found on the Law Society website in the Practice

---

Note on these topics of the 22nd October 2013, which has been approved by HM Treasury. There are also practice notes of interest to conveyancers in relation to 'Mortgage fraud' (31st July 2014) and 'Property and registration fraud' (11th October 2010); the latter guide was compiled in conjunction with the Land Registry.

2.18   The Bribery Act and accepting gifts from clients

2.18.1   The Bribery Act 2010 introduced significant new obligations on organisations to prohibit, and monitor for, improper payments. We are committed to conducting the business of the firm in an honest and ethical manner and, in particular, in accordance with the ten principles of legal practice which underpin the SRA Handbook. These include, most basically, a duty to uphold the rule of law (Principle 1).

2.18.2   It follows that we will never offer, pay or receive any improper payment, such as a personal cash payment or an inappropriate gift to an individual to place the work for their organisation with this firm.

2.18.3   Please note that it is not necessary for a payment to pass hands for a bribery offence to have been committed. Sections 1 to 5 set out the 'general bribery offences'. The main offence of giving or offering a bribe (s.1) is described in rather confusing terms as having two 'cases', the first being where a person:

> 'offers, promises or gives a financial or other advantage to another person, and [...] intends the advantage –
>> (i)   to induce a person to perform improperly a relevant function or activity, or
>> (ii) to reward a person for the improper performance of such a function or activity.'

2.18.4   The second case arises where a person:

> 'offers, promises or gives a financial or other advantage to another person, [knowing or believing] that the acceptance of the advantage would itself constitute the improper performance of a relevant function or activity.'

2.18.5   Further explanation is provided to the effect that in the first case, 'it does not matter whether the person to whom the advantage is offered, promised or given is the same person as the person who is to perform, or has performed, the function or activity concerned', and that in both cases it does not matter whether the advantage is offered, promised or given directly or through a third party.

2.18.6   Section 2 deals with the other side of the bribery transaction by prohibiting the request or receipt of a bribe, again confusingly set out in a number of illustrative cases. Under this offence it is necessary only to agree to receive or accept a financial or other advantage in circumstances where the person concerned should not do so, meaning that the crime will have been committed even if the payment or other benefit is not forthcoming.

2.18.7   Section 3 deals with the range of functions and activities that might be involved for possible liability under the Act, while s.4 sets out the provisions on when such an activity might be said to have been 'improperly' performed. Section 5 then completes this part of the Act by introducing a reasonableness test in relation to ss.3 and 4, reflecting the core problem of the legislation in attempting to differentiate between normally accepted business practice – especially in relation to marketing events – and what should be regarded as criminal behaviour. The offence of bribing a foreign official is dealt with separately within the Act in order to meet the specific requirements of the OECD Anti-Bribery Convention.

2.18.8   Notwithstanding the rather confusing definitions of the key offences by illustrative cases, the core offences are easily summarised: it is an offence to offer or request a bribe, regardless of whether that bribe, be it money, goods or other advantage, is actually paid or received. The relatively low threshold for criminality might therefore mean that illegal acts of bribery are encountered much more frequently than might be thought, as where a client offers a payment for their adviser to misrepresent the position in a matter or to lie in court.

Client entertaining

2.18.9   Our policy on gifts and entertaining is that we continue to undertake appropriate client entertaining activity as part of our marketing policy, but this is never to be lavish or open to misinterpretation under this policy. To take a potential client out to lunch would usually be permissible, but to take them on holiday would not (unless they are close friends or relations in any event).

Gifts from clients

2.18.10 Our policy on the receipt of gifts from clients or others is that there is a common sense limit of £50, or a case of wine of any reasonable value, to any item received and in no circumstances may any representative of the firm accept any cash gift. Likewise, there is no objection to your being the recipient of client entertaining by others as long as it is reasonable having regard to your role in the firm, your links with whoever is making any such offer and the value of what is being proposed. A register of gifts made by the practice and received is maintained by ??. Please notify them by email of .... (specify).

2.18.11 You must also note the provisions of O(1.9) of the Code of Conduct to the effect that where a client wishes to make a gift 'of significant value' to you or a relative, or to someone else at the firm or their family, the client must take independent legal advice. This is particularly relevant in relation to the drafting of wills for friends and family as the Code of Conduct does not specifically provide for an exemption in such situations as did the former 2007 Code (*see Law Society Practice Note on this topic of 20th January 2015*).

Money laundering

2.18.12 The [*partners/directors*] believe that the risks of bribery or corruption by the firm are very low and are adequately covered by the policy summary set out above. A greater risk is that we are dealing with a client who has either made or received improper payments. Since such payments are now criminal funds under the terms of the Bribery Act any such circumstances, or suspicions that they might be such, should be dealt with as a potential money laundering incident and so must be reported to [*name of the MLRO*] and will be dealt with under that policy (see Section 2.17 above).

2.18.13 The person responsible for this policy is [*name or title*]

2.19   Mortgage fraud

2.19.1   Conveyancers must be vigilant in relation to what has become the widespread practice of property and mortgage fraud in recent years. The risks to all firms undertaking conveyancing work – for seller or buyer and commercial or domestic – are very real; there are good firms that have been put out of practice through the indemnity insurance complications that tend to follow lenders' claims in particular.

2.19.2   Your first step should be to make sure that you are conversant with the Law Society guidance on:

- Mortgage fraud avoidance – As contained in its most up-to-date practice note on the topic (31st July 2014 or later); and
- Property and registration fraud – See the practice note of the 11th October 2010 (or later).

2.19.3   As these practice notes record, the patterns of property and mortgage fraud take many forms including:

- Application frauds – In which the deceit of the borrower as to their circumstances is a factor in the lender deciding to make an offer of advance, or on better terms than they would otherwise have done;
- Identity frauds – In which the client (perhaps acting in conjunction with fellow conspirators) produces false identity evidence with the sole objective of theft from the lender or the rightful owners of the property now or at some future stage; and
- Valuation fraud – Very often in conjunction with identity frauds and with the aim of defrauding the lender by leaving them with irrecoverable losses.

2.19.4   There have been particular warnings in recent years as to:

- Fraudsters producing false identity documentation to purport to be the seller of an unencumbered property, perhaps following a change of name process to assume the name of the rightful owner(s) – a particular risk with tenants in properties impersonating their landlord(s);
- Bogus firms – Fraudsters claiming to be solicitors or licensed

conveyancers but using false notepaper and changed telephone and address details so as to intercept the payment of funds;

- Sham transactions – Sales (usually at an over value) between co-conspirators to obtain larger loans than the transaction would support; and
- Intra-family frauds – Where both parties do not agree, for example, to a re-mortgage to cover outstanding debts.

Avoidance processes

2.19.5 Identity fraud remains the most pressing risk for law firms. You must follow our anti-money laundering processes with care, conveyancing being the highest risk work type of most mixed firms. Careful identity checking is also one of the prime requirements of firms in the CML Lenders' Handbook.

2.19.6 Be wary, and do not be taken in by plausible or bullying clients. Ask:

- **Why** us as the firm to act, especially if there is no local connection with the property or the client?
- **Why** this deal? Are there aspects that strike you as unusual?
- **Why** this price? We are not expected to be expert valuers but we should note obvious over values and under values (the former can suggest mortgage fraud and the latter money laundering).

As a result of the increased incidence of hacking attacks of phones and e-mails in conveyancing transactions you should always question any late change of representatives or banking details directly with those concerned (bearing in mind that the e-mails might have been infiltrated). Given the risk of bogus law firms operated by fraudsters you should also check the identity of any conveyancers on the other side of any transaction not known to you in the relevant professional directory, and further if you remain suspicious.

2.19.7 Other risks to consider are:

- Distant certification of a client you have not met – Are you sure that you know who has provided certification?

- Cloning of your profile – The SRA has suggested that firms should conduct regular internet searches of their identity;
- Imposter law firms (see also para. 3.1.4 in CML Lenders' Handbook – December 2014 version);
- Credibility of valuation advisers and valuation; and
- Property history – Rapid sales or variations in value?
- If you are not familiar with the conveyancers on the other side(s) of the transaction you should check their status and identity using the relevant professional directory.

2.19.8   See also the SRA website for any current versions of the 'warning card' on money laundering and property fraud.

2.19.9   Close attention needs to be paid to the duty of confidentiality if the firm is acting contemporaneously for a buyer and a lender. The professional position is as set out in chapter 4 of the Code. If there is any change in the purchase price, or if the firm becomes aware of any other information that the lender might reasonably be expected to think important in deciding whether, or on what terms, it will make the mortgage advance, the duty to the lender requires the firm to pass on such information to them, but with the consent of the buyer as a result of the duty of confidentiality that is owed to them. If the buyer will not agree to the information being given to the lender, then there will be a conflict between the firm's duty of confidentiality to the buyer on the one hand and the duty to act in the best interests of the lender on the other. The firm will then have to cease acting for the lender, and to consider carefully whether it could continue to act for the buyer.

2.20   Financial Conduct Authority ('FCA')

2.20.1   The Financial Services Agency ('FSA') was replaced by a combination of the Prudential Regulation Authority and the Financial Conduct Authority ('FCA') in April 2013. The more relevant of these bodies for solicitors' firms is the FCA to which most firms are accountable for some of their activities, namely the handling of investment business and advising on insurance under provisions relating to 'insurance mediation'. We are therefore included on the FCA's 'exempt professional firm' ('EPF') register and the Financial Services compliance officer is [name].

2.20.2   For the most part we are required to notify clients of our authorisation to provide certain services such as advice on the disposal of investments or the need for insurance in certain circumstances. In addition, you are required to provide the client with a 'demands and needs statement' wherever you are advising them to obtain insurance, on which see Appendix 22.

2.20.3   It is important to stress, however, that we are not permitted under the limited scope of our SRA authorisation in this area to provide mainstream investment advice and would be committing a criminal offence under the Financial Services and Markets Act 2000 if we were to do so. If a client does ask for a recommendation of a suitable financial adviser [*state your approach or any established contacts, if any, or explain the operation of your financial services department if you are one of the firms that offer this service*].

Consumer Credit Licences

2.20.4   A significant change was made to the licensing of consumer credit activity on the 1st April 2014 when the FCA succeeded the Office of Fair Trading ('OFT') as the supervisory and licensing body under the Consumer Credit Act 1974 for these purposes. Whereas the OFT had been content to permit law firms to undertake consumer credit litigation under the auspices of the so-called 'Part XX exemption (which exempts professional firms from the need to be regulated by the FCA if their consumer credit activities are incidental to their main areas of professional work) the FCA has taken a harder line approach which has made it more likely that law firms will need to be directly regulated by the FCA in relation to this aspect of their work, in addition to the SRA.

2.20.5   In the light of this development [*we have become/have applied to become FCA regulated as a firm that undertakes a significant amount of debt recovery work/in relation to our credit control and debt recovery processes*].

Part 4:   Client service

2.21   Complaints

2.21.1   We try hard to provide an excellent service to our clients. We hope that we will meet or exceed clients' expectations so that they will not feel the need to complain, but it has to be accepted that clients will sometimes do so, possibly because we have done something wrong or not done something that we should have done. Where this is the case and the complaint is merited, we need to take appropriate action such as offering the client an apology, a goodwill payment or compensation and learning from our mistakes. Our complaints procedure is available on request and should be offered to a client in circumstances where it seems likely that they might want it . The person responsible for this policy is [*name or title*] who is referred to in this policy as the ['*Client Care Manager/Partner*'].

Issues likely to result in complaints

2.21.2   Everyone needs to be aware of how a client may perceive our service so that any potential dissatisfaction can be prevented. Be aware that a client may give indications that he or she is not happy without wanting to use the word 'complaint', for example comments such as 'I was surprised by' or 'I was not expecting' can be an early warning and a complaint may be avoided by talking to the client at an early stage. The Legal Ombudsman has provided some useful information about the types of complaint that are referred to his office. We need to be particularly careful to avoid the following:

- Clients were not advised about alternative funding options which were available;
- Clients were not told about disbursements;
- Costs were more than the estimate but the client was not notified in advance;
- Delay;
- Discrimination;
- Errors in the bill;
- Failure to advise;
- Failure to follow instructions;
- Failure to keep the client informed of progress on their case/matter;
- Failure to progress the client's case or matter;
- Failure to provide information about costs;
- Failure to respond to telephone calls, e-mails or letters;
- Information was disclosed to a third party without the client's consent;
- Loss of, or damage to, documents, the client's property or the file;
- Refusing or failing to release files or papers;
- Something was charged more than once; and
- VAT was charged when it should not have been.

What is a complaint?

2.21.3   The Code now defines a complaint as being any expression of dissatisfaction that the complainant has suffered (or may do so) financial loss, distress, inconvenience or other detriment (see Glossary to SRA Handbook). However, a client may have a justifiable cause of complaint if the service they receive falls below our usual standard, even if it does not meet this threshold. Common sense suggests that problems that are immediately resolved (as where you point out to a client a letter confirming information that they claim not to have received) are not the sort of complaint that should be notified under this procedure. Please also bear in mind that the Legal Ombudsman will, in certain circumstances, entertain complaints from certain related parties who are non-clients of the firm and from people who have unreasonably been denied a service or offered a service inappropriately.

What you should do if someone complains

2.21.4   Everyone in the practice who has received training is authorised to deal initially with some complaints. These are known as 'informal' complaints. Specifically you are authorised to deal with an expression of dissatisfaction in relation to service standards – for example, a client says you have failed to respond to a letter or e-mail.

2.21.5   If an expression of dis-satisfaction can be resolved to the client's satisfaction at first instance, there is no need to do anything further.

Formal complaints

2.21.6   If the person raising the issue is not satisfied with the way you have dealt with their complaint initially, you must refer it for formal consideration as a 'formal' complaint. The following sorts of complaint must in any event be referred for internal investigation straight away:

- Any complaint raising issues of potential misconduct or negligence;
- Any complaint alleging discrimination or a breach of our policy on equality and diversity; and
- Any expression of dis-satisfaction which is made in writing
- When a complaint is passed directly to [*name or title*] and [*he/she*] will send the person a copy of our complaints procedure.

2.21.7   All formal complaints are recorded on a complaints monitoring form and held centrally by the ['*Client Care Manager/Partner*']. (S)he will open a file for every complaint, so that it is dealt with separately from a client's case or matter file.

2.21.8   The ['*Client Care Manager/Partner*'] will investigate complaints thoroughly and impartially, obtaining and considering evidence objectively. (S)he will respond to the client within the timeframe below:

Action	Timescale
Acknowledge complaint in writing and send a copy of the complaints procedure	Within two working days
Investigate the issues	Within 14 days of receiving the complaint whenever possible
Invite the person making the complaint to a meeting or to discuss the issues by telephone	On conclusion of investigation
Confirm the outcome of the meeting or telephone conversation in writing	Within three working days
If a meeting/telephone discussion is not possible or required: Investigate the issues and write to the person with the outcome	Within 21 days
Review and close the complaint	Within 8 weeks of receiving the complaint

2.21.9   If it is not possible to adhere to the deadlines indicated above, the ['*Client Care Manager/Partner*'] must write to the person raising the issues explaining why and providing a new date by which he or she will receive further contact. The ['*Client Care Manager/Partner*'] will:

- Attempt to meet the client's concerns;
- Identify the causes of the complaint;
- Offer an appropriate apology/redress/compensation/goodwill payment; and
- Instigate corrective action if appropriate, which may involve training, disciplinary action and/or changing office procedures.

2.21.10 At the conclusion of the internal investigation, the ['*Client Care Manager/Partner*'] will remind clients that they may ask the Legal Ombudsman to investigate, usually within six months.

2.21.11 The ['*Client Care Manager/Partner*'] will conduct an annual review of complaints received and provide the [*Risk Manager/COLP*] with a copy of the report.

2.22 Client feedback

2.22.1 To help us ensure that we provide services in ways that meet or exceed our clients' expectations, we invite [*all/a percentage of/a selection of*] clients to provide us with feedback by sending them a client questionnaire (see Appendix 14).

2.22.2 If a client is likely to instruct us on one or two cases or matters during a year, you should send out a client feedback form with the final letter at the end of each transaction. If a client is likely to instruct us on multiple matters during a year then you should send out a client feedback form every six months [*or vary if less frequent*].

2.22.3 If a client is of strategic importance (defined as a client billed more than £[*specify*] per year), in addition to sending out the client satisfaction form the ['*Client Care Manager/Partner*'] will offer to visit the client [*annually/every six months*].

Processing feedback questionnaires

2.22.4 Fee earners:

- Insert the file reference on the questionnaire; and
- Send it with a reply-paid envelope to the client with the final bill or the closing letter.

Returned questionnaires:

- Are sent to the ['*Client Care Manager/Partner*'] when the post is sorted; and
- A copy of a completed questionnaire is provided to the fee-earner.

2.22.5　The ['*Client Care Manager/Partner*'] carries out an annual analysis of all feedback received. A copy of his/her report is provided to all [*heads of department/partners/senior managers*] so that good practice can be shared and any required improvements can be planned and implemented.

2.22.6　A copy of the firm's complaints handling policy is [*on the intranet/available at (specify) – see Appendix 13*].

2.23　Legal aid

2.23.1　The firm is committed to the provision of a service to legally aided clients and holds contracts to do so in the areas of [*specify*]. The Contract Liaison Manager (LAA Standard Contract clause 2.3) is [*name*]. For the list of legal aid supervisors, see Section 1: 'Welcome to the firm'.

2.23.2　As we have a contract with the Legal Aid Agency, you should signpost people to other services where there is another practice or organisation who would deal with the client's enquiry more effectively, for example where:

- We cannot take on the work involved as a result of such issues as work overload or time limits; or
- The person needs advice or representation in a category of law in which we do not offer services.

2.23.3　The process of 'signposting' applies when non-clients approach us about legal aid services that we are unable or unwilling to provide, in which case we route them to other sources of advice or information. If we are unable to assist a member of the public, we should provide them with appropriate contact details. There is no need to keep records of signposting.

[*If you have identified firms of solicitors or other agencies to whom you send clients, you should include their details here or in a separate list.*]

2.23.4　If the person is likely to be eligible for legal aid, you may provide the *www.gov.uk/legal-aid* website address and/or for family, debt, benefits, housing, education or discrimination problems, the Civil Legal Advice call centre telephone number should be given [0845 345 4345 minicom 0845 609 6677] so that the person can find the most appropriate source of legal advice.

2.23.5   The Standard Contract Specification defines the transfer of an existing client in a current matter to another firm of solicitors as a referral. This might happen when conflict of interest becomes apparent after the start of the case, or because of professional embarrassment. Where the client is legally aided, you will need to ensure that the new firm has a legal aid contract.

2.23.6   In these circumstances we are under a duty to act in our client's best interests at all times and therefore only refer clients to other organisations that we believe will support our commitment to quality. Please note that paid-for referrals (see 3.20) are not permitted under the LAA Standard Contract clause 6 or O(9.6) in the Code of Conduct.

2.23.7   You must discuss with the client why it is appropriate to make a referral, ask if he/she has any preference and explain any cost implications, as far as possible. If there are any cost implications, you must confirm them in writing.

2.23.8   In order to identify referral patterns and needs for new services, you must record referrals on the central register. This records who made the referral, to whom and the reason for it. If it is not possible to find a suitable firm or agency, it must be noted.

2.23.9   The client should be invited to give feedback on the service received. If the client provides feedback, you should also record that on the central register.

SECTION 2

POLICIES AND STANDARDS

PART B: INTRANET FORMAT

> This is an alternative format for section 2 of the Manual dealing with policies and structures. For guidelines in its possible application and introductory drafting notes see the Introduction and pages 11–22 above.

This guide serves to:

- Summarise our approach to all work done within the firm and to set out details of the standards that we set for ourselves; and
- Provide a 'route map' to the more detailed policies and processes that are already contained within this intranet site and also to various relevant external sources.

Suggestions for improvements, updates or corrections are always appreciated and should be addressed to the appropriate [*partner/director/manager*] for that topic. If you are unsure as to the appropriate point of contact or what is required of you please consult [*name or title*].

You may also need to consult the related documents on the intranet dealing with:

- Case management;
- Office facilities;
- Staff handbook; and
- Accounts.

For more details on the responsibilities for updating the various parts of the Office

Manual see the 'Welcome to [*firm's name*]' document at [*give details of where to locate this on the intranet or elsewhere*].

Importance of compliance

We live and practise in an increasingly compliance-based professional and business culture. Failure to comply with the requirements of the regulators and statutes governing the conduct of solicitors could lead to various unwelcome consequences for the firm, including:

- Negligence claims by clients and others;
- Disciplinary action by the Solicitors Regulation Authority (the 'SRA');
- Increased premiums for our professional indemnity insurance;
- In the case of conveyancing, removal from lenders' panels;
- Reputational harm; and
- Criminal liability for the firm or for its personnel.

It follows that compliance with the practice's policies and procedures is a requirement of all personnel and failure to do so may be regarded as a matter of serious misconduct, which may lead to disciplinary action including termination of employment.

The [*partners/directors*] are committed to keeping all of the policies and procedures that comprise the Office Manual under continual review to ensure that improvements are made where possible. We are also committed to the provision of appropriate training so that everyone is properly trained to meet all of their responsibilities. If you feel unsure of what is expected of you, or how to do any element of your job, please consult [*a partner/your supervisor/your head of department/other*].

No.	Issue	Links
1	**An introduction to the firm**	
	To see a brief history of the firm and for details of our management structure see the 'Welcome to [firm's name]' document which forms part of our staff induction package.	Link to introductory part of Office Manual: Welcome to [Firm's name]
	For details of the terms of your employment, including your entitlement to benefits and other such details, and how we arrange training and our review processes, see the Staff Handbook.	Link to Section 6: Staff Handbook

2	**Our objectives as a firm**	
	We are committed to providing excellent service to our clients in terms of:	
	• Expertise – The firm is organised into specialist departments and it is important that all client work is undertaken within the appropriate department; • Concern – Our clients should feel that we are fully committed to providing them with the best service possible, and that advising them is something that matters to each and every one of us; and • Efficiency – One of the best ways to show concern is to be proactive on matters for which you are responsible and to communicate in a manner that is timely, intelligible and helpful.	
	[The firm provides a service to private paying and legally aided clients alike.] As evidence of our commitment to providing a quality service to clients we *[have been awarded/are in the process of applying for recognition under]* the Law Society's Lexcel scheme – a quality management award that is subject to independent adjudication. *[The firm holds the 'SQM' as administered by the Legal Aid Agency. We also hold a legal aid contract.]*	
3	**Professional standards and conduct**	
	[Name of firm] conducts itself in strict accordance with the SRA Handbook, which includes the SRA Code of Conduct ('the Code of Conduct') and also the SRA Accounts Rules. Please note that the rules of the SRA generally extend to all personnel working within the firm and not just the solicitors, as was previously the case. The SRA has indicated, however, that in relation to the steps it might take against non-solicitor members of staff 'the impact will vary depending on the nature of the work and the responsibility of the employee concerned.'	Link to www.sra.org.uk/ rules Link to 'SRA Principles 2011' in the Handbook, section 3.1
	Whatever your precise duties, it is important that you adopt the highest professional standards and you do not compromise the integrity of the firm in any actions you take either within your work for the firm or in the manner in which you conduct yourself in your personal life.	
	You are also required to notify *[name or title]* in the event that you are subject to any criminal enquiry other than regulatory offences such as parking.	
	There are various specific duties that are owed towards the SRA under the Code of Conduct, including obligations to co-operate with them (and with the Legal Ombudsman) and not to deter complaints.	

4	**Equality and diversity**	
	The firm has adopted a policy dealing with equality and diversity, as referred to in chapter 2 of the Code of Conduct. The policy contains:	Link to full policy – see Document 1 at the end of this section
	• A prohibition against acts of discrimination; and • Details of the *[partners'/directors']* commitment to achieve equality and diversity in all of the firm's dealings with clients, colleagues, external suppliers (such as counsel) and others with whom we have professional dealings.	Link also to chapter 2 of Code of Conduct if]possible and consider link to Equality Act 2010
	Training in this topic *[has been/will be provided and will be updated as appropriate. (Training in the topic, covering your policy also, is a Lexcel requirement – see 4.2.d.)]*	
5	**Client confidentiality**	
	One of the most important duties owed by solicitors and their staff to clients is the duty to maintain the confidentiality of all information received in relation to client matters, whatever its source. It might be tempting to discuss client matters outside the firm, but to do so could lead to disciplinary action against the firm by the SRA and so is likely to be treated as a serious disciplinary offence by the *[partners/directors]*.	Link to O(4.1) if possible
	There are very limited exceptions to the rule requiring us to safeguard client confidentiality, most obviously in relation to money laundering and terrorist financing, on which see section 6 of this document.	
	As a result of the approach of the SRA to the issues of conflicts of interests you are required to notify your *[head of department/supervisor/other]* if you have any personal knowledge of or any close connection to the client or others involved in any matter that you are working on (see Conflicts at section 6 of this document).	
	You should not discuss a client's affairs outside the office except with the express consent of a *[partner/director]* (other than in the course of carrying out the client's instructions).	

| 5 | Other than in the normal course of business you should not name clients or inform or confirm to a third party that the firm acts for a person unless that client has expressly given consent. Please note that this extends to enquiries from the police as to whether we are acting for a particular individual or concern – an increasing number of law firms report 'fishing expeditions' by the police along these lines. Our duty in law to respond to police enquiries is limited to our Anti-Money Laundering policy – see Section 15.

For similar reasons you must not answer any questions from the press or even confirm if we are acting for a particular client, let alone provide their address. Please refer any such enquiry to *[a partner/your supervisor/other]*.

Please also exercise care in how you dispose of unwanted correspondence and documents (including drafts and unwanted photocopies). Any papers, etc. which identify a client must be disposed of confidentially. *[Explain how confidential waste should be disposed of if special arrangements are in place.]*

Should you become aware or suspect that a breach of confidentiality has occurred, you must report the details to *[name or title]* immediately.

Please also be wary of conversations about client matters, both in the reception area and outside the firm (especially with mobile phone conversations in public places). Also be careful of carrying files that show information on the cover that would identify what we are doing and for whom (e.g. Mrs McGregor, 43 Acacia Avenue, Divorce). Do not leave files in unlocked cars, and in no circumstances in cars overnight. | Link to O(4.1) if possible |
| 6 | **Conflicts of interests**

The firm will not act where there is a conflict of interests as defined by chapter 3 of the Code of Conduct, or there is a significant risk that such a conflict might arise at a future date. The Code distinguishes between 'own' conflicts, where the client's interests could be seen to conflict with the interests of the firm or anyone within it, and client conflicts.

You must declare to *[name or title]* any personal interest – family, commercial, financial or otherwise – that might lead the client to suspect that we have not acted in their proper interests. This would also extend to any public office appointments you hold, | Link to chapter 3 of Code of Conduct if possible

Link also to relevant section of Case Management Manual (3.5) |

6	such as school governorships when we are acting against a school or college. Such conflicts are referred to as 'own' conflicts in the Code of Conduct.	
	Certain exceptions to the rule against acting where there is a conflict of interests exist in relation to client conflicts (but never own conflicts). These are:	
	• Where there is a substantially common interest between two or more clients; • Where a retainer can be agreed with two or more clients to confine the firm's role to aspects of the instructions that are not, or are not likely to become, in dispute; or • In acting for different parties with their informed and written consent where they are competing for the same asset and the conditions stipulated in the Code of Conduct are met.	
	Conflict searches A conflict search must always be carried out on our client database before new instructions to act for a new client or on a new matter are accepted. Remember that the quality of result is as effective as the information provided, especially in relation to linked parties (such as directors of companies to be represented).	Provide link to any such instructions and any conflict checking form
	Where there is a question as to whether a conflict of interests does exist the issue must be referred to *[name or title]*.	
	Property conflicts The ability of law firms to act for seller and buyer in the same transaction was curtailed but not ended by the new provisions on this point in the Code of Conduct – likewise in relation to instructions to act for both lender and borrower. The firm's policy on these issues is to be found *[state where]*.	See Appendix 7
	Confidentiality and disclosures In practice, most of the difficult issues to arise under conflicts are those where the conflict is not between clients but where we hold relevant information from another client or matter. Such conflicts of information are the domain of chapter 4 of the SRA Handbook. This provides that:	Link to chapter 4 of Code of Conduct if possible

| 6 | • There is an ongoing duty of confidentiality to clients and former clients that can only be waived in certain exceptional cases or by client consent;
• There is a duty to disclose to all clients all relevant information on that matter of which the fee earner is aware; and
• Work must be declined where the duty of confidentiality to one existing or former client would be put at risk by accepting instructions from another (i.e. the duty of disclosure to the new client would compromise the duty of confidentiality owed to another client or former client).

Information barriers
Information barriers do not overcome conflicts of interests but can permit us to act, or to continue to act, where the problem is one of relevant information being held in one part of the practice and it is withheld from another. Key to understanding their operation is that the duty to disclose all relevant information to clients – at O(4.2) of the Code of Conduct – is stated to be a personal obligation and confined to lawyers, i.e. the duty is to disclose that which that lawyer is aware of rather than the firm. You cannot therefore be censured for not disclosing issues that others in the firm might be aware of but you are not.

At an informal level this might involve ensuring that a new member of staff with experience of working for an opponent at another firm will not be assigned to a relevant matter. The firm does not operate under the formal information barriers employed in the largest commercial firms. *[or clarify if they do apply]*

Training
Training on the issue of conflicts will be provided to all relevant personnel. *[This is a Lexcel requirement – a training module is available via the Infolegal website]* | |
| 7 | **Environmental policy**

[Name of firm] is committed to acting responsibly in relation to environmental issues. The firm is working towards lessening its direct impact on the environment through its business practices and through the services it offers.

[For more information on this topic see www.legalsectoralliance.co.uk.] | Link to any environmental policy if you have adopted one |

8	**Part 2: Risk management**	
	Our approach to risk management	
	Risk is a fact of life for all professional and commercial organisations. The risk of undesired or unwelcome developments can never be eliminated, but it can be properly managed so as to avoid, reduce or mitigate that risk. Risk management is addressed as follows:	The former classification of risks as strategic, operational and environmental does not appear in Lexcel v6 but most firms will find it helpful to retain it. Lexcel now follows the SRA's view of risk as tends to be required in its risk review. Our recommended format at appendix 6 also retains this classification. A compliance plan is also required by Lexcel – see Appendix 5.
	• *Strategic* – The risks implicit in business developments are considered in the business planning processes adopted by the partners. *[State any processes whereby the business plan is shared with or communicated to staff if required.]*	
	• *Operational and regulatory* – Our client service standards, especially as set out in the accompanying Case Management Manual, address the established principles of risk management in law firms and our regulatory obligations as set out in the SRA Handbook and more generally.	
	• *Environmental* – We have all the same obligations as any other professional or commercial concern arising from our activities as employers of people and occupiers of premises. Our various obligations in relation to the use of our office facilities are set out in the accompanying Office Procedures Manual.	
	[See risk review/risk register matrix format at Appendix 6.]	
9	**Compliance Officer for Legal Practice ('COLP') and Compliance Officer for Finance and Administration ('COFA'): Reporting of non-compliances**	Link to r.8 of the SRA Authorisation Rules if possible
	It should be noted that the SRA Handbook introduced for all law firms an enhanced duty to report to the SRA any 'material' breach of the SRA rules, including the Accounts Rules. There is also an obligation to keep records of all breaches of the professional rules. Failure to make the necessary reports to the SRA will amount to a professional offence with potentially significant consequences for the firm and the personnel concerned.	The continued need for COLP and COFA in the smallest firms is now subject to a review by the SRA (November 2014). In the event that the requirement is relaxed it would be advisable to maintain the roles if not the titles as
	The firm's COLP is *[name, and add details of deputy if relevant – more likely in larger firms]* and the COFA is *[ditto]*.	
	Where you are unsure whether any problem that arises is relevant to the Code of Conduct or any other part of the SRA	

9	Handbook please consult with either of the above depending on the nature of the possible breach.	the concept of self-regulation is very clearly here to stay
	You should note that there is a duty on all personnel to co-operate fully with any investigation about any claim for redress (O(10.6)).	
10	**Potential claims against the firm**	
	The firm sets great store by the quality of its work. Nonetheless, errors will occur from time to time. Whatever the problem, delay in reporting it is likely to make things much worse and will be treated as a serious disciplinary issue by the firm. There are also professional obligations to point out certain circumstances to clients (when errors or omissions on our part could mean that they could bring a claim against us).	Link to O(1.16) if possible
	Any mistake or error made whilst acting for a client must be reported to *[name or title]* as soon as it is discovered.	
	The firm is committed to helping lawyers to resolve situations where errors have been made and will be supportive, providing that early notification is made.	
11	**SRA Accounts Rules**	
	For the most part compliance with the SRA Accounts Rules ('SAR') is achieved by the [Cashier/Accounts team] who [has/have] expertise in the obligations of how finances must be managed in a law firm. All others are required to follow the provisions of our Accounts Manual, but in addition please note the following issues where fee earners could, inadvertently, cause the firm to breach its obligations to the regulator.	Link to Section 4 of the Office Manual
	Rule 14 of the SRA Accounts Rules covers dealing with client accounts. Of particular relevance are:	
	• Rule 14(1): All client account receipts must be banked 'without delay' which is taken to mean on the same or next working day. Cheques are generally taken from the post when it is opened, but it is possible that the presence of a cheque might have been overlooked, or you may receive a cheque at a meeting with the client or via a hand delivery. It is essential that you forward or hand this cheque over to the *[Accounts Department/Other]* immediately upon receipt by you.	
	• Under Rule 14(3) we are obliged to clear all outstanding client balances 'promptly'. In particular, this means that	

11	unless there are clear and present underlying client instructions to explain why funds are in client account they must be returned to the client as soon as possible. This provision is closely linked to rule 14(5) which provides that law firms may not provide a banking facility to clients, in part because they are not legally permitted to do so under the Financial Services and Markets Act 2000 and in part because law firms could thereby become inadvertently involved in money laundering activities or aiding and abetting perverting the course of justice, as where funds are not being declared in divorce proceedings. It is essential, therefore, that you co-operate with the [Accounts Department/Other] in returning client funds when there is no adequate reason to justify the firm retaining them.	Link to SRA Accounts Rules (14(3)) if possible
	• Finally, rule 14(4) provides that if we are required to retain client monies at the end of a matter for some valid reason (e.g. in respect of possible warranty claims) the client must be informed of this in writing, along with an explanation for the retainer, and this correspondence must be updated at least annually.	
	On occasions we will be left with outstanding client balances where we cannot trace the client or perhaps are even unable to identify the client, as where an organisation has been taken over and it is unclear who the successor concern is. In these circumstances we are required to make reasonable attempts to contact the clients in order to account properly to them. Please note that to bill anything to the file in such circumstances – as for reviews or even the work undertaken in attempting to contact the client – will almost certainly be a breach of the SAR. Such actions have often triggered disciplinary action against firms and, in some cases involving larger amounts, strikings-off of those concerned. Where all reasonable attempts to locate the client have failed we are now permitted (since November 2014) to pay sums of up to £500 to charity, but on the basis that if the client will be refunded in full if they are subsequently identified and located. The charity/ies we use for such purposes is/are [Solicitors Benevolent Fund/other] which has undertaken to return any individual donation in these circumstances. If the figure involved is more than £500 specific SRA consent will be required before such a donation may be made.	
	Finally, please also note that we are required to account to the client for any commission received by the firm in relation to their instructions (e.g. insurance commission), regardless of the amount concerned. Commissions payable to the firm in such circumstances are nonetheless deemed to be 'client money' under SAR rule 12(2.f) and must be dealt with as such.	

12	Data protection	
	The firm's responsibilities under data protection legislation and the rules of conduct of the SRA are set out in our data protection policy. This policy deals with the responsibilities that we are subject to as data handlers and explains how we deal with data subject requests.	Link to DPA 1998
	In addition, the firm is legally and professionally obliged to ensure that it sets out clear procedures on the use of information and data, including the content and format of e-mails and responsible use of the internet. We are also subject to certain contractual commitments in this regard in relation to our access to the Land Registry portal for conveyancing work.	
	Our policy contains an 'acceptable use policy' which all personnel are required to sign. This not only sets out your agreement to use the firm's IT facilities in accordance with its provisions but also indicates your consent to the monitoring of e-mails received and sent by you.	Link to relevant part of Section 5 on Office Facilities and IT
13	Whistle-blowing	This is now a Lexcel requirement: see 4.9. The SRA intention in this provision is probably linked to O(10.7) and the obligation not to prevent anyone approaching the SRA or the Legal Ombudsman
	We have a 'whistle-blowing policy' as suggested by IB(10.10) of the Code of Conduct. This can be found in the Staff Handbook.	
	Please bear in mind that the operation of such policies in a law firm is still subject to our duties of client confidentiality. If, for example, we are representing a local business that has been charged with pollution offences the legislation would not excuse any partner or staff member approaching the press to tell them that the client had admitted their guilt to us.	
14	Health and safety	
	The [partners/directors] are committed to complying with the Health and Safety at Work etc. Act 1974, as amended. This involves a commitment to providing a safe place of work. Details of the firm's procedures under this policy are to be found in [the Office Procedures Manual/Section 5 of the Manual.]	Link to relevant part of Section 5 on Office Facilities and IT
	Your attention is drawn to your responsibilities to support this policy as by taking proper care of your working conditions and conducting yourself responsibly in relation to your colleagues and others.	

15	**Part 3: Financial crime**	
	Money laundering and terrorist financing	
	Money laundering arises as an issue whenever we encounter 'criminal conduct' that results in 'criminal property'. The key definitions are to be found in section 340 of the Proceeds of Crime Act 2002 ('POCA'):	Link to fuller policy – see Document 2 at the end of this section
	• Criminal conduct is anything which is an offence in the UK or would be if committed here; and • Criminal property is property that constitutes 'a person's benefit from criminal conduct or it represents such a benefit' (in whole or in part).	Consider also links to POCA, TA and MLR
	You must also remember the linked issue of terrorist financing which has very similar offences and the same need for disclosures to the authorities in certain circumstances. The former Serious Organised Crime Agency ('SOCA') was replaced by the National Crime Agency ('NCA') in 2013.	
	Disclosures to the NCA	
	In order to avoid the risk of personal liability any partner/director or member of staff (whatever your role) may need to make a disclosure of their concerns. The law involved is quite complex and will be covered in our training programme, but there is sometimes a duty to disclose as a result of information obtained in the course of practice and, in other situations, a need to do so in order to gain a defence to a possible charge.	
	As soon as you think that you have a problem under this heading you are encouraged to talk to *[the firm's Money Laundering Reporting Officer ('MLRO')/your head of department/other]*.	
	If a formal disclosure is required you will always discharge your responsibility to do so by contacting the MLRO as above. This will cover you against any non-disclosure liability as long as you follow any instructions given to you by the MLRO. You would make a formal report of your concerns [set out how – a form or e-mail?].	

15	*Identity checking under the Money Laundering Regulations 2007 ('MLR')*	
	Quite distinct from whether money laundering or terrorist activity is suspected we are obliged by the MLR to conduct customer due diligence ('CDD') on clients. These provisions do not apply, however, to certain areas of litigation, especially when we act for legally aided clients. The policy of the firm is therefore to undertake ID checks as required by our policy in all matters other than legal aid crime cases. *Or specify whether the MLR apply to your firm at all or state any other exceptions.*	
	Where the requirements apply not only must we, under reg.5 of the MLR, establish the identity of clients but we are also obliged to:	
	• Establish the identity of anyone associated with the client by way of 'beneficial ownership'; • Satisfy ourselves as to the 'nature and purpose' of the instructions; and • Subject our clients to 'ongoing monitoring'.	
	Beneficial ownership involves, in simple terms, an interest in more than 25 per cent of the entity involved. Any situation where we are acting for an agent raises similar issues in relation to the principal.	
	Ongoing monitoring involves maintaining up-to-date evidence of our clients and also considering whether instructions received are consistent with our knowledge and expectations of that client.	
	There are other obligations under the MLR which are spelt out in more detail under our full policy, including the need to maintain a training programme for all relevant personnel.	
	Non-compliance with the MLR is a criminal offence. In addition, the Law Society, through the SRA, has been nominated as the 'supervisory body' for solicitors in relation to the MLR, making a failure to conduct appropriate checks a matter of professional discipline under O(7.5) of the Code of Conduct.	
	Failure to comply with the Manual could lead to formal	

15	disciplinary action being taken against the individual as part of the firm's disciplinary procedures. In addition, please bear in mind that you could be exposing yourself to the risk of disciplinary or even criminal liability: you have been warned! If you require training on this topic contact *[name or title]*.	
16	**The Bribery Act and accepting gifts from clients** The Bribery Act 2010 introduced significant new obligations on organisations to prohibit, and monitor for, improper payments. The *[partners/directors]* are committed to conducting the business of the firm in an honest and ethical manner and, in particular, in accordance with the ten principles of legal practice which underpin the SRA Handbook. These include, most basically, a duty to uphold the rule of law (Principle 1). It follows that we will never offer, pay or receive any improper payment, such as a personal cash payment or an inappropriate gift to an individual to place the work for their organisation with this firm. For our more detailed policy on this topic, including the linked issues of client entertaining and accepting gifts from clients, see (link)	Link to Bribery Act 2010 and policy (document 3) Link to Principle 1 if possible
17	**Mortgage fraud** There are considerable risks to all law firms involved with conveyancing work, whether commercial or residential. The risks are that much the greater when acting for a buyer who is proceeding with a mortgage that they may have obtained through fraud, but firms acting for sellers are also prone to fraudulent activity as by fraudsters impersonating the rightful owners so as to sell or re-mortgage the property.	Link to Document 4 below. This is now a 'should' item in Lexcel v6 but will need to be in place when conveyancing work is undertaken.
18	**Financial Conduct Authority ('FCA')** The Financial Services Agency ('FSA') was replaced by a combination of the Prudential Regulation Authority and the Financial Conduct Authority ('FCA') in April 2013. The more relevant of these bodies for solicitors' firms is the FCA to which most firms are accountable for some of their activities, namely the handling of investment business and advising on insurance under provisions relating to 'insurance mediation'. We are therefore included on the FCA's 'exempt professional firm' ('EPF') register and the Financial Services Compliance Officer is *[name]*.	Consider links to Conduct of Business Rule in SRA Handbook if possible, also relevant part of the Case Management Manual on insurance mediation (3.19)

18	For the most part we are required to notify clients of our authorisation to provide certain services such as advice on the disposal of investments or the need for insurance in certain circumstances and do so through our *[client care letter/terms of business/other]*. In addition, you are required to provide the client with a 'demands and needs statement' whenever you are advising them to obtain insurance, as set out in the relevant section of the Case Management Manual. It is important to stress, however, that we are not permitted under the limited scope of our SRA authorisation in this area to provide mainstream investment advice and would be committing a criminal offence under the Financial Services and Markets Act 2000 if we were to do so. If a client does ask for a recommendation of a suitable financial adviser *[state your approach to any established contacts or provide link in next column or explain more if you do provide this service.]*	
19	**Part 4: Client service** **Complaints and client feedback** A copy of the firm's complaints handling policy is on the intranet. The *[Client Care Partner/other]* is *[insert name]*. Every engagement letter must have a clear statement pointing out to the client that there is a right to complain about the service provided or the level of the bill and to whom any complaint should be addressed – in the first instance, the matter handler. Please note that it is not only a breach of the firm's procedures to suppress a complaint but also potentially a disciplinary issue under the Code of Conduct. The Legal Ombudsman ('LeO') replaced earlier complaints handling arrangements in 2010. Complaints to LeO are only open to individuals and 'micro-enterprises' such as companies with no more than ten people or a turnover of £2m. and so it follows that the LeO service is not available to many of the firm's commercial clients. They could complain to the SRA instead but we are not obliged to point this out to them. The complexities of what we do have to tell our clients, and when, makes the use of the standard engagement precedents all the more important.	Link to complaints policy – see Document 5 at the end of this section Link to O(10.7) Link to Legal Ombudsman website

20	**Legal aid**	
	The firm is committed to the provision of a service to legally aided clients and holds contracts to do so in the areas of *[specify]*. The Contract Liaison Manager (LAA Standard Contract clause 2.3) is *[name]*. For the list of legal aid supervisors, see Section 1: 'Welcome to the firm'.	

The firm is committed to the provision of a service to legally aided clients and holds contracts to do so in the areas of *[specify]*. The Contract Liaison Manager (LAA Standard Contract clause 2.3) is *[name]*. For the list of legal aid supervisors, see Section 1: 'Welcome to the firm'.

As we have a contract with the Legal Aid Agency, you should signpost people to other services where there is another practice or organisation who would deal with the client's enquiry more effectively, for example where:

- We cannot take on the work involved as a result of such issues as work overload or time limits; or
- The person needs advice or representation in a category of law in which we do not offer services.

The process of 'signposting' applies when non-clients approach us about legal aid services that we are unable or unwilling to provide, in which case we route them to other sources of advice or information. If we are unable to assist a member of the public, we should provide them with appropriate contact details. There is no need to keep records of signposting.

[If you have identified firms of solicitors or other agencies to whom you send clients, you should include their details here or in a separate list.]

If the person is likely to be eligible for legal aid, you may provide the *www.gov.uk/legal-aid* website address and/or for family, debt, benefits, housing, education or discrimination problems, the Community Legal Advice call centre telephone number should be given [0845 345 4345 minicom 0845 609 6677] so that the person can find the most appropriate source of legal advice.

The Standard Contract Specification defines the transfer of an existing client in a current matter to another firm of solicitors as a referral. This might happen when conflict of interest becomes apparent after the start of the case, or because of professional embarrassment. Where the client is legally aided, you will need to ensure that the new firm has a legal aid contract.

We are under a duty to act in our client's best interests at all times and therefore only refer clients to other organisations

20	that we believe will support our commitment to quality (as is the case under O(6.1) in any event. Please note that paid-for referrals (see 3.20) are not permitted under the LAA Standard Contract clause 6 or O(9.6) in the Code of Conduct.	
	You must discuss with the client why it is appropriate to make a referral, ask if he/she has any preference and explain any cost implications, as far as possible. If there are any cost implications, you must confirm them in writing.	
	In order to identify referral patterns and needs for new services, you must record referrals on the central register. This records who made the referral, to whom and the reason for it. If it is not possible to find a suitable firm or agency, it must be noted.	
	The client should be invited to give feedback on the service received. If the client provides feedback, you should also record that on the central register.	

Appendix: Policies referred to above and not dealt with elsewhere in the Office Manual

Document 1: Equality and diversity (see Section 4)

This policy primarily addresses the 'protected characteristics' of the Equality Act 2010:

- Age;
- Disability;
- Gender reassignment;
- Marriage and civil partnership;
- Pregnancy and maternity;
- Race;
- Religion or belief;
- Sex; and
- Sexual orientation.

[Name of firm] is committed to avoiding discrimination on any of the above grounds in its dealings with clients and potential clients, other solicitors, barristers and third parties, and in relation to all current [partners/directors] and employees, including applicants for positions within the firm and all related recruitment activity. The [partners/directors] are also committed to promoting equality and diversity in all aspects of the firm's operations.

In addition to the firm's obligations not to discriminate against, harass or victimise those with a disability the firm is also subject to a duty to make reasonable adjustments to prevent those employees, partners and clients who are disabled from being at a disadvantage in comparison with those who are not.

Liability for acts of discrimination might extend beyond the individuals concerned to the owners of the firm. For that reason any breach is likely to be regarded as a serious disciplinary offence that might justify instant dismissal. Any complaint that a breach of this policy has occurred should be addressed to [*name or title*] without delay.

Training has been held on this topic and on this policy and will be repeated as necessary, to include the actual contents of this policy.

Disability considerations

Signing facilities will be provided by the firm at its own expense for clients who are in need of them. If a client has mobility problems [*state your arrangements here: do you have disabled access? If so, are you also able to offer toilet facilities? The primary obligation under the Equality Act is to make reasonable adjustments for disabled people, but limited to clients, colleagues and job applicants (i.e. not third parties such as counsel or opponents acting in person). If it is not reasonable for you to make the necessary adjustments to your offices you should consider offering home visits within a reasonable radius at no extra charge – to charge a disabled client who cannot access your offices more for your time in visiting them elsewhere could be seen to be direct discrimination against them on grounds of their disability. Much the same considerations apply to the issue of signing facilities.*]

Counsel and experts

If a client expresses a preference of an adviser that is based on any of the above grounds you should try to persuade them to modify their instructions. If they refuse to do so we may have to cease to act for them further.

Monitoring and review

This policy will be monitored periodically by the firm to judge its effectiveness and diversity monitoring will be conducted as required by the SRA through a questionnaire-based exercise. The firm has appointed [*name or title*] to be responsible for the operation of the policy. We will monitor the ethnic and gender composition of existing staff and applicants for jobs (including promotion) and the number of people with disabilities within these groups.

Document 2: Money laundering and terrorist financing (see Section 15)
Introduction

The firm must safeguard against becoming involved in the processing of illegal or improper gains for clients. As a professional practice the firm is particularly attractive to criminals wishing to convert gains to a respectable status. It is the policy of the firm not to assist them to do so. Breach of this policy could in any event be an unlawful act on the part of anyone concerned and could place the firm and/or its representatives at risk of criminal and/or civil proceedings.

We are also obliged to establish the identity of our clients as a result of the Money Laundering Regulations 2007 and also to screen all work to ensure that:

- We know the identities of other related parties who might be involved (those with a beneficial interest);
- We extend these searches to anyone paying us more than £10,000 by way of an 'occasional transaction'; and
- We are satisfied that we are aware of the nature and purpose of the instructions and that the work will not put us at risk of involvement in illegal or unprofessional conduct.

The partners have determined that all work conducted by the firm should be regarded as being covered by the Money Laundering Regulations with the consequential need to conduct identity checks in all areas of our practice. (*Or state if your practice is outside the scope of the MLR 2007 or any exceptions to certain areas of work in a mixed practice. If unclear on this issue see chapter 1 of the Law Society's Practice Note on Money Laundering at paragraph 1.4.5*)

Client checking ('CDD')

Fee earners must ensure that we obtain evidence of identity for all clients as soon as possible after contact is first established between the firm and the potential client, often with the assistance of receptionists and secretaries. The Law Society guidelines make the distinction between 'identification' (being told or coming to know a client's identifying details) and 'verification' (obtaining some evidence which supports this claim of identity). In general 'customer due diligence' (as it is referred to in the Money Laundering Regulations 2007) requires both elements to be addressed. The evidence of identity check must be undertaken by completion of forms ML1 and ML2 (Appendices 8 and 9) which must appear on the matter file in question.

Further guidance is provided here on a number of options. Although these requirements may seem onerous you should bear in mind that these checks are a legal requirement which could be enforced against us if we are in breach and that numerous firms have been penalised for falling victim to launderers and fraudsters. Where fraud is involved quite apart from the distress and inconvenience this will cause to our client this could lead to substantial increases in the firm's indemnity insurance costs: in some cases this has left firms unable to obtain cover at all (or at an affordable price) and has led to the consequential closure of the firm.

- Individual client met in person

  You should ask the client to bring the normal documentation as listed on form ML1 into the office for inspection and copying. The top half of form ML1 must be signed and dated by the person checking the documents along with the Passport/Driving licence checking form (form ML2). When undertaking this process please refer any concerns to a partner/director (e.g. you do not think that the photo is a likeness of the client presenting it). Where we are acting for co-clients we must certify each of them – it is not permissible for one to bring in the documents on the other where the person checking has not met that other client.

- Individual client not met in person

  Please note that every attempt should be made to meet the client in person to verify the evidence provided, but where this is not possible the client should be asked to obtain certification through local solicitors or other professionals. Certification is permissible if received from:

  o Other solicitors in private practice;
  o Accountants in private practice;
  o Mortgage brokers or other agents if regulated by the FCA and well known to us; or

o The Post Office's documentation checking service.

Wherever distant certification is obtained from another professional the adviser must make a check of the validity of the referring firm or organisation in a current directory such as the SRA website and print off the relevant entry if possible and place this on the matter file. Where the referrer is not well known to us you must also phone the person who has provided the certification to check if they did indeed do so: be sure to use the number in the professional directory rather than the number on the notepaper in front of you as that notepaper might be false and therefore part of the 'bogus firm' scam. Where repeat usage is made of a particular referrer (e.g. a mortgage broker who introduces multiple matters to the firm) there is no need to have this copy on every matter file.

Finally, we should also commission, with the client's agreement, an electronic search on the basis of copy documents and details provided.

- Companies

In the case of commercial clients a copy of the certificate of incorporation must be obtained at the outset of the first matter for that client, along with a companies search and evidence of the identity of at least two directors or officers, if possible, unless the representatives are known to the firm and have had personal ID checks undertaken already. Further checks may be needed in the case of non-domiciled companies. It is, in any case, important to check that those who purport to represent an organisation are actually entitled to do so.

PEPs and Sanctions

An electronic search should also be conducted wherever there is a risk that the client or someone else involved in the matter is or could be a 'politically exposed person' ('PEP') or might be on the UN/UK Sanctions list. You should question any client with a foreign connection (including UK passport holders who have recently been based abroad) if they have held a high ranking position in a foreign government or international organisation and/or conduct an electronic search.

Much the same considerations apply to anyone that might, from their activities or profile, appear on one of the sanctions lists. To check this for yourself go to

https://www.gov.uk/government/publications/financial-sanctions-consolidated-list-of-targets.

Third parties

It is becoming increasingly common for third parties to make payments to us, especially as more purchasers in conveyancing transactions obtain assistance from parents or other relatives. The approach of the firm is that the source of funds must always be known about in advance and where the sum is for a significant amount (again, a matter of judgement depending on the circumstances, but always where more than £1000 is to be received) questions must be made as to how that money was acquired. If 'savings' then you do need to profile how this person might have acquired this sum, such as detailing their occupation. Where possible check the information with a Google search and file any useful information that you find and/or request six months of bank statements to look for regular salary payments or unusual and large receipts.

Where more than £10,000 is to be received by us (whether directly from the third party or through the client's account) you must conduct an identity check as if the party was a client, save that it is permissible to undertake an electronic search only if the client or third party prefers. Be sure to maintain any evidence collected on the matter file together with an attendance note detailing what checks you have made and why.

If the client or third party resists your questions you may be apologetic but should point out that the firm has no option but to comply with the duties that are placed upon it by law. If the required information is not forthcoming please consult [*a partner/director/supervisor*] and it may well be that we will have to cease to act.

Form ML1

In line with Law Society advice it is permissible for a partner/director to 'sign in' a client they know well in all cases other than where the CML Handbook applies (even here see 3.1.5 of the Lenders' Handbook). In all cases the 'lawyer certification' part of the form must be ticked by a fee earner (not a secretary) and signed.

Ongoing monitoring

In relation to regular, established clients the firm will compile a directory of standing checks of identities. Even then the current address should always be checked in relation to any future instructions.

For those more occasional clients that have instructed the firm before, the usual CDD process should be conducted if there is a gap of three years since the end of the client's last matter with us, save that it is open to a [*partner/director*] to verify that the client is well known to him/her. Where possible we should be sure to be relying on up to date documents – i.e. passports should be current if possible. The full CDD process should therefore be repeated if possible where a passport has expired and must also be conducted whenever there is any doubt as to the identity of the client or the matter itself.

Records

The firm is obliged to maintain records for at least five years of:

- What has been done for the client; and
- Any disclosures made (completed form reference or name).

Please bear this in mind when deciding a destroy date when archiving files. In addition the firm must maintain ID evidence for at least five years from the end of the 'business relationship' or the close of the 'occasional transaction'.

Cash receipts

The mere fact that a client pays in cash or wishes to do so is not in itself a cause for suspicion. Nonetheless, the larger the intended cash payment, the more likely it is that the client actions are suspect. Substantial amounts of cash might be criminal in origin or are often the result of failure to declare income to HM Revenue and Customs and, as tax evasion, would amount to criminal conduct under the anti-money laundering regime.

The approach to cash receipts is therefore as follows:

- In the absence of any complicating factors the firm will accept sums of up to £500/£1000 in cash (complicating factors could include, most obviously, a capital declaration from a client in receipt of legal aid that they have less than this sum in capital).

- Sums of over £500/£1000 should not be accepted without the permission (to be noted on file) of the Money Laundering Reporting Officer ('MLRO') or, if (s)he is unavailable, another partner. [*Some firms have edited in higher cash limits in relation to their fees taking into account the defence of 'adequate consideration' under s.329 POCA and the frustration of turning away payment of their fees and expenses and having then to pursue them.*]

Where a significantly larger payment than you can accept is offered you must speak to [*name of MLRO*] and may have to complete a report form (ML4) in order that (s)he can consider if a disclosure should be made. Some judgement is needed here as the circumstances will vary from case to case, but it is envisaged that an offer of £??? or more of cash should always be reported by you to the MLRO.

Reporting to the National Crime Agency ('NCA')

A disclosure could be necessary for one of two reasons. First, the Proceeds of Crime Act 2002 (POCA 2002) s.330 imposes a duty to make a disclosure if, in the course of practice in the regulated sector, a person forms a suspicion (or should reasonably have done so) that money laundering is or could be occurring. The position is complicated by the fact that this is stated to be subject to legal professional privilege. The defence of privilege will mean that in most circumstances there is no need for the practice to make a report to the NCA on the basis of instructions received. This is not always the case, however, especially where third parties are involved, so please refer any concerns to [*name of MLRO*] in case a disclosure is required.

You are encouraged to have a discussion with [*name of MLRO*] at any time and you might then need to make a formal report by use of form ML4. Even if (s)he does not share your concerns it is your entitlement to send him/her a completed ML4 as in most cases this will be your defence to a charge that you have committed an offence under POCA.

Secondly, it should be noted that a disclosure might also be necessary to gain a defence to a charge under the principal offences under POCA 2002, ss.327–329, most probably that of 'entering into an arrangement' whereby money laundering is facilitated under s.328. There are similar offences in relation to terrorist financing in the Terrorism Act 2000, ss.15–18. Where a suspicion arises the firm may, subject to the complex provisions relating to legal professional privilege, need to make a disclosure and gain permission to continue to act. The rules on this requirement differ according to work type, so again please contact [name of MLRO] if any concerns arise.

Do not store a completed ML4 report form on the matter file to which it relates. This would create a risk that the client might see the disclosure report, especially if the file is sent out of the office. Please make sure that any of your colleagues who might become involved in the work being done on the file are informed that the issue of a possible disclosure to NCA has arisen so that they may also proceed with caution.

Responsibilities

As Money Laundering Reporting Officer [*name of MLRO*]'s duties are to:

- Ensure that satisfactory internal procedures are maintained;
- Arrange for periodic training for all relevant personnel within the firm;
- Provide advice when consulted on possible reports and receive reports of suspicious circumstances;
- Report such circumstances, if appropriate, to the NCA on behalf of the firm;
- Direct colleagues as to what action to take and not take when suspicion arises and a disclosure is made; and
- Report annually to the partners on the operation of the anti-money laundering policy and procedures.

It is the duty of all personnel within the practice to:

- Attend training arranged within the firm if required to do so;
- Conduct identity checks and other due diligence enquiries unless the MLRO signifies that this is not necessary in the particular case in hand;
- Report without delay all circumstances which could give rise to suspicion that the firm is being involved in some element of the money laundering process for a client;
- Be wary of payment arrangements different from those anticipated or deposits of cash into client account;
- Follow the directions of the MLRO when a disclosure has been made, bearing in mind the personal risk to the adviser of 'tipping off' the client in question either expressly or by implication; and
- Maintain the utmost caution in maintaining confidentiality for the client and the firm when suspicious circumstances arise.

In certain circumstances fee earners/advisers may or must report to the client that a disclosure will be made. They might also sometimes have the option in exceptional circumstances of informing a client that a disclosure has been made concerning another party or even the client themself, notwithstanding the offences of 'tipping off' and 'disclosing an investigation' (POCA 2002, s.333) or, in relation to work outside the regulated sector, 'prejudicing an investigation' (POCA 2002, s.342). There are, of course, significant risks in doing so and in all such cases the advice of the MLRO must be sought and his/her instructions must be closely followed.

Property lawyers should note the source of funds form (ML3) and use it as part of our duty to obtain information on the funds to be used in any purchase [*See appendix 10*].

Other resources

Helpful details on the obligations on all firms in relation to money laundering and terrorist financing can be found on the Law Society website in the Practice Note on these topics of the 22nd October 2013, which has been approved by HM Treasury.

There are also practice notes of interest to conveyancers in relation to 'Mortgage fraud' (31st July 2014) and 'Property and registration fraud' (11th October 2010); the latter guide was compiled in conjunction with the Land Registry.

Document 3: Anti-bribery policy
Section 16

The Bribery Act 2010 introduced significant new obligations on organisations to prohibit, and monitor for, improper payments. We are committed to conducting the business of the firm in an honest and ethical manner and, in particular, in accordance with the ten principles of legal practice which underpin the SRA Handbook. These include, most basically, a duty to uphold the rule of law (Principle 1).

It follows that we will never offer, pay or receive any improper payment, such as a personal cash payment or an inappropriate gift to an individual to place the work for their organisation with this firm.

Please note that it is not necessary for a payment to pass hands for a bribery offence to have been committed. Sections 1 to 5 set out the 'general bribery offences'. The main offence of giving or offering a bribe (s.1) is described in rather confusing terms as having two 'cases', the first being where a person:

> 'offers, promises or gives a financial or other advantage to another person, and [...] intends the advantage –

     (i)   to induce a person to perform improperly a relevant function or activity, or

     (ii) to reward a person for the improper performance of such a function or activity.'

The second case arises where a person:

'offers, promises or gives a financial or other advantage to another person, [knowing or believing] that the acceptance of the advantage would itself constitute the improper performance of a relevant function or activity.'

Further explanation is provided to the effect that in the first case, 'it does not matter whether the person to whom the advantage is offered, promised or given is the same person as the person who is to perform, or has performed, the function or activity concerned', and that in both cases it does not matter whether the advantage is offered, promised or given directly or through a third party.

Section 2 deals with the other side of the bribery transaction by prohibiting the request or receipt of a bribe, again confusingly set out in a number of illustrative cases. Under this offence it is necessary only to agree to receive or accept a financial or other advantage in circumstances where the person concerned should not do so, meaning that the crime will have been committed even if the payment or other benefit is not forthcoming.

Section 3 deals with the range of functions and activities that might be involved for possible liability under the Act, while s.4 sets out the provisions on when such an activity might be said to have been 'improperly' performed. Section 5 then completes this part of the Act by introducing a reasonableness test in relation to ss.3 and 4, reflecting the core problem of the legislation in attempting to differentiate between normally accepted business practice – especially in relation to marketing events – and what should be regarded as criminal behaviour. The offence of bribing a foreign official is dealt with separately within the Act in order to meet the specific requirements of the OECD Anti-Bribery Convention.

Notwithstanding the rather confusing definitions of the key offences by illustrative cases, the core offences are easily summarised: it is an offence to offer or request a bribe, regardless of whether that bribe, be it money, goods or other advantage, is actually paid or received. The relatively low threshold for criminality might therefore mean that illegal acts of bribery are encountered much more frequently than might be thought, as where a client offers a payment for their adviser to misrepresent the position in a matter or to lie in court.

Client entertaining

Our policy on gifts and entertaining is that we continue to undertake appropriate client entertaining activity as part of our marketing policy, but this is never to be lavish or open to misinterpretation under this policy. To take a potential client out to lunch would usually be permissible, but to take them on holiday would not (unless they are close friends or relations in any event).

Gifts from clients

Our policy on the receipt of gifts from clients or others is that there is a common sense limit of £50, or a case of wine of any reasonable value, to any item received and in no circumstances may any representative of the firm accept any cash gift. Likewise, there is no objection to your being the recipient of client entertaining by others as long as it is reasonable having regard to your role in the firm, your links with whoever is making any such offer and the value of what is being proposed. We maintain a register of gifts made by the practice and received which is maintained by ??? Please notify them by email of (specify).

You must also note the provisions of O(1.9) of the Code of Conduct to the effect that where a client wishes to make a gift 'of significant value' to you or a relative, or to someone else at the firm or their family, the client must take independent legal advice. This is particularly relevant in relation to the drafting of wills for friends and family as the current 2011 Code of Conduct does not specifically provide for an exemption in such situations as did the former 2007 Code (*see the Law Society Practice Note on this topic of 20th January 2015*).

Money laundering

The [*partners/directors*] believe that the risks of bribery or corruption by the firm are very low and are adequately covered by the policy summary set out above. A greater risk is that we are dealing with a client who has either made or received improper payments. Since such payments are now criminal funds under the terms of the Bribery Act any such circumstances, or suspicions that they might be such, should be dealt with as a potential money laundering incident and so must be reported to [*name of the MLRO*] and will be dealt with under that policy (see Section 2.17 above).

The person responsible for this policy is [*name or title*]

Document 4: Mortgage and property fraud policy
Section 17

Your first step should be to make sure that you are conversant with the Law Society guidance on:

- Mortgage fraud avoidance – As contained in its most up-to-date practice note on the topic (31st July 2014 or later); and
- Property and registration fraud – See the practice note of 11th October 2010 (or later).

As these practice notes record, the patterns of property and mortgage fraud take many forms including:

- Application frauds – In which the deceit of the borrower as to their circumstances is a factor in the lender deciding to make an offer of advance, or on better terms than they would otherwise have done;
- Identity frauds – In which the client (perhaps acting in conjunction with fellow conspirators) produces false identity evidence with the sole objective of theft from the lender or the rightful owners of the property now or at some future stage; and
- Valuation fraud – Very often in conjunction with identity frauds and with the aim of defrauding the lender by leaving them with irrecoverable losses.

There have been particular warnings in recent years as to:

- Fraudsters producing false identity documentation to purport to be the seller of an unencumbered property, perhaps following a change of name process to assume the name of the rightful owner(s) – a particular risk with tenants in properties impersonating their landlord(s);
- Bogus firms – Fraudsters claiming to be solicitors or licensed conveyancers but using false notepaper and changed telephone and address details so as to intercept the payment of funds;
- Sham transactions – Sales (usually at an over value) between co-conspirators to obtain larger loans than the transaction would support; and
- Intra-family frauds – Where both parties do not agree, for example, to a re-mortgage to cover outstanding debts.

Avoidance processes

Identity fraud remains the most pressing risk for law firms. You must follow our anti-money laundering processes with care, conveyancing being the highest risk work type for most mixed firms. Careful identity checking is one of the prime requirements of firms in the CML Lenders' Handbook.

Be wary, and do not be taken in by plausible or bullying clients. Ask:

- **Why** us as the firm to act, especially if there is no local connection with the property or the client?
- **Why** this deal? Are there aspects that strike you as unusual?
- **Why** this price? We are not expected to be expert valuers but we should note obvious over values and under values (the former can suggest mortgage fraud and the latter money laundering).

Furthermore, as a result of the increased incidence of hacking attacks of phones and emails in conveyancing transactions you should always question any late changes of representatives or banking details (see Appendix 34).

As a result of the increased incidence of hacking attacks of phones and e-mails in conveyancing transactions you should always question any late change of representatives or banking details directly with those concerned (bearing in mind that the e-mails might have been infiltrated). Given the risk of bogus law firms operated by fraudsters you should also check the identity of any conveyancers on the other side of any transaction not known to you in the relevant professional directory, and further if you remain suspicious.

Other risks to consider are:

- Distant certification of a client you have not met – Are you sure that you know who has provided certification?
- Cloning of your profile – The SRA has suggested that firms should conduct occasional internet searches of their identity;
- Imposter law firms (see also para. 3.1.4 in CML Lenders' Handbook – December 2014 version);
- Credibility of valuation advisers and valuation; and
- Property history – Rapid sales or variations in value?

- Whether the conveyancers on the other side(s) of the transaction are known to you and, if not, whether they may be bogus.

See also the SRA website for any current versions of the 'warning card' on money laundering and property fraud.

Close attention needs to be paid to the duty of confidentiality if the firm is acting contemporaneously for a buyer and a lender. The professional position is as set out in the Code of Conduct 2011 at chapters 3 and 4. If there is any change in the purchase price, or if the firm becomes aware of any other information that the lender might reasonably be expected to think important in deciding whether, or on what terms, it would make the mortgage advance available, in such circumstances the duty of disclosure to the lender requires the firm to pass on such information to them, but with the consent of the buyer as a result of the duty of confidentiality that is owed to them. If the buyer will not agree to the information being given to the lender, then there will be a conflict between the firm's duty of confidentiality to the buyer and the duty to act in the best interests of the lender. The firm will then have to cease acting for the lender, and to consider carefully whether it could continue to act for the buyer.

Document 5
Complaints policy and client feedback (see Section 19)

We try hard to provide an excellent service to our clients. We hope that we will meet or exceed clients' expectations so that they will not feel the need to complain, but it has to be accepted that clients will sometimes do so, possibly because we have done something wrong or not done something that we should have done. Where this is the case and the complaint is merited, we need to take appropriate action such as offering the client an apology, a goodwill payment or compensation and learning from our mistakes. Our complaints procedure is available on request and should be offered to a client in circumstances where it seems likely that they might want it . The person responsible for this policy is [*name or title*] who is referred to in this policy as the ['*Client Care Manager/Partner*'].

Issues likely to result in complaints

Everyone needs to be aware of how a client may perceive our service so that any potential dissatisfaction can be prevented. Be aware that a client may give indications that he or she is not happy without wanting to use the word 'complaint', for example comments such as 'I was surprised by' or 'I was not expecting' can be an early warning and a complaint may be avoided by talking to the client at an early stage. The Legal Ombudsman has provided some useful information about the types of complaint that are referred to his office. We need to be particularly careful to avoid the following:

- Clients were not advised about alternative funding options which were available;
- Clients were not told about disbursements;
- Costs were more than the estimate but the client was not notified in advance;
- Delay;
- Discrimination;
- Errors in the bill;
- Failure to advise;
- Failure to follow instructions;
- Failure to keep the client informed of progress on their case/matter;
- Failure to progress the client's case or matter;
- Failure to provide information about costs;
- Failure to respond to telephone calls, e-mails or letters;
- Information was disclosed to a third party without the client's consent;
- Loss of, or damage to, documents, the client's property or the file;
- Refusing or failing to release files or papers;
- Something was charged more than once; and
- VAT was charged when it should not have been.

What is a complaint?

The Code now defines a complaint as being any expression of dissatisfaction that the complainant has suffered (or may do so) financial loss, distress, inconvenience or other detriment (see Glossary to SRA Handbook). However, a client may have a justifiable cause of complaint if the service they receive falls below our usual standard, even if it does not meet this threshold. Common sense suggests that problems that are immediately resolved (as where you point out to a client a letter confirming information that they claim not to have received) are not the sort of complaint that should be notified under this procedure. Please also bear in mind that the Legal Ombudsman will, in certain circumstances, entertain complaints from certain related parties who are non-clients of the firm and from people who have unreasonably been denied a service or offered a service inappropriately.

What you should do if someone complains

Everyone in the practice who has received training is authorised to deal initially with some complaints. These are known as 'informal' complaints. Specifically you are authorised to deal with an expression of dissatisfaction in relation to service standards – for example, a client says you have failed to respond to a letter or e-mail.

If an expression of dis-satisfaction can be resolved to the client's satisfaction at first instance, there is no need to do anything further.

Formal complaints

If the person raising the issue is not satisfied with the way you have dealt with their complaint initially, you must refer it for formal consideration as a 'formal' complaint. The following sorts of complaint must in any event be referred for internal investigation straight away:

- Any complaint raising issues of potential misconduct or negligence;
- Any complaint alleging discrimination or a breach of our policy on equality and diversity; and
- Any expression of dis-satisfaction which is made in writing
- When a complaint is passed directly to [*name or title*] and [*he/she*] will send the person a copy of our complaints procedure.

Recording and reporting complaints

All formal complaints are recorded on a complaints monitoring form and held centrally by the ['*Client Care Manager/Partner*']. (S)he will open a file for every complaint, so that it is dealt with separately from a client's case or matter file.

The ['*Client Care Manager/Partner*'] will investigate complaints thoroughly and impartially, obtaining and considering evidence objectively. (S)he will respond to the client within the timeframe below:

Action	Timescale
Acknowledge complaint in writing and send a copy of the complaints procedure	Within two working days
Investigate the issues	Within 14 days of receiving the complaint whenever possible
Invite the person making the complaint to a meeting or to discuss the issues by telephone	On conclusion of investigation
Confirm the outcome of the meeting or telephone conversation in writing	Within three working days
If a meeting/telephone discussion is not possible or required: Investigate the issues and write to the person with the outcome	Within 21 days
Review and close the complaint	Within 8 weeks of receiving the complaint

If it is not possible to adhere to the deadlines indicated above, the ['*Client Care Manager/Partner*'] must write to the person raising the issues explaining why and providing a new date by which he or she will receive further contact.

The ['*Client Care Manager/Partner*'] will:

- Attempt to meet the client's concerns;
- Identify the causes of the complaint;
- Offer an appropriate apology/redress/compensation/goodwill payment; and
- Instigate corrective action if appropriate, which may involve training, disciplinary action and/or changing office procedures.

At the conclusion of the internal investigation, the ['*Client Care Manager/Partner*'] will remind clients that they may ask the Legal Ombudsman to investigate, usually within six months.

The ['*Client Care Manager/Partner*'] will conduct an annual review of complaints received and provide the [*Risk Manager/COLP*] with a copy of the report.

To help us ensure that we provide services in ways that meet or exceed our clients' expectations, we invite [*all/a percentage of/a selection of*] clients to provide us with feedback by sending them a client questionnaire (*see Appendix 14*).

If a client is likely to instruct us on one or two cases or matters during a year, you should send out a client feedback form with the final letter at the end of each transaction. If a client is likely to instruct us on multiple matters during a year then you should send out a client feedback form every six months [*or vary if less frequent*].

If a client is of strategic importance (defined as a client billed more than £[*specify*] per year), in addition to sending out the client satisfaction form the [*'Client Care Manager/Partner'*] will offer to visit the client [*annually/every six months*].

Processing feedback questionnaires

Fee earners:

- Insert the file reference on the questionnaire; and
- Send it with a reply-paid envelope to the client with the final bill or the closing letter.

Returned questionnaires:

- Are sent to the [*'Client Care Manager/Partner'*] when the post is sorted; and
- A copy of a completed questionnaire is provided to the fee-earner.

The [*'Client Care Manager/Partner'*] carries out an annual analysis of all feedback received. A copy of his/her report is provided to all [*heads of department/partners/senior managers*] so that good practice can be shared and any required improvements can be planned and implemented.

A copy of the firm's complaints handling policy is [*on the intranet/available at (specify)*] – *see Appendix 13*].

SECTION 3

CASE MANAGEMENT

Note: This section provides guidance in relation to using the draft procedures that follow.

Introduction

The aim of this section is to work through all of the stages of running a file, including some of the supervisory and risk management processes that are not covered elsewhere in this Manual. The core process of fee earning is common to all forms of practice – taking the client's instructions, confirming them and then processing them until the matter has been completed and archived. However, when examined in more detail there are, of course, numerous differences arising from the type of work and client in question, along with the extent to which the firm employs case management systems as opposed to more traditional file management processes. This section is based on an essentially paper-based system and so will need more extensive amendment if your firm is one that has adopted an electronic file management system.

This section envisages that there will be one main case management section with the departmental or work area variations being set out in a set of departmental instructions, on which see appendix 15. This approach promotes the concept of there being one common way of doing things within a mixed firm whilst also recognising that there are different issues for each specialisation. This approach is also likely to prove more user-friendly than including long sections of interest to some, but not most, of the users (dealing with conflicts in conveyancing matters is a good example). Finally, the appendix approach is also a convenient format for setting out the lists of work undertaken and the risks that are inherent for the profile of firms as required by section 5 of Lexcel.

3.1   Supervision
3.15   Inactivity checks

3.16   File reviews

This introductory section cross refers to the section on risk management and supervision in the Policies and Standards Manual (Section 2). It appears here as this sets the scene for the proper control of files and should be read in conjunction with the related procedures for file checking and independent file reviews at sections 3.15 and 3.16.

3.2   Enquiries from potential clients

3.3   Accepting and declining instructions: Consumer Contracts Regulations 2013

Without a doubt the most significant change to be addressed within this section of the manual in this second edition of the book is the implications of the Consumer Contracts (Information, Cancellation and Additional Charges) Regulations 2013 (SI 2013/3134) which took effect on the 13th June 2014. These regulations go some way beyond the previous Distance Selling Regulations 2000 and the Cancellation of Contracts made in a Consumer's Home or Place of Work etc. Regulations 2008 (the "Doorstep Selling Regulations"). The risks for law firms of losses from non-compliance through inability to enforce claims for fees are now much greater: there is also the risk of criminal liability for non-compliance in relation to off-premises contracts, but much as was the case under the former 2008 regulations in any event.

The three situations that are covered by the new regulations are:

- "On-premises contracts" – covering most instructions taken from private clients;
- "Distance contracts" – in certain instances where there is no meeting with the client; and
- "Off-premises contracts" – replacing the similar provisions in relation to doorstep selling.

Unfortunately the provisions do not lend themselves to a simple plan of action for all firms and some decisions will have to be made as to how strictly the firm wishes to adhere to the new requirements. This is because the precise circumstances when the more heavily regulated distance and off-premises contracts will arise is far from clear in the context of a solicitor's practice.

On-premises contracts

Contracts formed in the normal way, where instructions are taken in the office (whether there is a meeting with the client or not) will be regarded as "on-premises". Here no points of any great relevance should arise as long as the usual client retainer information and confirmation of terms of business processes as required by chapter 1 of the Code of Conduct are provided. It is particularly important that the firm addresses:

- the scope of the retainer(as required by Outcome 1.12 of the Code);
- costs information (Outcome 1.13);
- the firm's complaints handling process (Outcomes 1.9-1.10); and
- details of the client's right to terminate the retainer and the consequences if they do so, along with your rights to cancel (Outcome 1.3).

The definition of on-premises contracts makes this type of consumer contract the sweep-up class – in other words a contract will be on-premises unless it is a distance or off-premises contract, and the great majority of matters undertaken for private clients will be on-premises contracts. Where, however, there is a meeting with the client in the early or pre-instructions stage of any such matter away from the offices of the firm there is a risk that it might become an "off-premises" contract.

Distance selling contracts

For many years firms had complied with the earlier Distance Selling Regulations 2000 by having an appropriate warning notice in their terms of business document, and the Doorstep Selling Regulations by obtaining the client's written agreement to the work going ahead. The requirements now are:

- The difference between private and commercial clients was previously quite clear but a "consumer" is now "an individual acting for purposes which are wholly or mainly outside that individual's trade, business, craft or profession". This might be unclear if acting for a self-employed client whose instructions relate partly to their business activities and partly to their private client requirements.

- Where there is the greatest room for confusion is quite what amounts to a distance contract. Most firms formerly addressed this with a clause about cooling off rights in the terms of business document but the formalities are now much greater. The key point is that instructions which are received by phone, e-mail or fax where there is no meeting with the clients will still be "on-premises" as long as they are not concluded under an "organised distance sales or service provision scheme". These terms are not defined in the regulations but seem to imply some form of outreach initiative. The Law Society has suggested that this might typically involve "mail order, online sales and telesales", all of which would be unusual within most firms (and, to a certain extent, could be in breach of the ban on cold calling private individuals under Outcome 8.3 of the Code in any event). Under this interpretation the definition of "on-premises" therefore refers more to where the contract is agreed rather than whether the client was, at any stage, on the firm's premises in the process of agreeing the retainer. Given the continuing uncertainty as to when a distance selling contract arises we have provided alternatives in the draft manual and firms will have to decide which approach to adopt.

- The cooling off period now extends to 14 calendar days in the case of both distance and off-premises contracts, in contrast to the former periods of seven working days for distance selling and (confusingly) seven calendar days for doorstep selling. In both cases the onus will be on the consumer to notify the "trader" (as the law firm will be for these purposes) of their wish to cancel the contract as long as they have been notified of their rights under the regulations.

- There are some important formalities to note in relation to commencing work within the 14 calendar days period in cases of distance and off-premises contracts. Whereas under the Distance Selling Regulations consent to continue with the work could be presumed the firm will now have to have received "an express request" (r.36) for the work to commence within the cooling off period for distance contracts also. Where the regulations apply and fee earners do not obtain a specific request in this regard from the client there will therefore be a risk of having to write off the fees that are incurred during the earliest stages of the matter.

Critically, in cases of delay in providing the required information within the first 12 months of taking instructions the 14 days cooling off period will run from the time that the notice is served, so it will probably be a case of "better late than never" if the non-compliance emerges during a file review or in the course of general supervision during the first year of the life of the file, if relevant.

Off premises contracts

It is also difficult to decide with any certainty as to when an off-premises contract may have arisen. There will be numerous situations where the distinction will be blurred, for example:

- There is an initial meeting at the client's home when the services which are available are explained but it is left to the client to phone or write in with confirmation of their wishes for the firm to act
- The initial meeting occurs within the office but the retainer letter is delivered and signed at a subsequent meeting at the client's home
- The client phones to ask about your services on a matter and you send out your retainer letter and terms of business document confirming what you will do. You subsequently meet to take fuller instructions.

The first two of these situations would be likely to be regarded as off-premises but not the third, the key point being when and where the contract is made. In the third situation an off-premises contract might arise, however, if at the follow-up meeting additional instructions outside the retainer which has been delivered are taken and acted upon. The issue of the precise point at which an off-premises contracts will arise will vary case by case and the safer course of action, therefore, is likely to be to comply with the notice requirements for off-premises contracts whenever there is a pre-retainer or immediate follow-up meeting outside the firm.

There is also the prospect of an off-premises contract arising where there is an "excursion" at a neutral venue, but only where the venue was of the adviser's choosing. The Law Society advises caution on differentiating too narrowly on who has organised the meeting and suggests, for example, that it is safer to regard meetings in hospital as being covered by the requirements of the regulations even though it would not be the solicitor who would have chosen this venue.

The required forms

The forms provided in the appendices at the end of this section by way of template are based on the Schedules to the regulations and the Law Society advice on issues to be covered. The references to "sales" sound quite alien to the activities of law firms **but the wording is mandatory under the regulations**. Schedule 2 provides guidance on the "information relating to distance and off-premises contracts" as required by r.10(1:a) and schedule 3 provides at part A the "model instructions for cancellation" and at part B the "model cancellation form". The instructions for cancellation require adaptation for each type of business and we have opted for the "service contract" format at note 6, which fellow pedants will see contains a typographical error within the regulations in that the word "us" needs to be inserted to make sense of the model clause provided. The format of the cancellation form needs to be as set out in Part B of schedule 3 – see r.10(1:b). Although the form needs to be provided in the prescribed format its use by clients is optional and the client's notification can be valid if communicated clearly by other wording or means.

There is more flexibility in how the required information is provided in the case of distance contracts as opposed to off-premises contracts but the safest option is to confirm the retainer, terms of business, commencement and cancellation forms in hard copy in all cases.

Under the former regime doorstep selling required more paperwork than was necessary in situations of distance selling, but the same paperwork is now required for any situation involving distance or off-premises contracts.

There is less flexibility in how you provide the necessary information in an off-premises contract: the client must be supplied with a copy of the signed contract, or confirmation of the contract in your retainer letter, on paper or some other "durable medium" before the performance begins of any service provided under the contract. In practice it will be advisable to ensure that all the paperwork is provided in hard copy in any situation of distance or off-premises contracts.

There is no one definitive way in which to incorporate the necessary changes, and much will depend on the profile of the firm, but in all cases any lingering reference to the Distance Selling Regulations 2000 should be deleted from your retainer letter or terms of business.

If most of the retainer letters sent out go to private clients it may be as well to have one format of notification to all clients. You may wish to include in your terms of business document wording such as the following to replace any reference to the Distance Selling Regulations 2000: "If you are a client instructing us other than in the course of business the provisions of the Consumer Contracts Regulations may apply to the work we undertake for you and you may be entitled to cancellation or 'cooling-off' rights in certain circumstances. You will be advised where this is the case." This is, however, just one way for firms to address their responsibilities and it will be necessary for each firm to consider its potential exposure to the regulations and the most appropriate response for it.

3.4 File opening and transfers

It is important to set out any special arrangements for handling enquiries from existing or potential clients. There is generally no obligation to accept work where required to act, though there are certain statutory restrictions on the ability of advocates to turn work away. Clearly, any refusal to act must not risk being seen to be in breach of your equality and diversity policy; grounds on which firms generally decline to act are set out in section 3.3.

3.5 Conflicts of interests

The policy considerations on conflicts of interests are set out in Section 2 of this Manual. The emphasis here is the sort of checking procedures required to screen for conflicts – both at the outset of any matter and as it progresses – in order to ensure that problems are identified and acted upon as soon as possible. In this regard outcomes 3.1 and 3.2 of the Code of Conduct ('the Code') are relevant, in relation to 'client conflicts' and 'own conflicts' respectively.

3.6 Outset of the matter or case

The rather long list of issues that must or should be covered is as a result of section 6.2 of Lexcel which does seem now to run counter to the SRA's more purposive approach in chapter 1 of the Code of Conduct. In practice most of these items will be better covered through standard terms and conditions documents or engagement letters, but certain of the core issues – those relating to what the firm will do for the client and to what objective – will have to be individually drafted. Lexcel 6 has made the issues of the client's objectives and the cost-effectiveness of the matter items to be covered only "where appropriate", but note that "timescale" must always still be addressed, even if only to say that no useful advice can be provided on this point.

3.7 Referrals from others

This area was one of the more significant changes effected by the revised version of the Code of Conduct in the SRA Handbook. Formerly referrals of work between lawyers were the subject of 'fee sharing' arrangements but this distinction no longer applies and chapter 9 on referrals is expressly stated to apply to referrals between lawyers also. There is a need to set out any paid-for agreement to refer work under O(9.7): likewise, the information provided to clients on such arrangements should be 'clear and in writing' under IB(9.6) and in a format which is suitable for that client.

3.8 Risk management at the outset

Risk management was elevated to the status of being one of the Principles in the SRA Handbook. Principle 8 provides that you must:

'run your business or carry out your role in the business effectively and in accordance with proper governance and sound financial and risk management principles'.

Although not referred to as such in the Handbook or the Code, the concept of risk screening is a requirement under Lexcel – now at 5.12. An issue in many firms is the number of different risk profiles to be undertaken in the light of the different obligations that also arise under the Money Laundering Regulations 2007. These can be listed as:

- General risk – Is the work of a type the firm does and wishes to undertake? If so, are there special risk factors in this case that need to be safeguarded against?
- Financial risk – Can you be sure that you will be paid for this work? Do you need money on account and/or a company search?
- Authority risk – Does this individual have the authority to act for the client organisation?
- Identity risk – Can you be sure you are dealing with the person that you think you are?
- Ownership risk – Are there beneficial interests that you have failed to identify?
- Matter risk – Can you be confident about the nature of the instructions and the source of funds?

Where possible these assessments should be combined into one integrated form so people do not have the frustration of completing multiple forms.

In relation to the 'general' risk profile the standard process is to band work into being 'normal' or 'high' risk, in which case thought does need to be given as to what will be done if a file is designated as being high risk [*See the sample file opening form at appendix 17*].

3.9 File maintenance
3.10 Traceability, including papers and other items supplied by the client

There are certain core standards of file maintenance that can be set out relatively easily but more detailed requirements are probably better set out in the departmental instructions. An issue of growing importance in many firms is the issue of electronic filing and the adoption of suitable protocols to ensure that all information can be located in the event of it being required during the matter, or thereafter if further instructions or a claim or complaint are received by the firm.

3.11 Confidentiality

This section cross refers to the policy on this topic in Section 2: Policies and Standards.

3.12 Planning and progressing matters

It is essential that all clients are presented with a strategy for dealing with their matter. This will usually be contained in the engagement letter but there may be occasions when a separate case plan is required, as where a team of people is assembled to work on that matter. There are some specific requirements for separate case plans in legal aid work which are covered in Section 7: Legal Aid as they are too extensive to include in this section.

The case plan must be kept up to date and communicated to the client in an appropriate manner.

3.13 Costs updates

3.14 Continuing risk management

The main principles here are that the firm that is committed to providing a good level of service will be proactive in its management of the matter or case and that the client must be informed as soon as it appears that a costs estimate already provided is likely to be exceeded. There has been a good deal of case law on the position of the law firm attempting to enforce its fees when it is in breach of the various regulatory requirements. It may well be that the firm has not only to notify the client of the changed circumstances but also to explain why the earlier estimate proved to be inaccurate (see *Reynolds v Stone Rowe Brewer* [2008] EWHC 497 QB).

3.17 Undertakings

Undertakings provided by the firm are, of course, a key risk management consideration. The standard provisions are for partner/director sign-off other than for the routine and fast-moving undertakings that enable conveyancing transactions to proceed. A central register of undertakings is not a specific requirement of Lexcel or the SQM but might be helpful in some firms.

3.18 Key dates reminder system

With missed time limits remaining one of the prime causes of claims against firms, the need for a back-up system in addition to the main entry in the matter file should need little justification. Modern electronic diary systems have largely replaced the former departmental diaries, but by no means universally so. The choice of system is less important than whether or not it works and the need for everyone to enter all listed dates is stressed. A partially reliable system is arguably worse than no system at all.

The arrangements for the monitoring of the key date entries must be set out under Lexcel requirements. [*For sample lists of dates for common areas of legal work see appendix 16.*]

3.19   Insurance mediation

This section again refers to Section 2 of the Manual. The main point in this section is to remind the fee earner of the need for a 'demands and needs statement' (Appendix 22) when advising that a particular insurance product is taken. The full requirements will arise where the firm routinely recommends one form of policy, such as a particular defective title or after the event insurance policy, but are generally avoided where the firm instead refers on to a broker.

3.20   Recommendations and commissions received

Chapter 6 of the Code of Conduct deals with the situation where recommendations or referrals are made to third parties, including other lawyers or financial services providers. It is provided at O(6.2) that clients must be fully informed of any financial or other interests that arise in these circumstances, and so it would be necessary to detail an introduction fee which the firm will have if referring that client elsewhere. Note that a 'client', for these purposes, is defined by the Glossary to the Handbook so as to include prospective clients, and so will apply when non-client enquirers do little more than ask about the service in question.

3.21   Instructing counsel and experts

Legal aid practitioners have found themselves out of pocket when they have paid experts' fees out of payments received 'on account' from the Legal Aid Agency, only to find those fees reduced on assessment at the end of the case, perhaps several years later. It is advisable to protect your firm against this eventuality in your letter of instruction.

The Law Society issued a practice note (24th January 2012) on the use of interpreters in criminal cases, which may be of interest.

3.22 End of the case/matter

The issue of how long to store files for before they are destroyed is an issue increasingly raised by firms. There is an argument for retaining property purchase files indefinitely so as to have evidence in the event of a longstop claim, or the converse could also be argued. Many years ago the Law Society did produce an advisory table of file storage times but the only advice now provided by it on this issue is to be found in its practice note in relation to wills and probate. Factors relevant to your policy could include the fact that people move house on average every 7-10 years and problems will usually come to light, if at all, on a subsequent sale or transfer. This is an issue that might be worth putting to your brokers, with their advice seeming often to be to keep the full file for 15 years or a compromise period of 12 years.

SECTION 3

CASE AND FILE MANAGEMENT

Introduction

This section of the manual sets out the main rules by which fee earning work is supervised and conducted. It is supplemented by a series of 'departmental instructions' which contains details of the special features and aspects of each area of work within the practice [*See Appendix 15*].

3.1 Supervision

3.1.1 Details of the supervisors of all work performed by the firm can be found in Section 1.4. If you are a supervisor it is your responsibility to ensure that suitable levels of supervision are maintained in your [*department/team*] having regard to the numbers of persons that you have responsibility for and their level of experience and that there is continuity of cover at all times. You must also ensure that work is allocated and, if needs be, re-allocated in a suitable manner. You should also note that there are particular requirements in the Code of Conduct relating to the effective supervision of reserved legal work and immigration (O(7.7)).

3.1.2 Supervision procedures include:

- Incoming post is seen by a supervisor or a partner (unless otherwise agreed);
- Monthly review of work in progress figures, with particular emphasis on apparently inactive files;
- Regular monitoring and review of the work done under their control;
- Exercise of delegated functions in legal aid work;
- 'Open door' periods for consultation in the day and discussion of

work priorities and the opportunity to raise problems for discussion and assistance;

- Availability for consultation by telephone and e-mail when not in the office; and
- Regular team or departmental meetings.

For legal aid specific requirements in relation to supervision see Section 7.

3.1.3   The supervisors will maintain details of the persons who are authorised to sign outgoing post, but the general principles are that:

- All post will be checked for your initial six monthly probationary period (unless otherwise agreed); and
- You are unlikely to be authorised to sign post unsupervised until you have been admitted for [*one year/two years*].

[*Either*]

3.1.4   [*Outgoing/All*] e-mails are monitored in the same way as the post signing rules as above.

[*or*]

3.1.4   It is not feasible to monitor e-mails in the same way as hard copy post, so e-mail checking is covered under our supervisory file review procedure and is largely a matter of trust on a day-to-day basis. You must consult your [*Head of department/supervisor*] if you are unsure what to do at any time (regardless of whether you are subject to the post signing rules above or not) and must bring to their attention any message which might be of concern or interest to them. See also 5.15.

3.1.5   You are reminded of the firm's policies in relation to e-mail monitoring at 5.15 and the need to inform the Compliance Officer for Legal Practice ('COLP') or Compliance Officer for Finance and Administration ('COFA') of any potential non-compliance with this Manual or the relevant professional rules (1.3.11).

3.1.6   It is the responsibility of the [*Heads of Department/supervisors*] to maintain:

- lists of work that will and will not be undertaken within their area of the practice; and
- lists of the generic risks associated with their area(s) of work and ensure that any changes to such lists are brought to the attention of any relevant personnel.

Such lists can be found in the departmental appendices at appendix 15.

3.2   Enquiries from potential clients

3.2.1   We recognise that anyone contacting the practice could be a client or potential client and we therefore treat all callers with courtesy and respect. This includes responding to calls as soon as possible, or returning them promptly if asked to do so.

3.2.2   In accordance with our risk management policy, we limit the types of matters and cases that we will take on (2.10.2). We might also prefer to decline to act (and in some cases would be obliged to do so) on such grounds as:

- There is, or could be, a conflict of interests, professional or commercial (see 2.8);
- Previous adverse experience with that client , including that they have not paid or have resisted paying a bill;
- We do not have sufficient time, resources or expertise to provide that client with a good level of service; and
- We have grounds to believe that the client is being subjected to duress or undue influence.

3.2.3   If declining to act we should provide the enquirer with such information as we are able. If there appears to be a conflict, please refer to your supervisor if you have any doubt about what to say.

3.2.4   Each head of department will ensure that switchboard/reception knows whether their department is able to take on new clients and can put potential clients in touch with an appropriate person without delay.

3.2.5 For details of the obligations in relation to signposting and referrals in legal aid areas of work see 2.23.2.

3.3 Accepting and declining instructions

[Practices have different policies for accepting instructions. In some, a supervisor must authorise acceptance; in others, any fee earner may accept instructions in principle. You should amend the paragraph(s) below.]

[Either]

3.3.1 Any *[fee earner/solicitor/partner/director]* may accept instructions, but subject to such considerations as:

- Current capacity;
- Expertise;
- Conflict checks;
- Our equality and diversity policy; and
- The availability of adequate funding.

[or]

3.3.1 The consent of a *[partner/director]* is needed to the opening of any file and is evidence that they believe that this is a matter that can be taken on and assigned to the fee earner who is named as the person acting.

3.3.2 All new matters – whether from new or existing clients – are subject to an initial risk assessment (see Section 3.8).

Deciding to decline instructions

3.3.3 If we cannot accept someone's instructions, he or she should be informed as soon as possible. In litigation cases in particular the enquirer should be sent a letter of non-instruction to explain that although we are unwilling to take their matter on a different view might be taken by other advisers, and that in declining to act we are not providing them with advice as to the merits of their case. Legal aid enquirers should also be provided with signposting information (see 2.23.2).

3.3.4   The Consumer Contracts (Information, Cancellation and Additional Charges) Regulations 2013 (SI 2013/3134) implement the remaining elements of the EU Consumer Rights Directive. Unfortunately solicitors' practices fall within the definition of "traders" under the regulations. The new provisions apply to all private clients, defined as a "consumer" for these purposes, if they are "an individual acting for purposes which are wholly *or mainly* outside that individual's trade, business, craft or profession". Our emphasis by italics shows that certain clients whom we might regard as being commercial clients by virtue of the department instructed might fall under the definition if their personal circumstances also form a main element of the work to be done for them.

There are three classifications under the regulations which determine the action that is required to be taken.

- Where we are instructed in the office in the normal way there are few requirements beyond compliance with chapter 1 of the Code of Conduct and the need for information on the retainer, the costs of the matter, the client's right to cease acting at any time and our complaints handling information.

- If the private client instructs us remotely – i.e. by phone, letter or e-mail following an "organised distance sales or service provision scheme" – they will be classed as having a "distance" contract. If this is the case they will have a 14 days cooling off period and must have notice in the format which follows to this effect. If they do not receive this notice they may decline to pay our fees for a maximum period of 12 months plus the statutory 14 days. Furthermore, if we are to be sure that we will be paid for any work done within the first 14 days following our confirmation of the contract we must have received a request from the client for us to commence work within the 14 day period.

- The third situation is where a representative of the firm meets with the client but not at our premises – an "off-premises" contract. An off-premises contract will only arise where the meeting occurs at the client's home or where the firm has arranged the meeting venue, but it is probably safer to apply the requirements wherever the first meeting to explain what we can do for the client or where we agree to act occurs away from the office. Here the same paperwork is required and must either be given to the client (and signed as appropriate by them) at the meeting or be sent to them as soon as you return to the office. This documentation consists of the Cancellation Notice, the Commencement of Work Request and the Cancellation of Work Request. If delivering these forms to the client, in person or by post, you should explain that we may only commence work on their matter within the 14 days cooling off period if we have the Commencement of Work Request Form from them (or they would be entitled to refuse to pay for the work we do for them during this time).

The Law Society has issued a practice note on this topic which can be viewed on its website under "Practice Support"

Choose one of:

We do not consider that we will customarily be involved with distance contracts *or*

We consider the following situations within the firm should be regarded as distance contracts (*list*):

We will address the main changes required by [*specify: circulation of amended terms of business documentation? Have different forms of TOB documents or have signature box at the top of each version and require the fee earner to tick if the regulations apply, in which case include Commencement and Cancellation forms? See further guidance in introductory text. For forms see the appendix to this section of the manual and the Infolegal factsheet on this topic*]

Please be sure to address these new provisions – we are unwilling to risk criminal conduct for the firm or its personnel (however unlikely a prosecution might seem) or the substantial loss of fees we might suffer from non-compliance.

If you have any questions as to the note or how we will need to address the regulations please ask [*name or title*].

3.4   **File opening and transfers**

3.4.1   In order to open a file [*explain your process – is a form sent to the accounts department or do fee earners obtain their own client/matter number? If you are making this available through your firm's intranet, we suggest you link to the current form in use at your firm or refer to the form as at Appendix 17*].

3.4.2   It is important for the effective operation of our file management system that we know about all file transfers. If, for any reason, the supervising [*partner/director*] or the fee earner handling the matter changes please tell [*name or title, and refer to any process involved – if a transfer form is in use, provide link or set out copy at an appendix*]. If such a change is made, the client must be informed.

3.4.3   The client matter numbering system contains important data as to the instructions, including the identity of any third party funder.

3.4.4   In legal aid work, we need to be able to identify all 'linked' cases for a single client. [*See Section 7 for more information about linked cases in crime.*]

3.5   **Conflicts of interests**

3.5.1   We cannot act where there is a conflict of interests, other than in the exceptional cases that are outlined in our conflicts policy (see Section 2.8). We could have a conflict because:

- A client's interests could be in conflict with another, or there is a significant risk that this might be the case ('client conflict'); or
- A client's interests could conflict with our interests as a practice or with the interests of an individual within the practice, or there is a substantial risk that this might be the case ('own conflict').

3.5.2   In order to check for conflicts of interests you should [*specify procedure – accounts database check or other*].

3.5.3   The steps to be followed when checking for potential conflicts are:

- Before confirming acceptance of instructions, check the name of any person whose interest might conflict with our client's on our database, to ensure that he or she is not already a client;

- Record the name(s) checked on the file/case management system;
- Record the outcome of the check; and
- If it appears that there is or may be a conflict, please consult your supervisor who will decide if we can accept the instructions or refer the issue on to [*name or title*].

3.5.4   The overriding principle is that we must be able to act in the best interests of every client and so must avoid all such conflicts (O(3.4-5)) and also that we undertake suitable checks for conflicts or potential conflicts before we accept instructions. We provide training and guidance on avoiding conflicts and, if you are in any doubt, you must refer the issue to [*name or title*].

3.5.5   Examples of what would amount to a conflict of interests are set out in each of the departmental instructions.

3.5.6   You may not be able to eliminate the possibility of conflict arising during a case through an initial check. Keep the possibility of conflicts in mind and consult [*name or title*] if necessary.

3.6   Outset of the matter or case

3.6.1   It is essential that we understand as fully as possible the client's situation and their objectives. You must therefore note carefully the client's initial instructions and ensure that they are recorded on the matter file, using any checklists that have been adopted in your department or team.

3.6.2   When confirming the instructions and the basis on which we will act you should address the following:

- The client's requirements, and objectives if appropriate;
- An explanation of the issues involved (including cost benefit where appropriate) and the options available;
- What you will and will not do and the level of service;
- The next steps to be taken, and by whom;
- How long the matter or case may take to conclude;
- How the case will be funded (including advice on whether the client might qualify for legal aid);
- The level of service we will provide;

- Your responsibilities;
- The client's responsibilities;
- Your name and status;
- The person responsible for overall supervision of the matter;
- How, and with whom, to raise any problem with the service provided;
- The basis of our charges and how charges may be increased;
- Payment terms;
- That we may have a lien for unpaid costs; and
- Any potential liability for another party's costs or likely payments to others.

3.6.3   Many of these issues will be dealt with in our standard terms of business and/or client care or engagement letters.

3.6.4   It is also important to provide the 'best possible information, both at the time of engagement and when appropriate as their matter progresses, about the likely overall cost of their matter' (O(1.13)). You should therefore include an estimate for the matter as a whole, or for the next stage in more complex matters. Where you cannot sensibly provide this level of information until you have undertaken some prior work on the matter you should explain this to the client and then be sure to provide further advice on the likely costs as soon as you are able to do so: do not simply include a notional sum instead. It is considered good practice in such situations to suggest to the client that they may wish to set a costs limit that you will not exceed without their further agreement.

3.6.5   You are also required to consider the cost-effectiveness of all matters where appropriate (IB(1.13)), particularly in relation to costs risks in litigation matters, and raise any such concerns with your client if they do arise. You must also deal with the various funding options that are open to clients.

Standing terms of business

3.6.6   There is no requirement to confirm the terms of business where they are already well known to the client, as is most likely to be the case with regular clients who instruct us on work of a repetitive nature. If you think that any of your clients do not need the usual client care information at the outset of every matter you undertake for them, please provide their details to [*name or title*] who maintains the list of all such [*exemptions/key clients*].

Outset of legal aid cases

3.6.7   There are additional issues to be confirmed to the client in legal aid cases (*See Section 7: Legal Aid, paragraph 3.6.7, which will assist in adapting this section to your needs*).

Contingency fees

3.6.8   There is no general prohibition against the use of contingency fees in non-contentious work, but in contentious work any agreement must be in a format permitted by legislation and the SRA, in which case any required information must be provided (see IB(1.17)).

3.7   Referrals from others

3.7.1   There are some important considerations that need to be addressed when we receive work from a referred source, whether or not we pay for such introductions. Following the changes introduced by the SRA Handbook in 2011 this applies also to referrals received from other lawyers, which were previously subject to different rules on 'fee sharing'. Paid for referrals are not permitted in the case of crime and legal aid work or in relation to banned fees for personal injury cases under LASPO. All paid for referral agreements must be in writing.

3.7.2   Our policy in relation to paid-for referrals is [*specify*]. Records of the agreements that we have with any such paid-for sources of work are maintained by [*name or title*]. Where we have paid for referrals we must ensure that the clients are informed in writing of any financial or other interest that we have in the manner in which the work has been introduced to us, including any fee sharing agreement that we have with other lawyers if they are the introducers. In all cases of referred work we must be able to act in the best interests of all clients and independently of any external pressure.

3.7.3   The main considerations if you are in receipt of work that has been referred to you (whether paid or unpaid) are that:

- Our ability to provide the client with independent advice must not be compromised in any way; and
- The work must not have been obtained by the introducer in such a

manner that would breach the SRA's publicity rules (in particular that there must have been no cold-calling of individuals by phone or in person (see O(8.3)).

- If you have any concerns as to the above you must raise them with [*name or title*].

3.8 Risk management at the outset

3.8.1 You will be aware of our risk management policy (see Section 2, Part 2: Risk Management for more information). A risk management assessment must be undertaken at the outset of any potential case or matter and recorded on [*insert as appropriate – it could be part of your case management system, it could be recorded on your file opening form or it could be recorded on a separate risk management form*].

3.8.2 You must give consideration as to whether these instructions could fairly be regarded as being high risk. You must notify [*your supervisor/your Head of Department/name/title*] if you think this could be the case. Any special factors in this regard are set out in your departmental instructions, but in general you should always consider such issues as:

- Timescale – the period within which we must respond or the client wishes to have concluded the matter;
- Foreign law;
- Unusual complexities that might be beyond our expertise; and
- Transfers of matters from elsewhere, especially if the client is unhappy with the handling of their matter to date or has already been in contact with the Legal Ombudsman.

3.8.3 If a matter is regarded as being unduly high risk it must be turned away (see Section 3.3 above on accepting and declining instructions). If a matter is high risk but it is felt possible to safely deal with it through taking suitable precautions you must refer the instructions to [*name or title – usually the risk partner or a head of department*] in order that they can determine what extra measures are appropriate in that case.

3.8.4 If a matter is regarded as being high risk, but not so much so that we should decline to act, [*specify. Consider controls – list of all high risk matters with head of department or COLP, greater involvement of counsel and more regular reviews, or other?*]

3.9 File maintenance

3.9.1 All files must constitute as full a record of dealings on that matter as possible and be kept in an orderly and secure manner, including in accordance with any electronic case management protocols. Your files must 'tell the story' of the matter so that a colleague can pick it up in your absence and talk authoritatively to the client or the other side in your absence. This also involves maintaining files in a consistent and predictable manner, following any rules to this effect contained in the relevant set of departmental instructions for your work.

3.9.2 Please also note that numerous actions against solicitors' firms have been based on a failure to maintain adequate attendance notes (which might take the form of a contemporaneous e-mail to the client). The usual practice of the courts is to side with the client's recollection of any discussions that have not been recorded, rather than with the adviser, the reason being that the adviser might have been confused as to which client they had that discussion with whereas the client will be more likely to have discussed that point only once. The rule must therefore be that you must record any conversation of note on the file, either by an attendance note or an e-mail.

3.9.3 If you are a secretary you should also produce attendance notes where a caller or visitor to the firm provides you with relevant information, such as that they have received some important documents or that they wish to change information that they have already provided. Please be sure to bring this to the fee earner's attention and make sure that it is placed on the matter file.

3.10 Traceability, including papers and other items supplied by the client

3.10.1 You must ensure that all papers, documents and items in relation to client work are traceable within the office through their being filed or stored on the matter file at all times. This will also mean keeping all filing up to date and following any protocols on document and messaging storage. If we are storing bulky items and papers which are not kept within the file you must clearly record this information on that file. You must tag any items of evidence that are in our possession, or other physical items which we are required to retain for the client, with a secure label showing the matter number and the client's name.

3.10.2   If a client or their representative supplies any documents or other materials for use in any case or matter you must consider their suitability and you must make arrangements for their secure storage. In accordance with O(1.16) of the Code you will probably need to report any loss or damage to them, in which case you should first notify [*name or title*]. You should copy any sensitive items where their loss could cause particular difficulty.

3.10.3   For wills and deeds storage arrangements see 5.9.

3.11   Confidentiality

3.11.1   Protection of confidential information is a fundamental feature of the solicitor/client relationship. You must ensure that you take all reasonable care to safeguard confidential documents and information, especially when away from the office. Please therefore:

- Be careful about mobile phone calls that might identify the client or reveal other sensitive information, especially when in public places or on public transport;
- Do not leave documents or electronic devices in unlocked cars, or overnight; and
- Make sure that you observe our information security policy (see 5.13).

When it may be permissible to breach confidentiality

3.11.2   The general rule is that no information may be given about clients, even that they may have instructed us, without their permission (subject to some possible exceptions set out below). See also Section 2: Policies and Standards.

3.11.3   There are some circumstances in which it may be permissible to breach the normal duty of confidentiality. If you think we may need to do so you must discuss the issue with your supervisor. Examples of circumstances where it may be permissible or a legal requirement to breach confidentiality include:

- Where breaching confidentiality may be necessary to prevent the client or a third party committing a criminal act that you reasonably believe is likely to result in serious bodily harm;

- Where there are exceptional circumstances involving children, where you should consider revealing confidential information to an appropriate authority. This may be where the child is the client and the child reveals information which indicates continuing sexual or other physical abuse but refuses to allow disclosure of such information;
- Where a warrant permits a police officer or other authority to seize confidential documents; and
- In the case of a publicly funded client, you may be under a duty to report to the Legal Aid Agency information concerning the client which is confidential and privileged, for example where it comes to light that a client has not provided accurate information about his or her means.

Confidentiality and money laundering

3.11.4 A disclosure to the National Crime Agency ('NCA') will not breach the duty of confidentiality owed to a client provided there were reasonable grounds to suspect that money laundering was taking place and our procedures have been followed. However, because inappropriate disclosure to any person of information relating to potential money laundering activities could amount to the offence of tipping off, internal confidentiality is essential. You must not inform the client, the other side or any other person about any disclosure that has been made without the Money Laundering Reporting Officer's ('MLRO') express prior authority (see Section 2.17).

3.11.5 On the position of disclosures to the lender on issues concerning the purchaser client in conveyancing matters see 2.19.9.

3.12   Planning and progressing matters

3.12.1 The client must be presented with a plan of action or 'matter plan' explaining what it is that we are planning to do on their behalf. In most cases this will simply consist of advice provided in a letter or e-mail confirming their instructions. In complex cases (such as those involving a team from different departments) a formal case plan may be drawn up and agreed with the client.

3.12.2 [*See 3.12.2 in Section 7 for details of legal aid cases requiring a case plan to enable you to adapt this section to your needs.*]

[Either]

3.12.3   You should respond promptly to requests for contact from the client and others. The firm operates the following service levels [*state here any response times that you are committed to (there is no need to do so under Lexcel but some firms choose to do so as part of a client charter or client care promise)*].

[or]

3.12.3   The firm does not operate strict response times but we should always aim to respond to the client as quickly as possible, having regard to the urgency and importance of the matter so far as the client is concerned.

3.12.4   You must keep the client informed of the following:

- Progress or reasons for lack of progress;
- Developments in relation to costs and risk;
- Changes in the cost benefit to the client;
- Any adverse costs order;
- Any change of fee earner or supervisor; and
- If there is any material change to our complaints handling procedures.

3.12.5   The client must also be informed of any change of the fee earner acting in their matter and/or the person responsible for its supervision. You should do so in writing and preferably before any such change occurs.

3.12.6   If any issue arises which makes you consider whether you should cease acting for a client, you should discuss it with [*name or title*]. The Code of Conduct suggests at IB(1.10) that you should explain to the client the options open to them to continue to pursue their matter in such circumstances.

3.13   Costs updates

3.13.1   You must monitor the developing costs position on all matters other than those that we are undertaking on a fixed fee basis. The requirement is not so much to provide six-monthly updates on the developing costs position as to notify the client as soon as it appears that you are likely to exceed a costs estimate that has already been provided. Not only do the courts tend to disallow costs claims that have not been updated in actions to enforce the payment of fees but it is likely that any such failure could also be seen as a breach of O(1.13) of the Code.

3.13.2   Where possible you should also explain to the client any changed circumstances that will explain why any earlier estimate will no longer apply.

3.13.3   To assist you in this task [*explain any alerts that fee earners might receive – many systems provide this sort of automatic notification when the fee earner has reached a stated percentage of the estimate figure*].

3.13.4   [*For legal aid cases, see Section 7 – 3.13.4.*]

3.13.5   [For crime cases, see Section 7 – 3.13.5.]

3.14   Continuing risk management

3.14.1   You need to be aware of any changed circumstances that would lead you to conclude that the risk profile of a matter could have changed. This might involve greater risk to the firm or the client, as where unfavourable advice is received from counsel or the client's financial circumstances change. Whenever any such change of circumstances might have occurred you must consult your supervisor [*name or title*] as soon as possible.

3.14.2   Any adverse costs orders made against the firm must be promptly reported to [*name or title*] as soon as possible and to the client.

3.15   Inactivity checks

3.15.1   You must take adequate steps to ensure that there is no undue delay on any matter for which you are responsible. This can be achieved by a weekly check of your filing cabinet or a suitable bring-forward system [*or state your preferred method*].

3.15.2   There are also regular review meetings between fee earners and their [*heads of department/supervisors – set out more details if this is the case*].

3.15.3   Note that in legal aid cases, claims for payment should be made within three months of the right to claim at end of a matter or case. Fee earners should ensure that they close cases promptly so that this can be done.

3.16 File reviews

3.16.1 We operate a system of regular file review checks in all departments and extending to [*partners'/directors'*] files also. The file review system is the responsibility of [*name or title*] who will [*explain any checks to ensure that the process is being maintained*].

3.16.2 The frequency of file reviews is as follows [*there is no required frequency under Lexcel – these are common provisions but are by no means mandatory on the one hand, or necessarily adequate on the other. Legal aid practitioners need to note that there are stipulated minimum numbers and frequencies for file reviews, particularly in crime, and these will need to be taken into consideration when determining your own procedure. See Section 7 (3.16.2) for more information*]:

- Partners and other senior lawyers – one file per quarter; and
- Other fee earners – one file per month.

Files are selected on the following basis: [*specify how – at random or selectively from matter print outs? Note that Lexcel 6 requires you to explain your file selection criteria and the number and frequency of file reviews. You may wish to address such issues as seniority, size of caseload, duration of cases. See Lexcel 5.11 (a-b)*]

3.16.3 A file review sheet [*see various formats at Appendices 18-21*] will be completed whenever a file review is undertaken. Copies of this form will be put onto the matter file and into [*central/departmental*] records. If corrective action is required it is the responsibility of [*name or title*] to ensure that this is undertaken within the time specified and in no case will this be longer than 28 days. The reviewer must then verify to his or her reasonable satisfaction that the corrective action has been performed and then sign off the form at or before the next monthly review.

3.16.4 The Head of Department or Supervisor must monitor all file review data. In addition a review of file review data is undertaken [*annually/quarterly by name/title*] and forms part of the annual review of risk data (see 1.7).

3.17   Undertakings

3.17.1   Care is needed in relation to the giving, monitoring and discharge of undertakings. The Glossary of the SRA Handbook defines an undertaking in broad terms as any statement made by the firm or one of its representatives in the course of practice to someone who reasonably relies upon it. There is no need for the word 'undertaking' to be used and we are still liable for anything that we have undertaken to do even if we are unable to do so (e.g. discharge a debt where we are not in funds ourselves).

3.17.2   The sanctions for non-compliance with an undertaking are both contractual and regulatory, failure to honour an undertaking being a potentially serious disciplinary offence which may result in proceedings being taken against a defaulting party in the Solicitors Disciplinary Tribunal.

3.17.3   For these reasons the giving of any undertaking requires a [*partner's/director's*] consent or approval. The only permitted exceptions to this rule are as set out in the department appendices and are limited to the giving of routine conveyancing undertakings and oral undertakings that are offered to court.

3.17.4   When an undertaking is given you must keep a record of it on the file, inform the client of the existence of any undertaking and record that notification on the file. In addition you must clearly record the undertaking by [*placing a sticker on the file and any continuation file on that matter and/or entry to Outlook calendar or notification to Risk Manager, head of department or other*].

3.17.5   You must monitor all outstanding undertakings, particularly those which involve the performance of an act before a given date, and ensure that you continue to operate within that timeframe.

3.17.6   If an undertaking contains a specific date requirement, you must enter that date in your own diary and in the key dates diary so as to ensure compliance with that requirement.

3.17.7   You should also ensure that the discharge of undertakings is confirmed by a [*partner/director*] and noted by [*partner/director signature on the file undertaking sticker or summary sheet and/or entry to Outlook calendar, etc.*].

3.18   Key dates reminder system

3.18.1   It is essential that we maintain a fully reliable back-up system by way of key dates reminders. The list of what constitutes key dates will be found in each set of departmental instructions [*See Appendix 15*] but in general is any date which, if missed, could give rise to a loss to the firm and any other dates which it is convenient to add to any such list.

3.18.2   You must ensure that the date in question is prominently noted in your file [*as on a file summary sheet if you use these in your firm*] and in [*your personal Outlook diary system/the central or departmental diary system, etc.*].

3.18.3   Where appropriate, you must ensure that there are suitable 'countdown' dates as well so that you, or in your absence a colleague, have adequate prior warning of date-specific commitments. There is little point in being alerted for the first time of the fact that a limitation period in litigation expires the following day, for example.

3.18.4   It is your responsibility to monitor and action any key dates reminders [*alternatively set out details of the diary monitor system if one applies in your firm*]. In your absence, planned or otherwise, it is the responsibility of your [*head of department/supervisor/buddy or other*] to check your entries and ensure that suitable action is taken. This system can only work if you **always** enter the required dates in your reminder system.

3.19   Insurance mediation

3.19.1   We are allowed to provide advice on 'investment activity' (such as selling shares or transferring securities) under the auspices of the Financial Conduct Authority and our status as an 'exempt professional firm' under the Financial Services and Markets Act 2000 (see Section 2.20). There are some important related provisions dealing with 'insurance mediation', which consists of advising, arranging or assisting in the administration or performance of insurance contracts. In addition to the need to notify clients of our status in relation to such advice you must provide the client with a 'demands and needs statement' (see Appendix 22). This statement must be provided at the time that the advice is given and cannot be contained as a standard clause in our terms of business document or engagement letter. You must set out details of:

- What you already know about the client and the matter;
- Details of their relevant existing insurance, if any;
- The client's requirements from any policy and the appropriate level of cover; and
- The suitability of the policy that you are recommending.

3.19.2 If you are recommending a particular policy you will have to say whether the recommendation has been made with or without 'fair market analysis' of the available policies. There is generally no obligation to provide a demands and needs statement, however, where (as is more normally the case) we refer the client on to an insurance broker and do not act as the broker ourselves.

3.20 Recommendations and commissions received

3.20.1 There are some important considerations arising from chapter 6 of the Code which you must bear in mind if you are referring clients to third parties. Note that the former restriction requiring that referrals should only be made to independent financial intermediaries was replaced by a revised O(6.3) in early 2013. You must:

- Make the recommendation in the best interests of the client and in such a way that our independence is not compromised (O(6.1));
- Inform the client of any financial interest that we may have in that business (O.(6.2));
- Ensure that clients are in a position to make informed decisions as to how to pursue their matter (O.(6.3)); and
- No prohibited referral fees are paid (O.(6.4)).

3.20.2 The payment of commission income has become much less common in recent years, but if we do receive any such payment as a firm (whether described as commission, a discount on the usual price or other) we must account to the client in full for any such receipt regardless of the amount. If we propose to retain any such sum, or part of it, the client has to agree to this and we would need to be able to justify this in the light of the work that we have done in obtaining it.

3.21 Instructing counsel and experts

3.21.1 When we instruct counsel or other outside experts it is essential that they support our commitment to providing the best levels of service to our clients.

We also have a responsibility to check any advice received and consider its suitability. There is a prohibition in the Code of Conduct against outsourcing reserved legal activities to unauthorised persons.

Choice of adviser

3.21.2   The choice of adviser should always be based on finding the best source of advice possible, having regard to any fee constraints and availability. Many clients rely on us to choose the most appropriate counsel, expert or other professional to assist on their case. However, it may be appropriate to consult the client before instructing someone; for example, if they have used the services of a barrister or other specialist in the past, the client may prefer to use the same person again. The firm maintains a list of approved counsel and experts [*explain arrangements – firm-wide or departmental – including how suggestions for additions or removal should be made and to whom. See Appendix 23.*]

Client information

3.21.3   When instructing experts, you should tell the client how long they might take to respond. In most cases the client will pay the fees, either to us as a disbursement or through the operation of the statutory charge in legal aid matters. Where clients have a financial interest, the cost of the service must be explained to them and confirmed in writing.

3.21.4   You must confirm to the client in writing the name and status of the person being instructed. Where the client expresses a preference that is contrary to the firm's equality and diversity policy their instructions will be challenged. If the instructions are not varied the firm should decline to act further in the matter. In all cases, however, a client may require that a particular medical examiner is not to be used on grounds of previous personal experience.

Instructions

3.21.5   In all cases you need to ensure that the barrister or other expert is fully briefed in order that their advice will be reliable and comprehensive. You will need to provide instructions through letter, brief, telephone conversation or at a meeting. Where instructions are provided verbally they must be confirmed subsequently in writing. In all cases a note of instructions or a copy of them must appear on the matter file.

Evaluation of advice

3.21.6 You must consider the suitability of any advice provided and request supplementary or amended content where appropriate. If, having done so, you are still concerned about the standard of advice provided you should notify [*name or title*] and review whether payment of the fee should be withheld in full or in part. You might also wish to recommend that that person's details are removed from the approved list [*see Appendix 23 for experts and counsel recommendation form*].

Payment of fees

3.21.7 Experts' fees are paid as soon as we are in funds to do so and usually before the end of the case unless a deferred payment arrangement is in place.

3.21.8 In legal aid cases, you must make application for payment on account of disbursements where possible. In addition, the expert must be advised of:

- Any maximum hourly rate applying;
- Any activities that the LAA will not fund (e.g. a cancellation fee where notice of cancellation is given more than 72 hours in advance);
- Requirements for an estimate;
- Procedure to be followed in respect of invoicing;
- Provision of receipts;
- Notification required if an estimate may be exceeded;
- Notice that fees will be assessed by either the court or the LAA; and
- That we will not be responsible for any fees over and above those finally assessed and paid.

3.22 End of the case/matter

3.22.1 At the end of the case or matter you should confirm the following to the client in writing:
- The outcome if required;

- Any further action that the client is required to take in the matter and what (if anything) we will do (and not do, e.g. provide reminders of future key dates such as rent review notices); and
- Arrangements for storage and retrieval of papers (and any charges).

3.22.2   You must also:

- Account to the client for any outstanding money;
- Return any original documents or other property belonging to the client (save for any items which we agree to store);
- Advise the client about whether they should review the matter in future and, if so, when and why;
- Obtain feedback on our service (see Section 2.22: Client Feedback for more information); and
- Carry out a concluding risk assessment and notify [*name or title*] if you feel that the client might fairly complain or make a claim in relation to the work we have done for them on that file.

[*See the file closing section of the file summary sheet at Appendix 24 for a sample file closing checklist.*]

3.22.3   You should mark the file with a destruction date. If you are unsure about an appropriate storage/retention period, please consult your supervisor. You should archive the file as soon as possible, taking into account the likelihood of further or immediate follow-up work. In order to archive a file [*set out your arrangements here*].

3.22.4   If you need to request any file to be retrieved from archiving [*set out your arrangements here and details of any charges that apply if this service is outsourced*].

3.23   Releasing files to another firm

3.23.1   If you are asked to release a current file to another firm you must notify [*name or title*]. The client should be asked to confirm the request formally and in writing, whether to themselves or by onward transmission to another firm. In all cases the file must be checked for its suitability for release and internal notes which are the property of the firm should be removed. [*Consider how and where any such requests are filed for future reference.*]

Notice of a right to cancel your contract with name of firm pursuant to The Consumer Contracts (Information, Cancellation and Additional Charges) Regulations 2013

Right to cancel

You have the right to cancel this contract within 14 days without giving any reason.

The cancellation period will expire after 14 days from the day of the conclusion of the contract.

To exercise the right to cancel, you must inform us by email to your e-mail address, by fax to number ??? or by post to [insert name and full postal address] your decision to cancel this contract by a clear statement (e.g. a letter sent by post, fax or e-mail). You may use the attached model cancellation form, but it is not obligatory to do so.

To meet the cancellation deadline, it is sufficient for you to send your communication concerning your exercise of the right to cancel before the cancellation period has expired.

Effects of cancellation

If you cancel this contract, we will reimburse to you all payments received from you, including the costs of delivery (except for the supplementary costs arising if you chose a type of delivery other than the least expensive type of standard delivery offered by us).

We may make a deduction from the reimbursement for loss in value of any goods supplied, if the loss is the result of unnecessary handling by you.

We will make the reimbursement without undue delay, and not later than –

(a) 14 days after the day we receive back from you any goods supplied, or
(b) (if earlier) 14 days after the day you provide evidence that you have returned the goods, or
(c) if there were no goods supplied, 14 days after the day on which we are informed about your decision to cancel this contract.

We will make the reimbursement using the same means of payment as you used for the initial transaction, unless you have expressly agreed otherwise; in any event, you will not incur any fees as a result of the reimbursement.

If you requested us to begin the performance of services during the cancellation period, you shall pay us an amount which is in proportion to what has been performed until you have communicated us your cancellation from this contract, in comparison with the full coverage of the contract.

This Notice is dated [insert date].

CONTINUATION OF WORK REQUEST

Please complete, detach and return this form to us IF YOU WISH US TO **COMMENCE WORK** WITHIN 14 DAYS OF CONCLUDING YOUR CONTRACT WITH US.

Please note that we will be unable to start work on your instructions until we have received this notice from you.

If you sign and return this form you will still have the right to cancel this contract within 14 days of the date of this form but you will be required to pay a reasonable amount for the work done up to the point at which you notify us of the cancellation.

....

To name and address of firm, e-mail and fax number

I/We hereby give notice that I/we wish you to **continue to act** in relation to my/our contract for the supply of the following services:

Date of retainer letter and writer's reference ....

Your name ....   Your name ....
(Client 1)   (Client 2)

Date of signature ....   Date of signature ....

Any additional clients please sign and date here and/or overleaf

Date received by name of firm ....

CANCELLATION OF WORK REQUEST

Please complete, detach and return this form to us IF YOU WISH US TO **CEASE** ACTING ON THE INSTRUCTIONS YOU HAVE PROVIDED ONLY.

Under the Consumer Contracts (Information, Cancellation and Additional Charges) Regulations 2013 you have the right to cancel your instructions in this matter within 14 days of the confirmation you have received from us. Please use this form only if you wish to **cancel** your instructions to [name of firm] to act on your behalf.

Please note that on receipt of this signed form we will cease to act on your behalf and will no longer be responsible for safeguarding your interests in this matter.

On receipt of this form you will be responsible for all fees incurred up to the point of cancellation if you previously requested us to make a start on your matter.

....

To name and address of firm, e-mail and fax

I/We hereby give notice that I/we **cancel** my/our contract for the supply of the following services:

Date of retainer letter and writer's reference ....

Your name ....   Your name ....
(Client 1)   (Client 2)

Date of signature ....   Date of signature ....
Any additional clients please sign and date here and/or overleaf

Date received by (name of firm)..

SECTION 4

ACCOUNTS MANUAL

Note: This section provides guidance in relation to using the draft procedures that follow.

Introduction

It is important to get the level of the Accounts Manual right for the firm. The starting point is to consider for whom the Manual is intended, whether it is the accounts team or the 'users' of the accounts department, most obviously the fee earners, secretaries and administrators. In the great majority of firms it is the latter form of Manual that will be required, rather than a more advanced Accounts Rules Guide for the specialists providing that function. The Manual should be drawn up on the basis that the specialists are aware of their responsibilities, and if this is not the case then it should be addressed as a training need. This draft has therefore been drawn up as an 'accounts users' Manual'.

The main focus of this part of the compliance documentation should be the range of basic transactions that arise from fee earning work. In all probability the basic principle of the separation of client and office monies will be understood by all and, given the risk of disciplinary action by the SRA for Accounts Rules breaches, most firms will ensure that anybody who does not understand such basics – new or temporary personnel most obviously – is unable to process transactions without proper checks and safeguards being in place.

In addition to the finance procedures set out in this chapter of the Manual there are further points which are important for fee earners to note at section 2.13 of Chapter 2: Policies and Standards.

Quality standards

The requirements of the main quality standards in relation to accounts are not great – for the most part the need is simply to have a set of financial control procedures. This can be found in:

- The 'Compliance Plan' that is recommended good practice in the guidance

to the Authorisation and Practising Requirements of the SRA Handbook;
- Section 2.5 of Lexcel; and
- Section C2 of the SQM, and clause 4 of the Legal Aid Agency's Standard Contract.

There are also more specific requirements in Lexcel in relation to the processes of billing clients and credit control at section 2.4, with a specific requirement that credit limits are set for 'new and existing clients'. Whether this is meant to be applied to clients in relation to all of their matters globally or on every matter that the firm is handling is unclear, and the provisions are more likely to apply as a form of matter control in most firms – i.e. an estimate is set for the anticipated work to be done on that matter. There seems to be no reason why this provision should not be exempted in fixed fee and externally funded work, legal aid most obviously.

The need for a time recording system features in Lexcel at section 2.3 as a 'should' item and the Legal Aid Agency Standard Contracts, clause 7.16 (7.17 in the Crime Duty Provider Contract). The requirements concentrate on the need for accurate billing data where the fees are time-based, but do also refer to the monitoring of work in progress values where this is not the case. The Standard Contract (clause 17.16(g)) requires that firms are able to show a financial value of work in progress. What this means in practice, and what your Contract Manager will expect, depends on the category of law and level of work.

Contract Managers will expect to see a financial value for civil and family work (especially certificated work, where there is a need to keep track on financial limitations) and police station and magistrates' court work. The Legal Aid Agency ("LAA")'s Head of Contract Management confirmed in 2011 that the Commission does not expect a financial running record in standard fee Crown Court cases.

There is also a need for certain management accounting processes to be adopted: profit and loss accounts and balance sheets should be compiled, along with budgets for future income and expenditure and cash flow monitoring.

Legal aid practitioners will be aware that the LAA has increasingly made its contract a regulatory tool, and that its providers may need to produce evidence of financial viability in specified formats (see for example the Financial Assessment Criteria in the 2015 Crime Tender). In addition, the legal aid scheme has its own detailed rules for applying for payments on account and billing.

The SRA Accounts Rules 2011

Although responsibility for compliance with the SRA requirements on financial management should be capable of being entrusted to the accounts department (or those providing support as an outsourced or bought in service) all partners at least, and preferably more besides, should have an awareness of the main principles of the SRA Accounts Rules ('SAR') and the main changes to this area of practice that were introduced by this part of the SRA Handbook in 2011.

The SAR have been drawn up in line with the outcomes focused approach that runs through the SRA Handbook in general, but are much more rules-based than the Code of Conduct. One of the ten principles that underpin the entire regime is relevant:

'You must protect client money and assets.' (Principle 10)

The outcomes that are relevant to the financial management of law firms will include that client money is safe and that the public can have confidence that this will be the case, that there will be proper safeguards in place and that client funds are used for proper purposes only.

Under the former rules all funds received were either client or office monies. There is now a third category of 'out of scope' funds, which arises in alternative business structures (ABSs) in relation to their activities that are not subject to the control of the SRA. A multi-disciplinary practice, for example, would have out of scope money in relation to client work being undertaken by surveyors or accountants within the business, rather than by their lawyer colleagues who would be subject to SRA regulation. The former category of 'controlled trust money', by the way, was abolished in earlier changes to the former Solicitors' Accounts Rules in 2009.

One of the most common causes of disciplinary actions by the SRA is the withdrawal of client funds without proper authority. Three conditions must always be satisfied for such a withdrawal, namely:

- There must be sufficient funds held in client account in relation to the matter in question;
- The reason for the withdrawal is one of the reasons set out at s.20 SAR (or the withdrawal is on SRA authority; and
- The authority for the withdrawal is signed by an 'appropriate person'.

The range of permitted signatories for client account withdrawals is wider under the SAR and s.21(1) suggests that the firm should have 'procedures for signing on client account'. The draft procedures that follow suggest the usual arrangement whereby partners/directors only may authorise withdrawals and in many firms this is limited to the (often named) equity partners only. However, this is open to amendment as seems suitable by each user, in which case it is worth consulting guidance note (i) to the rule on the factors that should be taken into consideration before deciding what other arrangements might be appropriate. A related change introduced by the SAR is that the authority may now be electronic, though it is envisaged that most firms will continue with the previous requirement to have a physical signature by one of the authorised signatories. The Rules now provide that there is no requirement to keep hard copies of electronic authorities for client account withdrawals as long as the information is capable of being reproduced reasonably quickly in printed form for at least six years. In practice most firms will prefer written records and should have a voucher system in place. These may be custom designed forms specific to the firm, or bought in vouchers as supplied by Oyez, amongst others. Lexcel firms should also note that this the issue of cheque authorisations has become part of that standard with 2.5 now providing that there needs to be a procedure covering financial transactions and 'authorisations'. Although this term is defined to mean 'permission to approve expenditure to pre-defined levels' the intent seems to have been to reflect rule 21(1) of the SAR.

Billing (4.14)

The section on billing envisages the normal practice of billing generally on account of costs. In most cases it will be unlikely that an interim bill will be final for the period it relates to, meaning that the firm will be unable to enforce it as a debt and, moreover, the client will be able to challenge it at any stage before receipt of a 'final' bill, even if they have paid it at an earlier stage.

It is important to note that unless specific wording or an agreement to the contrary is adopted an interim invoice will not be final for the period that it relates to, especially in relation to contentious work. There is, however, the alternative of issuing 'interim statute bills' which are complete, self-contained bills for the period that they relate to. For an analysis of the different types of bills see *Winchester Commodities Group Ltd v R D Black & Co* [2000] BCC 310. There is something of a 'heads and tails' element to the choice of billing format: if the bill is a general interim bill the firms will be unable to sue upon it, but they can revisit the issue at a later stage and charge more for the period that it relates to if it is fair to do so.

Client interest (4.17)

The other main change of note to the SAR in 2011 was the abolition of the former rule allowing firms to retain sums of up to £20 of interest earned on client monies, or according to the formula set out in the 1988 rules (e.g. £1000 held for eight weeks, etc). In line with the outcomes focused approach on which much of the SRA Handbook is based all firms are now required to adopt a policy which they believe to be suitable in all the circumstances, and so depending on the nature of the firm, its clients and the amounts of money that are typically held in client account and for how long. The circumstances where it is not necessary to pay interest are set out in s.22(2) and include the situation where legal aid monies are held in client account.

In practice most firms will follow the suggestion found in the guidance notes to this part of the rules that a 'de minimis' £20 rule will apply, and this is the approach adopted in the procedures that follow. The same guidance also states that it is important to keep any such figure under review in the light of changing interest rates and this notice also appears in the draft procedure below. Commercial firms in particular may wish to vary this limit to a higher sum in which case the guidance to be found at rule 23 should be taken into account.

Since monies placed on specific deposit are required to be paid net of tax all such amounts must be paid to clients – see note (i)(d) to rule 22 changes in the SAR. All firms should ensure that their policy on the payment of interest is set out in their retainer letters or terms of business documentation as a result of the specific requirement at s.22(3) that the policy on the payment of interest must be brought to the client's attention.

ACCOUNTS MANUAL

4.1   Introduction

4.1   It is important that you follow these procedures so we can be sure that we comply with the SRA Accounts Rules 2011 ('SAR'). It is the responsibility of the fee earner with conduct of a matter to ensure that the accounts staff have the fee earner's authority and clear instructions before any transactions are processed, especially those relating to client account.

4.2   Responsibility for financial management

4.2.1   The [*finance partner/person with responsibility for financial management*] is [*name*].

4.2.2   In accordance with the SRA Handbook, [*he/she/other*] has been nominated as the firm's Compliance Officer for Finance and Administration ('COFA'). In this respect [*his/her*] duties are to:

- Monitor for compliance with the SAR;
- Maintain records of any such non-compliances; and
- Report to the SRA any material breach of the SAR.

4.2.3   It is the responsibility of all personnel to ensure that they follow these finance control procedures and report to [*name or position*] any suspected or actual non-compliance with these requirements.

4.2.4   In addition to the preparation of annual profit and loss and balance sheet reports, [*name or position*] is responsible for the preparation of forward budgets for income, expenses and capital expenditure. The financial performance of the firm is monitored against these budgets [*monthly/at each partners' meeting/other*] in order that corrective measures can be taken in the event of adverse trends or other developments, as is cash flow. The financial performance of the firm is therefore monitored as required by IB(10.2) of the Code of Conduct and any serious financial problems would be reported to the SRA as required by O(10.3).

4.2.5   [*Name or position*] is responsible for the preparation and monitoring of the client account reconciliation as required by s.29(12) of the SRA Accounts Rules, by comparing the balances of all client accounts with the liabilities to clients, allowing for any unpresented items and preparing a reconciliation report to explain any differences that emerge from the process. This process is undertaken monthly, with the intervals between it being undertaken never exceeding five weeks. This reconciliation statement is signed by [*name or position*] or, in their absence, [*name or position*].

Part A: Payments in and out of the firm's bank accounts

4.3   Cheques and other receipts into client account

4.3.1   All monies received for payment into client account must be banked on the day of receipt whenever possible, or on the following day at the latest. To achieve this you must ensure that cheques, cash and banker's drafts are passed to cashiers with a completed voucher [*or form reference*] as soon as possible or by 12:00 on the day following receipt at the very latest. You must ensure that you retain the duplicate voucher [*or form reference*] on the matter file.

4.3.2   Since we are not allowed to use one client's funds to support another client's matter it is essential that cheques that have been requested from clients or lenders arrive in time for us to be sure that they have cleared the banking system. This means that clients must be asked to provide us with any such payment at least six days in advance of the day the funds will be required. By way of example, if a conveyancing purchase is due to complete on Friday 25th June we should look to bank the funds no later than Friday 18th June. Special clearance will be required for cheques received later than the sixth day prior to completion. Charges for such special clearance may be recharged to the client provided that this is made clear in the terms of business. Although most mortgage lenders will transmit funds by CHAPS, cheques received from lenders may be treated as cleared funds and used on the day of banking.

4.3.3   In the event of the absence of a fee earner it is the responsibility of the secretary to check the incoming post of the absent fee earner to ensure that any cheques are processed as required by the SAR.

4.3.4   [*Set out here any details of how your client account receipt form should be completed or provide an illustration.*]

4.3.5   The firm's client account is held at:

> Bank and branch details
> Sort Code:
> Account No.

4.4   Cheque receipts into office account

4.4.1   All monies received for the firm's costs and for disbursements that have already been paid by the firm, along with any other office account payments, must be paid into office account on receipt. Care must be taken with mixed receipts containing unpaid professional disbursements to ensure that these are either paid out within two working days or transferred to client account.

4.4.2   [*Set out here any details of how your office account receipt form should be completed or provide an illustration.*]

4.4.3   Please ensure that you retain the duplicate voucher [*or form reference*] on the matter file.

4.4.4   The firm's office account is held at:

> Name and branch details
> Sort Code:
> Account No.

4.5   Third party cheques

4.5.1   Where a cheque is received which is payable to a third party it must not simply be attached to the file until used. You must instead complete a [*describe receipt form or specify what must be noted in a memo*] and pass this along with the cheque to the accounts department.

4.5.2   You will receive in return a receipted voucher [*or receipt form reference*] which you should attach to your file until such time as the cheque is required.

4.5.3   To send off the cheque, take the voucher [*or receipt form reference*] back to the accounts department who will exchange it for the original cheque which you may then dispatch.

4.6   Payments out (client and office accounts)

4.6.1   Requests for cheques are made on vouchers [*or describe forms for client and office accounts, or describe by colour*] and should show the following: [*Specify*].

4.6.2   [*Set out here any details of how your payment form should be completed or provide an illustration.*]

4.6.3   All cheque requests must reach the accounts department by no later than [*time*] if you wish to guarantee having a cheque on the same day that the request is made. Except in cases of emergency all cheque requests received after [*time*] will be processed on the following day.

4.6.4   If you are requesting a cheque on client account it is your responsibility to ensure that the necessary sums are in the account and are cleared. Cheques to cover disbursements should be paid from the office bank account, not client account, and funds transferred from client account if they are available and we have the client's approval to do so.

4.6.5   Any payment from client account requires the signature of [*a partner/one of the following partners – see introduction to this chapter*]. Office account payments may be authorised by [*specify*].

4.7   Legal aid receipts and payments

4.7.1   Monies received from the Legal Aid Agency as regular payments must be paid (and will normally be paid electronically directly) into the firm's office account.

4.7.2   For monies received for or on account of disbursements, reference must be made to Rule 19 of the SAR.

4.8   **Cash**

4.8.1   As a result of the obligations that law firms are subject to we operate a cash handling limit of [*£500/£1,000 per transaction/28 days are common limits*]. The handling of cash involves more risk to the firm in any event, not least in taking large amounts to the bank; for both reasons, payments out or receipts of cash should be discouraged even if they are within the overall limit.

Receipt of cash

4.8.2   If you are asked to receive cash ask a colleague to assist, preferably a member of the accounts staff. A receipt must be prepared by the accounts department and handed to the client. Cash receipts from third parties will be exceptional and will require the consent of the MLRO.

4.9   **CHAPS**

4.9.1   CHAPS stands for 'Clearing House Automated Payments System', used for the telegraphic transfer of monies electronically.

4.9.2   [*State any arrangements for this system within the firm and the firm's policy on how the charges are dealt with: note IB(1.21) on not inflating disbursements such as telegraphic transfer fees and describing them as such to cover what actually amounts to the firm's charges for its time and service.*]

4.9.3   If you are a fee earner who is requesting a CHAPS payment it is your responsibility to ensure that cleared funds are available before submitting the CHAPS instruction to the accounts department.

4.9.4   [*State the firm's policy on CHAPS charges – are they passed on to the client at cost or recharged at a different rate and classed as profit costs – what do the terms of business say?*]

4.10   **Bankers' drafts**

4.10.1   A banker's draft is a document similar to a cheque but drawn on the bank itself against a cleared cash balance, giving the payee confidence that payment is guaranteed. All requests for outgoing banker's drafts must be made to the accounts department at least one working day before the day that they are required. The main use of a bank draft will be where it is not possible to transmit funds electronically, or where payment in a foreign currency for a specific sum is required.

4.10.2 Our policy is [*to re-charge the banker's draft fee as a disbursement/make a charge of £? as profit costs to include the disbursement charged to the firm by the bank*].

4.11 Petty cash

4.11.1 [*State arrangements for petty cash, including any form that has to be completed and submitted for reimbursement.*]

Part B: Billing and credit control

4.12 Credit limits

4.12.1 At the start of every private paying matter which will not be undertaken on a fixed fee basis (i.e. in all matters where the fees are uncertain at the outset, even if the subject of an estimate) the fee earner must include in the matter opening form a billing 'reserve' figure which must then be kept under review. As soon as it becomes clear to you that this limit will be exceeded you must contact the client to explain why that figure will no longer apply and set a new estimate figure. [*In some firms an automatic prompt will be provided to warn that this limit is being approached, in which case set out here when this will occur and what actions the fee earner then needs to take.*]

4.13 Time recording

4.13.1 It is the policy of the firm to record [*all fee earner time/all chargeable time/time in all matters where billing will depend upon it, etc*].

4.13.2 You record time by [*describe your process – timesheets for the accounts department to process or direct input by fee earners*]. In areas of work such as domestic conveyancing where most work is conducted to fixed fee estimates the policy of the firm is [*not to record time/occasional time recording is sometimes conducted for management information*].

4.14 Billing

4.14.1 Our policy on the need for money on account of costs and interim billing is set out in the [*terms of business document/retainer*] letters. Payments on account of disbursements must be obtained in advance wherever possible.

4.14.2   You must present clients with their final bills as soon as possible after the completion of a matter and where possible within 14 days, making sure that all unbilled work in progress is taken into account. In transactional work final bills should be presented prior to the completion of the matter so as to enable the bill to be paid upon completion.

4.14.3   Bills on clients' matters must always be addressed to the client and must show the client's address. Where a bill is payable by a third party, it should be made out to the client's name at the client's address, which should then be followed by the words "Payable by ..." and give the third party's name and address.

4.14.4   [*It would be helpful here to set out more about who does what in your billing procedures, including the authority that fee earners have to write off time before settling billing amounts. Is a partner's consent to or signature on all bills required?*]

Legal aid receipts

4.14.5   Legal aid receipts are credited direct to our bank account.

4.14.6   Accounts will identify the payments relating to individual matters and prepare the relevant copy bills for processing, and enter the bills so that the financial accounts will reflect the fact that the payment has been received.

Legal aid disbursements

4.14.7   You may apply for 'prior authority' in respect of any legal aid disbursement planned over £100. Payment on account of disbursements can and should be claimed for disbursements under legal aid certificates. See also below for claiming payment on account of costs under legal aid certificates.

4.15   Amendments to bills

4.15.1   If you discover a mistake on a bill subsequent to its being sent out you must request a credit note from the accounts department and settle a revised bill for the client.

4.16   Legal aid billing

4.16.1   The rules for legal aid billing are complex. The following is a brief introductory outline.

Legal Help/Family Help (Lower) matters

4.16.2   You should send the file for costing as soon as the matter is finished or a full certificate is granted following prior Controlled Work (unless there is any remaining work that would not be covered under the certificate but would be covered under Controlled Work). The Controlled Work will then be claimed in the next monthly online Controlled Matter Report Form ('CMRF') submitted to the LAA. Individual files are not routinely assessed but may be called for audit on a sample basis.

4.16.3   If costs on a Controlled Work matter exceed three times the fixed fee, they are called 'exceptional cases' if the case is an Access to Justice Act 1999 case (pre 1 April 2013), or 'escape fee case' if the case was opened under legal aid funding from 1 April 2013. The files are submitted to the LAA and they are individually costs assessed.

Full Legal Aid Certificates (Civil)
Payments on account

4.16.4   You can (and must) claim a payment on account of profit costs after a certificate has been in force for three months. After that you can claim every six months (although you are limited to two claims in a 12 month period). You can also claim payment on account of disbursements as these are incurred.

Final bills

4.16.5   Legal aid bills are assessed by either the LAA or the court. LAA assessment applies in standard and graduated fee cases and in other cases where costs, disbursements and counsel's fees do not exceed £2,500. If costs exceed £2,500 they are assessed by the court. However, note that if there is an element of costs between the parties, the bill will be assessed by the court regardless of the size of the bill.

4.16.6   If the client has financial interests by way of monies or property gain, or the client has paid legal aid contributions, you must give the client notice of his or her right to object to the claim for costs. After expiry of a period of 21 days the file will be returned to the fee earner for signing and submission of the claim for costs. If costs are reduced on assessment there is an appeals procedure.

4.16.7   In cases which cannot be assessed by the LAA, the bill will need to be lodged at court and assessed by a District Judge. Assessments are generally on the papers only, unless a hearing is requested. Appeals against reductions have short deadlines (seven days to notify counsel and 14 days to appeal in total from the receipt of the returned bill).

4.16.8   Where there is an element of inter partes costs, the bill must be served on the other side before assessment takes place. They have three weeks in which to accept the bill, or serve points of dispute. If agreement is not reached, a hearing will take place before a District Judge or Costs Officer.

4.16.9   If the client has a financial interest, he or she will have the right to object to the bill, as above.

Police station and magistrates' court fees

4.16.10 Online claims are submitted to the LAA every month in respect of standard fee cases, as for legal help civil cases, above. Non-standard fee cases are submitted for individual assessment.

Crown Court cases

4.16.11 These are almost all paid under the Litigator Graduated Fee Scheme and the Advocates Graduated Fee Scheme. They are sufficiently complex for the LAA to have issued a spreadsheet for lawyers to use to calculate their costs.

Legal aid: Interim payments – Crown Court Litigator Graduated Fee Scheme – Crime

4.16.12 Litigators may apply for interim payments in Crown Court cases where the representation Order was granted on or after 2 October 2014. Payment may be claimed in cases where there has been an effective PCMH, except for either way offences where the defendant has elected for a Crown Court trial. A second interim payment may be claimed where a trial has commenced and is estimated to last for 10 days or more.

4.16.13 Payments on account of disbursements are available for disbursements where prior authority has been granted and the disbursement is over £100.

4.17   Client interest

4.17.1   As required by s.22(3) of the SAR the firm has adopted a policy on the payment of client interest which the [*partners/directors*] believe will treat clients in a manner that is fair and reasonable. Since tax will have been deducted at source on any funds held on designated client account all such receipts of interest are paid to the client net. The current policy in relation to sums earned by way of interest in relation to funds held in general client account can be found in the terms of business. The policy on the payment of interest to clients is kept under regular review.

4.18   Credit control

4.18.1   The firm's terms of business allow [*time/number of days*] for the payment of bills.

4.18.2   If payment has not been received after [*time*] the accounts department will send an initial reminder notification to supplement your own attempts to obtain payment. Letters will be sent automatically unless stopped by [*specify who has authority to stop the process*].

4.18.3   [*Describe your follow-up processes of further reminders and then debt recovery action.*]

4.18.4   Write-offs of bills that have been sent out by [*describe your procedures*].

4.19   Debit/credit card payments

4.19.1   [*Set out here any provisions for clients to make payments to the firm by credit cards and how receipts are processed. Many firms will not accept payments for disbursements in this manner because of the deductions made by card companies.*]

CHAPTER 5

OFFICE FACILITIES AND INFORMATION TECHNOLOGY

Note: This section provides guidance in relation to using the draft procedures that follow.

Introduction

This chapter of the Manual, like the Accounts chapter, will probably need more extensive amendment than others to reflect the different practical arrangements that will exist in all firms. If yours is a multi-office firm you will also need to consider how to reflect the arrangements for your different locations.

Health and safety

The need for a policy on this issue is well known and is addressed in the section on policies in Section 2. Here the greater concern is the more detailed procedures that are required to make sense of that policy. All firms need a designated 'responsible person' whose role and functions are set out in a range of statutory instruments such as the Management of Health and Safety at Work Regulations 1999 (SI 1999/3242) and the Workplace (Health, Safety and Welfare) Regulations 1992 (SI 1992/3004).

In relation to fire safety issues, likewise, the Regulatory Reform (Fire Safety) Order 2005 (SI 2005/1541) replaced the former fire certificate procedure with an obligation on all firms to appoint a 'responsible person' who will need to conduct or organise a fire risk assessment, which they can only do if they have been suitably trained to do so. Quite apart from the obvious concerns to meet the responsibilities to colleagues that the partners or directors will have, there are potentially serious penalties in the event of a fire causing injury or loss of life if the firm has not met its obligations in this regard.

Outsourcing

A section on outsourcing is unlikely to appear in the manuals in place in most firms and has been included in response to O(7.10) of the SRA Code of Conduct, which makes most of the requirements reflected in this procedure. Outsourcing is an increasingly used business strategy, common examples being IT support, secretarial services and paralegal support. The main concern is need to ensure compliance with the duty of confidentiality at O(4.1), with IB(4.3) suggesting that firms should only outsource services where they have taken steps to ensure that client confidentiality can be maintained. Although not part of the Code's requirements we have extended the suggested arrangements to include the commercial confidentiality of information relating to the firm.

Information technology

It is difficult to see how any law firm could claim to be exempt from the Data Protection Act 1998 and the consequential need to register as a processor of data with the Information Commissioner. It is worth noting that a number of practitioners have been convicted in recent years for failure to do so. See the 'Resources' section of the Introduction for details of a webinar on this topic (as required by Lexcel at section 3.1.i). The main issues to consider here are:

- The uses to which information technology ('IT') will be put, in the form of an IT plan;
- An assessment of the 'information assets' of the firm, i.e. those items for which it has responsibility; and
- The appropriate usage of communications technology such as e-mails, the internet and, increasingly, social media.

The whole issue of information management, and of cyber-security in particular, will quite clearly become an increasing concern for law firms in the months and years to come. The SRA reports increased incidences of attacks on the integrity of law firms' IT systems including, most worryingly, the banking systems with them. A growing number of firms have experienced the successful infiltration of client account so as to divert purchase monies in transactions to the fraudsters' accounts. More generally the Information Commissioner has issued criticism of the level of data controls that are relied upon by the legal profession – see "Information Commissioner 'sounds the alarm' on data breaches within the legal profession" at www.ico.org.uk which recommends, amongst other things, increased use of encryption for confidential data and acceptance that passwording in itself is inadequate protection in the event of the loss or theft of hand-held devices.

In this regard see also the more specific requirements that have been added to Lexcel in relation to the information security policy required at 3.1, now extending to details of firewalls, configuration of network devices and details of all software programmes that are used. Under Lexcel 6 firms also need a register of all their software and a plan for monitoring and updating it. Legal aid practitioners are increasingly needing to use the internet as an integral part of case management, for example; to submit civil applications and bills, to lodge applications for legal aid and to correspond with other parties in the case through the criminal justice system secure email system.

The use of e-mail and the internet raises a number of legal considerations which practices need to incorporate into their policies. In particular, partners/directors/senior managers need to decide whether, and to what extent, they will or may monitor e-mail and use of the internet.

The Human Rights Act 1998 provides a 'right to respect for private and family life, home and correspondence'. Case law suggests that employees have a reasonable expectation of privacy in the workplace and ACAS recommends that employers should provide their staff with some means of personal communication which is not subject to monitoring. Firms should make sure employees know of any monitoring or recording of correspondence (which includes e-mails, use of the internet and telephone calls).

The Information Commissioner's code of practice *Monitoring at work: an Employer's Guide* states that any monitoring of e-mails should only be undertaken where:

- The advantage to the business outweighs the intrusion into the workers' affairs;
- Employers carry out an impact assessment of the risk they are trying to avert and workers are told they are being monitored;
- Information discovered through monitoring is only used for the purpose for which the monitoring was carried out;
- The information discovered is kept secure; and
- Employers are careful when monitoring personal communications such as e-mails which are clearly personal.

Social media

Western Europe leads the way for social media usage in the legal sector, with a particularly high level of activity in the UK. The main challenge presented to law firms by the growth of facilities such as Twitter, Facebook and LinkedIn is that of safeguarding client confidentiality under O(4.1) of the Code of Conduct. This threat has to be seen as being very real since revealing to third parties that a named person is a client without their permission could amount to a breach of this duty. Another increasingly common problem is that of poor judgement, since it is all too easy to fire off an instant comment which, once posted, is unlikely to be capable of being retracted. A related concern is the comments that personnel can make about their employers in chatrooms, risking reputational harm for the practice itself.

The Law Society has issued a practice note on this topic (20th December 2011) which can be found on the Law Society website. The thrust of this note is to recommend the adoption of a suitable social networking policy, whilst recognising that a formal written policy might not be necessary in smaller firms, but as required under Lexcel v6 in any event.

Most firms would be well advised to address this issue if they have not done so already. The main steps are to appoint someone to take responsibility and then to set out what is permitted within the firm in relation to client information and communication, and also to set out the limits on what might be said about the firm, perhaps as an amendment to employment contracts.

OFFICE FACILITIES AND INFORMATION TECHNOLOGY

Part 1: Health and safety

5.1   Policy

5.1.1   Our policy is to provide safe and healthy working conditions, equipment and systems of work for all employees, and to provide adequate training and supervision. We also operate with consideration for the health and safety of people who are not our employees, when using our premises. See also 2.16.

5.2   Responsibilities

5.2.1   The [partners/directors/managers] retain overall responsibility for establishing and monitoring health and safety arrangements. The health and safety representative (see 1.3.7) has responsibility for implementing this policy. (S)he carries out a health and safety assessment annually and records the findings, taking any action required.

5.2.2   All employees must co-operate to achieve a safe and healthy workplace and take reasonable care of themselves and others. Any employee encountering a health and safety problem that they cannot resolve must inform the health and safety representative immediately. All health and safety incidents must be reported internally so that we are aware of all problems and can take any steps required to prevent them happening again.

5.2.3   As part of our induction training programme, all new employees are given details of the health and safety policy, and training is arranged as appropriate with respect to the hazards which we have assessed as relevant to our practice. A health and safety poster is displayed [state where].

5.2.4   If you experience any problems with heating/lighting, please inform [name or title].

First aid

5.2.5   Our trained first aiders are [*insert*].

5.2.6   A first aid box is located [*state where*]. [*Name or title*] is responsible for stocking it.

Accidents

5.2.7   The accident book is kept [*state where*]. The health and safety representative or, in his/her absence, any other of the [*partners/directors*] will record any accident involving injury, including any first aid treatment given, in the accident book as soon as possible after the accident.

5.2.8   If an accident is reportable under the Reporting of Injuries, Diseases and Dangerous Occurrences Regulations 1995 (RIDDOR), for example death, injuries resulting in seven days or more off work, occupational diseases or dangerous occurrences, the health and safety representative will make a report via the Health and Safety Executive website. The HSE may pass on information to the Environmental Health Department of the local authority.

Fire safety

5.2.9   A fire evacuation drill is held at least once a year. A copy of the fire evacuation policy is displayed [*state where*] and in reception.

5.2.10   [*State colour*] fire extinguishers for extinguishing fires other than electrical fires are situated [*state where*]. A [*state colour*] fire extinguisher for extinguishing electrical fires is situated [*state where*].

Hazards

- Only those staff who have been trained to do so, and who have protective clothing/suitable equipment, may use potentially hazardous chemicals.
- All staff will have their workstations assessed to ensure good posture and avoid glare and reflections on the screen. You are expected to take breaks and/or change activity regularly.

- Eye tests are provided for those who need them. We pay for spectacles if these are needed specifically for display screen use (or a portion of the cost depending on the prescription).
- If you use a laptop, we will train you how to carry out an assessment so that you can use it safely and comfortably away from the office. When used in the office, a laptop should be used with a docking station, full size screen, keyboard and mouse.
- [Name or title] will carry out a regular visual inspection of plugs and cables, inspecting for loose connections and faults. If you see any defective plugs, discoloured sockets, damaged cables, switches, etc. you must take them out of use and report them to [name or title] at once.
- Please ensure you do not move electrical equipment and leave wires trailing. Be sure to wipe up all spills (or arrange for it to be done) immediately.
- If a light bulb needs to be changed, or you need something from a high shelf, use a ladder or steps and use them safely. Chairs and tables are not suitable for these purposes.
- If you work at home, we will show you how to carry out an assessment on your workstation to ensure good posture.

Personal safety

5.2.11 If someone tries to steal from you, whether inside or outside the office, do not resist. Tell your supervisor or any senior manager as soon as possible so that the matter can be reported to our insurers/police.

5.2.12 Thankfully, violent incidents are extremely rare but, if you are concerned, you should [*practices have different ways of dealing with this. Some have panic buttons in conference rooms; others alert colleagues by telephone using an agreed phrase, such as 'Could you bring in the precedents file'. You will need to insert your practice here*].

5.2.13 If you are going on any external visit, especially to a client for the first time, consider whether you should take someone with you. It is also preferable to try to meet new contacts (on the first occasion at least) in a public venue rather than their private premises. Your personal safety must be your first priority.

Remember: when in doubt, get out – your personal safety is more important than an offended client!

5.2.14 Before you go, ensure someone else in the office is aware of the following:

- Your mobile number;
- The client's name, address and telephone number;
- The time and date of the visit;
- The time you expect to be back at the office; and
- If you will not be coming back to the office, arrange a time to telephone in at the end of a visit.

5.2.15 At the end of the visit, go back to the office or telephone by the time you indicated. If you are concerned about anything arising from the visit, tell your supervisor.

Work related stress

5.2.16 Work is generally good for people and we hope that you will enjoy your job at the firm. Most of us will enjoy some degree of pressure in our work and it is probably a main ingredient of our job satisfaction. Pressure, however, can easily turn into stress, this being a natural reaction to too much pressure. The Health and Safety Executive's formal definition of work related stress is:

'The adverse reaction people have to excessive pressures or other types of demand placed on them at work.'

5.2.17 If you feel that you are becoming stressed please talk to [*name or title*]. We will work with you to find ways of making your job more manageable. If the source of your problem is your relationship with your supervisor, please use our dignity at work policy (6.10).

Part 2: Office facilities
5.3 Security

Burglar alarm

5.3.1 The alarm is linked to the local police station. If you need to start work early or leave late and will need to set or turn off the alarm, please contact [*insert*] for information.

5.3.2   The keyholders for alarm purposes are [*insert*].

Reception

5.3.3   The reception area is our shop window and we need to ensure that it is well presented and comfortable, this being part of the [*Receptionist's/Other's*] responsibilities. Please be sure to project the right image of the firm whenever you are in the reception area by avoiding inappropriate conversations with colleagues and respecting the need for client confidentiality if you do meet there briefly with clients.

5.3.4   Visitors, whether clients or others, should be escorted to and from reception.

[*If you use a visitor pass system, you may want to include a reference here.*]

Interview rooms

5.3.5   We have a limited number of interview rooms. To book one please [*insert appropriate wording here*].

Parking

5.3.6   Parking spaces are always at a premium. Unless you have been allocated a staff parking space, only authorised visitors are allowed to park in our car park. If your client or other visitor requires a parking space, please [*insert appropriate wording here*].

5.4   Telephones
[*You will need to adapt this to reflect the system you use. A sample procedure is shown below.*]

5.4.1   Our main land line number is answered from [*9:00-5.30, Monday to Friday*]. We aim to answer all callers [*within three rings/as soon as possible*].

5.4.2   In addition, fee earners [*may/should*] make their direct dial numbers available so that clients and others can contact them directly outside of office hours if necessary.

5.4.3   If you need to work undisturbed, you may route your calls to voicemail but you must ensure that calls are returned within a reasonable time. If a secretary or other colleague will be taking your calls please ensure that they know when you are likely to return calls in order that they can convey this information to the caller, and then be sure to do so. This simple act of teamwork will usually prevent most follow-up calls.

5.4.4   If you are away from the office please ensure your phone is answered or leave a clear 'out of office' voicemail message. Do remember to update this as necessary: it does not inspire confidence to be told that today's date is in fact a week or more ago!

5.4.5   Fee earners who are often away from the office are provided with mobile telephones. These must not be used if you are driving unless you have suitable 'hands-free' equipment.

5.5   Stationery and supplies

5.5.1   These are kept [*state where*].

5.5.2   [*Name or title*] is responsible for ordering stationery and supplies. [*Insert here any particular instructions you may have.*]

5.6   Photocopying

5.6.1   [*Explain any file charging system in place.*] Any problems with photocopiers should be notified to [*name or title*].

5.6.2   If you are considering sending photocopying to an external organisation, please refer to our outsourcing policy (see 5.11). This is important as, if you do not comply with it, you and we may breach our professional obligations to a client.

[*Insert here any particular instructions you may have.*]

5.7   Post and DX

5.7.1   DX should be used in preference to Royal Mail wherever possible, as it is cheaper and can be more reliable.

5.7.2   Post and DX should be taken to the [*post room/reception*] by [*time/regularly throughout the day and no later than ... for dispatch that day, or explain how collection system works*].

5.8   Fax

5.8.1   E-mails and attachments have substantially replaced the use of fax machines, but they do remain an important tool for the transmission and acceptance of documents, especially when needing to have a note of the time of transmission. Fax machines are located [*state where*].

5.8.2   When sending a fax, be extremely careful to ensure that you are directing it to the right number as breaching confidentiality by sending it to the wrong place could easily breach our professional obligations, and could also result in censure by the Information Commissioner (see below).

5.8.3   Any faxes received must be given to [*the addressee/the appropriate supervisor*] without delay.

Part 3:   Document management and library

5.9   Wills and deeds

5.9.1   Draft wills are stored on the matter file in the usual way, but once they are signed they must be entered into the wills management system which is [*explain your firm's arrangements for retaining wills in safe storage and the keeping of any register, to include how it is noted that wills have been sent from the firm on request (by recorded delivery or collection from someone who is known to the firm or who has supplied ID information). State whether a charge is made for this service if your firm is not to undertake the probate and check your firm's terms of business on this point.*]

5.9.2   It is permissible for fee earners to retain deeds on live matters that are being worked on in their normal filing system, but you should have regard to the following while doing so:

- Avoid taking them out of the office where possible;

- Take great care of them when this is necessary;
- Store them in your filing cabinet when not in use, and especially overnight.

5.9.3 If we are asked to keep deeds in our possession for safe keeping our policy is to do so for clients where we have worked on a matter relating to that property [*state your charging policy, if any – many firms provide this as a free service but then charge a retrieval fee if the deeds are taken elsewhere in relation to any further transactions*].

5.9.4 Deeds that are no longer being actively worked upon (whether the matter file has been archived or not) must be deposited with [*name or title*] for safe keeping. [*Explain process as above for wills – in many firms it is the same process.*]

In order to retrieve deeds from storage [*explain*].

5.10 Library

5.10.1 We possess a range of relevant books and other research resources. The person with overall responsibility for these materials, including the purchasing of new titles and editions and withdrawal of obsolete materials, is [*name or title*].

5.10.2 You will find a list of available titles and their whereabouts in the office at [*insert*]. Please be sure to return all titles when not in use to avoid wasted time for others.

5.10.3 We are subscribers to [*insert details of any external research and precedent database systems, in which case clarify who may make searches and any passwording systems in place.*]

5.11 Outsourcing

5.11.1 There are restrictions on the ability of law firms to outsource reserved legal activities (O(7.9)). We need to ensure, whenever we outsource a business function that is critical to the service we provide to clients, that we have taken proper safeguards to check the credentials of any individuals, agencies or other concerns that we are dealing with and have agreed suitable arrangements with them to ensure that they are committed to upholding the professional duties that we are subject to – the duty of confidentiality in particular (O(4.1)). This section does not, however, apply to the instructions of barristers and other experts, on which see 3.21.

5.11.2   We currently outsource the following functions. The person responsible for that arrangement is also shown. It is the duty of the person named as having responsibility for the activity listed for monitoring the quality, effectiveness and suitability of the service provided.

Activity	Contractor	Responsibility of

5.11.3   All outsourcing arrangements must comply with O(7.10) of the Code of Conduct and agree to the following provisions in their terms of engagement with the firm (to be agreed as a rider to their existing agreement if necessary):

'As a solicitors' practice we are regulated by the Solicitors Regulation Authority ('SRA') and, as such, are subject to strict duties of client confidentiality under its Code of Conduct (which can be inspected at www.sra.org.uk/handbook). In accordance with O(7.10) we are required to ensure that you agree to the following provisions in relation to all work done by you for and on behalf of this firm, namely that you will:

- Maintain in strict confidence all client information of which you become aware, including the identity of any clients of the firm, and also any commercial information on this firm;
- Conduct suitable checks on any personnel that you employ or retain who have responsibility for, or access to, the information you have access to on our behalf; and
- Provide to the SRA such information as it may request, or permit the SRA or its agents to inspect your records (including electronic records) or enter your premises in relation to the services provided to this firm and/or our clients.'

5.11.4   Any outsourced service arrangement will be cancelled in the event of serious concerns arising as to the continuing suitability of that person or organisation. Any such concerns must be reported to the [*name or title – probably COLP*] in which case it might be necessary to report the breach to the SRA and perhaps the client.

Part 4: Information management

5.12   Information technology

5.12.1   Like most businesses, we are heavily dependent on our hardware and software systems. We maintain a register of all the software we use and we have a plan for monitoring and updating our software.

We have procedures for the safe configuration of network devices (these are the components that join our network together and allow us to access files/printers/mobiles etc.). We have firewalls to protect our systems; but if any malicious software should get through, we have additional software to detect and remove it.

If you experience any hardware or software problems, you should contact [*state whom*]. [*Alternatively, explain outsourced IT arrangements if these are in place.*]

5.12.2   The uses made of ICT within the firm are:

- Word processing;
- Financial management and accounting;
- Database information; and
- [*Etc*].

5.12.3   The person with responsibility for the creation and review of the firm's IT plan is [*name or title*]. The future planning of the use of IT within the firm forms part of the business planning exercise (see 1.3.3) [*or spell out here how a separate IT plan is developed and maintained. Lexcel firms need to consult section 3.1 of that standard and the additional requirements now stated for procedures covering information security to include:*

- *the retention and security of the information assets;*
- *the use of firewalls; and*
- *network configuration.*

There is more emphasis on greater controls over software including the need for a plan for updating and monitoring the software used, a register for all software in use (presumably excluding the operating systems) and the removal of infected items. There is likewise the need for procedures to 'manage user accounts'. Since these issues would be of concern to the IT department only they would not be expected to form part of the office manual and the following procedures are limited to those of general concern to users. See, however, Appendix 34.

5.13   Information management policy and processes
Policy and responsibilities

5.13.1   We are committed to maintaining the highest standards of data quality and security. This policy, and associated procedures and practices, are designed to protect data integrity and ensure security and appropriate access.

5.13.2   The person with overall responsibility for data management is [*name or title*]. (S)he is also responsible for organising ongoing training on data protection principles and procedures for all personnel in the practice (see below), and for carrying out an annual review of this policy.

5.13.3   Data consists of any information in electronic format, or any hardware or software that makes the storage and use of such information possible. It also includes paper files where they contain information about individuals, for example:

- Databases;
- Externally accessed databases;
- CDs;
- Video;
- Recorded magnetic media;
- Photographs;
- Digitalised information;
- Electronic communication systems; and
- Personnel files.

5.13.4   We comply with all relevant legislative and regulatory provisions governing the management and storage of data in both electronic and paper formats. We are registered with the Information Commissioner for all necessary activities under the Data Protection Act 1998. We comply with data protection principles, i.e. that all data covered by the Act (which includes not only computer data but also personal data held in a filing system) is:

- Fairly and lawfully processed;
- Processed for limited purposes;
- Adequate, relevant and not excessive;
- Accurate;
- Not kept longer than necessary;
- Processed in accordance with the data subject's rights;
- Secure; and
- Not transferred to countries without adequate protection.

5.13.5   Paper files and other records or documents containing personal/sensitive data are kept securely and retained for as long as – but no longer than – necessary. *See 3.22.5 for guidelines on storage periods for client files. See 6.23 for guidelines on storage periods for staff records.*

5.13.6   The data contained in our network, including e-mails, is backed up and stored off site on a daily basis. [*You may want to add more information on back-up and electronic archiving processes.*]

Information assets – Practice

5.13.7   The information assets that we are under a duty to safeguard include:

- Client data, whether in electronic or hard copy format;
- Personnel data, including personal contact and other details on [*partners/directors*] and any sensitive data obtained from our recruitment or diversity monitoring processes; and
- The firm's own confidential data, such as management policies, plans and reports, finance records and contracts.

Lexcel requires a register of 'relevant information assets' to be maintained 'of both the practice and the clients' and then procedures for their safeguarding. There needs, in addition, to be a procedure for their retention and disposal.

Safeguarding information

5.13.8   Staff must adhere to our confidentiality policy at all times when dealing with information relating to clients and other sensitive information which we hold.

We also operate procedures for safeguarding the integrity of electronic documents. [*You will need to specify the procedures you use for archiving and arranging access to stored electronic documents.*]

Responding to data access requests

5.13.9   The Data Protection Act provides certain rights for individuals to make 'data subject requests' for details of the information that we hold on them. If you do receive any such request please pass it to [*name or title*]. As an employee of the firm you are also a 'data subject' with an entitlement to know what data we hold on you.

Risk assessment in relation to data protection

5.13.10 We carry out regular assessments of risks in relation to the data we hold. This forms part of our Business Continuity Planning process.

Protection and security guidelines

- Do not install any software unless it has been authorised and can be supported on our system.
- Do not disclose your password to anyone.
- If someone else finds out your password, change it.
- Do not use other people's log-ins.
- Log off when you leave your PC or workstation unattended.
- Ensure above all that no member of the public has access to our system when you leave your PC or workstation.
- Always secure laptops and mobile devices in unattended offices.
- Do not take equipment, data, information sources or software off-site unless you have written authority to do so.
- To preserve the integrity of data, ensure it is transferred between laptops/mobile devices and the main system as soon as possible.

Keeping and storing data for individual use

5.13.11 Keep master copies of important data on the network server and not on your PC's local C drive or data sticks. Data will not be backed up unless it is on the network server and so it is at risk.

5.13.12 Ask for advice from [*name or title*] if you need to store, transmit or handle large quantities of data, particularly images or audio and video. These large files use up disk space very quickly and can bring the network to a standstill.

5.13.13 Similarly, do not copy files that are on the network server into your personal directory unless you have good reason (i.e. you are updating them or you need a copy for a special purpose) since this uses up disk space.

Land Registry requirements

5.13.14 We are subject to certain contractual obligations regarding information security in relation to our status with the Land Registry and our access facilities to the Portal system. The firm is obliged to ensure that only authorised staff have access to the Land Registry systems and that the main IT system is not open to interference. If you need access to the Land Registry Portal system, or guidance on the use of it, please consult [*name or title*].

5.13.15 If you are one of the authorised users you are subject to certain obligations. These include:

- You must protect your computer when leaving it unattended;
- You must not share your password; and
- You must ensure that like controls are in place if you are working from home or away from the office.

5.13.16 We are required to nominate a 'Responsible Person' (RP1) and an 'Administrator' (BA) to operate the Land Registry Portal arrangements. These are:

- [*Name*] is the firm's designated RP1; and
- [*Name*] is the firm's designated BA.

5.13.17 Replacements must be made to the above appointments should they become necessary and you should also note that we are under an obligation to report actual or suspected security breaches to the Land Registry.

Breaches of data or information protection policies

5.13.18 Please note that breaches of our information security policies and procedures will be subject to our disciplinary procedures, depending on their seriousness and whether or not they are deliberate.

Training

5.13.19 It is the responsibility of [*name or title*] to provide training on the issues of data protection and information security and our policy in this area of our activities. This is done [*specify how*].

5.14 Use of the internet and e-mails

5.14.1 The internet and communication via e-mail are vital business and professional tools. The following guidance is provided to help you use them appropriately and reduce, as far as possible, the risks that can be associated with them.

[*Name or title*] has overall responsibility for ensuring that we meet all legislative and regulatory requirements in the use of e-mail and the internet and our own guidance on good practice. (S)he undertakes an annual review of our policy.

Use of the internet

5.14.2 Every member of staff is provided with an internet user account requiring a user name and password which is unique to him/her. Passwords are changed regularly. We would regard the following as the usual and permitted uses of the internet:

- Legal research;
- Client or practice research; and
- [*Specify any other acceptable uses*].

5.14.3   You should note that viruses are often imported through downloading files and programmes from external sources. You must not download executable files without taking advice from [*name or title*].

5.14.4   Please note that the deliberate accessing of offensive, obscene or indecent material on the internet, such as pornography, racist or sexist material, violent images or incitement to criminal behaviour is prohibited (unless this is necessary in the course of client work).

5.14.5   You must be aware of copyright and licensing restrictions that may apply to downloaded and forwarded material, whether internet or e-mail, and including unauthorised software, games, etc.

5.14.6   Any breaches of our internet policies will be subject to:

- Our equality and diversity policy (see 2.6);
- Our policy on dignity at work and bullying (see 6.10); and, in some cases,
- Our disciplinary procedures (see 6.21).

5.14.7   Please note that use of the internet is monitored by [*the partners/directors/IT Manager other*].

5.15   E-mail protocols

5.15.1   When you publish or transmit information externally, be aware that you are representing the firm and could be seen as speaking on our behalf. Make it clear when opinions are personal. It is important to note that there are important requirements made in the SRA Code of Conduct (O(8.5)) as to the information that must be contained in any e-mail message sent by the firm and for this reason the use of the current e-mail footer is mandatory in all cases.

5.15.2   Use of facilities for leisure or personal purposes (e.g. sending and receiving personal e-mails, personal phone calls, playing computer games and browsing the internet) is permitted in break times as long as such usage is reasonable and otherwise in accordance with our acceptable usage policy. In particular it must not:

- Incur specific expenditure for the firm;

- Impact on your performance of your job or role;
- Bring the firm into disrepute;
- Breach the confidentiality of the firm's information assets or those of its clients;
- Adversely affect network performance by using large amounts of bandwidth (e.g. by downloading/streaming of music or videos); or
- Impact negatively on the availability of resources needed for business use (hardware or network).

Use of e-mail

- Always consider whether e-mail is the right medium for the communication. Although it appears to be an informal communication tool, in fact it has the same authority as any other communication to and from the firm. Anything sent by e-mail should be regarded as published information.
- Avoid sending an e-mail which might inadvertently create a contract or undertaking, for example. Also beware of defamatory comments in relation to colleagues or other parties (deliberate or otherwise). Abrupt, inappropriate and unthinking use of language can lead to a bullying tone and possible offence to others, and may even amount to harassment.
- In long e-mail trails, people often forget potentially sensitive material contained nearer the start and, by transmitting it, the data becomes your responsibility.
- If you need to discuss a complex or confidential matter, a telephone call may be more effective. In many formal matters, conventional correspondence may be more appropriate.
- It is good practice to check your inbox at regular intervals during the working day and provide timely responses to messages received, and save e-mail attachments before working on them to prevent the risk of your work being lost.
- If you have to send e-mails to a significant number of recipients, it is important that recipients do not perceive your message as spam, so only send e-mails to people who need to know.
- Consider also the use of the 'undisclosed recipients' function if it would be preferable to withhold the details of all with whom you

are dealing (as on a marketing message to various clients where the disclosure of client identities would be a breach of confidentiality).

- Only use the 'reply to all' function when appropriate. Internally, be careful sending 'thank you' messages; busy recipients may not thank you for another message in their inbox.
- Never forward virus warnings to others without checking first with [*name or title*]. Usually such warnings are fakes.

Personal e-mail

[*You will need to amend this section in the light of your policy decision regarding the personal use of the firm's e-mail system; see above.*]

5.15.3 The firm's e-mail system is legally the property of the firm. This allows us wide-ranging rights to access mail as part of an official investigation, such as for discrimination, harassment or health and safety. You may use the e-mail address given to you by the firm to send limited amounts of personal e-mail but please note that it is subject to inspection by the [*partners/directors/managers*].

5.15.4 However, you may wish to set up a free account with a provider such as Hotmail, Google or Yahoo. You are allowed to access personal e-mails at work in accordance with our policy on e-mail and internet access. Personal mail accounts should always be accessed using web interfaces to avoid possible problems of having multiple mail clients on your work computer.

Storage and destruction of e-mails

[*You may wish to amend the following according to your firm's own policies.*]

5.15.5 Client e-mails must be stored in the client's electronic file. All client e-mails must be printed off and a hard copy kept on the file for billing purposes [*or modify if electronic storage is preferred*].

5.15.6 We have set a limit on the size of data that can be kept in an inbox. Therefore, you are responsible for clearing your inbox regularly. If you do not, you may not be able to send or receive e-mails.

5.15.7 The firm keeps back-ups and electronic copies of e-mails as set out in our information management policy.

Encryption

5.15.8 Sensitive data should not be sent unprotected over the open internet via e-mail. If sensitive data is to be e-mailed, it should be via an attachment (i.e. not in the body, header or subject line of the e-mail) and that attachment should be encrypted. The encryption key should not be shared in the same transmission. It should be shared with the intended recipient separately, e.g. by phone or other method.

Spam

5.15.9 We have spam filters, but spam does sometimes get through. If you are suspicious about an e-mail message, for example because you do not recognise the name of the sender, it should not be opened, especially if it has attachments. Another common practice involves persons adopting the same e-mail name as a contact that you might have in order to encourage you to open their (generally) marketing messages. Similarly, caution is needed where the message is from a familiar source but there is no text in the message. If you have any doubt, you should delete the message without opening it, or phone the apparent sender to check if the message is actually from them.

Absence from the office

5.15.10 Ensure your e-mail is being dealt with or leave a clear 'out of office' message.

5.16   Social media – General policy on permitted use

5.16.1 [*Insert name*] has overall responsibility for ensuring that we meet all legislative and regulatory requirements in the use of social media and our own guidance on good practice. (S)he undertakes an annual review of our policy.

5.16.2 Only people who are authorised and trained to do so may participate in social media on behalf of the practice. When you publish or transmit information externally, be aware that you are representing the firm and could be seen as speaking on our behalf. Make it clear when opinions are personal.

5.16.3   Personal use of social media is permitted in break times as long as such use does not:

- Incur specific expenditure for the firm;
- Impact on your performance of your job or role;
- Break the law;
- Bring the firm into disrepute; or
- Breach confidentiality of the firm's information assets or those of its clients.

Any breaches will be subject to our disciplinary procedures.

5.17   Our website

5.17.1   [*Insert name*] has overall responsibility for ensuring that we meet all legislative and regulatory requirements in the use of the firm's website. (S)he undertakes an annual review of our policy.

5.17.2   (S)he approves all content and authorises publishing and removal of content, including:

- Ensuring content is up to date and secure;
- Ensuring content does not infringe copyright;
- Specifying conditions for downloading material;
- Ensuring any publicity conforms to the SRA Code of Conduct;
- Ensuring that it is accessible to people with disabilities; and
- Ensuring there is a privacy notice explaining how any data collected from visitors will be managed by the practice.

Linking

5.17.3   [*Name or title*] will decide whether we should permit any links to be made from our website to any others.

CHAPTER 6

STAFF HANDBOOK

Note: This section provides guidance in relation to using the draft procedures that follow.

Introduction

The aim of this section of the Manual is to set out the details of all the policies and processes that affect the rights and responsibilities of the employees of the firm. In practices opting to upload their procedures onto their intranet this might have a 'staff handbook' icon on the desktop, whereas if you are adopting a more traditional manual format we suggest that this is Section 6 of the Office Manual. Employment law is, of course, fast-changing and you should satisfy yourself that the suggestions made here are in line with your duties in law to your employees or colleagues. This is particularly the case with the various statutory entitlements that are covered in 6.14-6.22.

The parts of this section that are most relevant to Lexcel and the Legal Aid Agency's quality standards including the SQM are those dealing with personnel management systems and training, as they have requirements in relation to such issues as recruitment, job descriptions, staff induction processes and training in general. Both Lexcel and the SQM also require performance reviews (appraisals) to be in place, to include partners. The requirement for exit procedures is a relatively recent addition to Lexcel that will not be found in the SQM or the related legal aid SQM/contract requirements.

For ease of reference this section is divided into three parts as follows:

- Part 1: Personnel management systems;
- Part 2: Training; and
- Part 3: Employment policies and entitlements.

Part 1: Personnel management systems

The various provisions of this section will now seem familiar to most firms, especially if they undertake legal aid work under the SQM requirements or are accredited to Lexcel. Much still depends on the device of job descriptions, now referred to as 'role profiles' in Lexcel (section 4.4). The terms used in most organisations are 'job descriptions' to cover the needs of the role in question (usually through a statement of the main purposes of the role and then a summary of the main duties) with the 'person specification' covering the skills, qualifications, experience and abilities for that job. Some sample precedents are provided in the appendices relevant to this section.

There is, of course, a considerable amount of legislation that affects the relationship of employer and employee and the involvement on this of any employment lawyer within your firm will be helpful. One of the most important considerations is the Working Time Regulations (1998) which cover not just the length of the working week but also holiday entitlement (see 6.12.1). There is also a statutory entitlement to unpaid emergency leave under s.57A(1) of the Employment Relations Act 1996 which has a bearing on the discretion that most firms will want to exercise in relation to requests for compassionate or unpaid leave in general (see 6.13.7-8 below).

Drafting the job description is also the first stage of the recruitment process. For these purposes it is useful to distinguish between:

- Recruitment – The process of identifying a position that needs to be filled, planning for it and attracting a field of candidates; and
- Selection – Choosing the best candidate and then agreeing terms with them if they do accept your offer.

It is important that you bear in mind the potential for unwitting breaches of your equality and diversity policy in restricting the pool of potential applicants during the recruitment stage. Does a fee earner really need to have a driving licence, for example, so as to exclude blind and visually impaired people from that job? This might perhaps be justifiable for a licensing advocate who is required to represent national retailers at hearings up and down the country every week, but such instances in the law are likely to be exceptional. In this respect it is important to remember your duty to make reasonable adjustments, not just for clients, but for 'personnel' also. Likewise, there were fears when age discrimination provisions were introduced that advisers referring to the need for certain periods of post qualification experience would fall foul of this strand of discrimination law, but there seems now to be general acceptance that stipulating the more common periods of two or three years PQE is unlikely to be unlawful.

Undertaking more careful checking of job applicants has become increasingly common practice in recent years and is a specific requirement of the Law Society's Conveyancing Quality Scheme (CQS). There are strict liability offences for employing those who do not hold work permits when they are required, and the prospect of professional censure if someone is employed who has been struck off or suspended as a solicitor, or if an order has been made by the SRA that a non-solicitor should not be employed in legal practice. The sample procedure that follows envisages fairly full checking processes, and care should be taken if you choose to relax these. The SRA has provided warnings as to the risks of the use of false identities by law firm personnel in relation to mortgage fraud; various firms have discovered this to their cost when fraudsters have obtained jobs in their conveyancing departments (see, for example, *Pulvers v Chan* [2007] EWHC 2406 (Ch)).

Appraisal schemes have also become very much more commonplace in recent years, but they do benefit from change from time to time to keep the process fresh. Scoring based systems, under which the appraiser 'marks' the performance of the appraisee to a range of factors, are now uncommon and are probably best seen as a throwback to the days of performance related pay as it operated in the 1980s; 'comments-only' schemes have since become more commonplace. The review process should be seen to be an essentially two-way process and not some form of end of year school report. There is now a reference to a 'performance management policy' in Lexcel at section 4.8: this is an attempt to suggest that the (usually) annual review meeting should not be a 'one-off' but should be part of a more integrated approach to the review and management of that person's development in, and contribution to, the firm.

Part 2: Training
It makes sense that a knowledge-based profession should display a commitment to training and that this should be seen as something more important than the mere process of collecting sufficient hours or points. This was the reasoning of the SRA in their decision to phase out the mandatory CPD scheme in 2015, thirty years after it was first introduced. It is important to note that the abolition of CPD does not mean that training has become an optional extra for firms – far from it: there is instead now a more personalised requirement for everyone in the practice (regardless of their status) to receive the training they require to do their job effectively given the need to provide a "proper" standard of service (Principle 5 – see also O.7.6). In Lexcel see 4.3 and the need for a "learning and development policy".

Training should always have a clear purpose in mind, and so works best where a need for that development has been identified. In most firms this emerges from the performance review or appraisal process, as envisaged in this section. It should also follow that if a need for training has been identified then there should be checks as to whether the training provided has actually worked to fill that need, through an evaluation process (see Lexcel 4.3.c and the appendices for a training evaluation form). If the training was poorly conducted, or the contents were misdescribed in some way, the training need will still exist and so will require further action to be taken. Note also the change from the need for a training and development policy at 5.5 of Lexcel v5 to now a 'learning and development policy' at 4.3 of Lexcel v6. Training and learning being different sides of the same coin this change is unlikely to have any great practical significance but it is useful to stress that the whole purpose of training is for those in attendance to meet their development needs.

In relation to legal aid work, there are minimum numbers of training hours for all caseworkers and supervisors. In addition, accreditation to certain panels is required in some areas of law in order to be able to do the work at all, for example to qualify as a police station representative or magistrates' court duty solicitor, or to do immigration or asylum work, or as a route to increased fees. See Section 7(6.9) for more information.

The SQM (D2.3) requires individual training plans (see Appendix 21), as opposed to Lexcel which requires an organisation-wide learning and development plan (Lexcel v6 4.3d).

Finally, most firms have sought to economise on this element of their operations in recent years. Better planning of training provision can lead to more cost-effective provision and many firms have found that it is indeed possible to 'get more for less' by administering suitable controls.

Part 3: Employment policies and entitlements

This part sets out the policies other than training that are core to the employer/employee relationship, along with the approaches commonly adopted by many firms to the mass of issues that arise for consideration from time to time with most personnel.

The Dignity at Work policy should be seen as an accompaniment to the equality and diversity policy, but is very much more general in its scope than the 'protected characteristics' of the Equality Act. The 'requirement' for a whistle blowing policy might not be strictly seen as such since it emerges from an indicative behaviour within the Code (IB(10.10)) but it might, in practice, be difficult for larger firms in particular to justify not having adopted one. Lexcel firms do not have this option, however, as there is now stated to be a need for a whistle-blowing policy at 4.9 of Lexcel v6.

The Shared Parental Leave Regulations 2014 (3050) provide for greater flexibility in relation to the entitlement to parental leave for both parents. The full entitlement is quite complex and one of the best sources of further information on this topic can be downloaded from the ACAS website. In common with most of the other statutory entitlements covered in this part of the Manual whoever is responsible for the operation of any such scheme will need further specialist guidance on the operation of your employment systems.

Another new requirement to Lexcel (4.10) is the need for a flexible working policy which is covered in this chapter at 6.18. This seems merely to bring the legal obligations on employers under the relevant provisions of the Employment Rights Act 1996 and the regulations made under them into the arena of issues that might be assessed at audit. There is a 26 weeks qualification period in the statutory provisions and this would presumably be permissible under Lexcel also.

The scope of this policy was extended quite considerably by the Flexible Working Regulations which took effect on the 30th June 2014. Whereas the entitlement was at first limited to those with specified caring responsibilities there is now the right for most workers to make a "statutory application" to vary the working hours or arrangements if they have worked for the employer for at least 26 weeks. As employer you are required to handle the request in a "reasonable manner" and, in particular, give careful consideration to the request and deal with it promptly. The maximum period allowed by law for the application to be responded to is three months, but you might wish to state a shorter period in your policy 6.18.

The application may be rejected on various grounds, most commonly because the extra costs of the planned arrangements will damage the business or it will not be possible to re-allocate the work amongst other members of staff. There might also be a lack of work of a certain type to do in the proposed hours, as with a receptionist who wishes to start work well before the office opens, for example, and where their duties are limited to greeting visitors to the office.

There is no statutory right of appeal but including an appeals process might provide evidence of any applications having been handled in a fair and reasonable manner. This is probably more feasible in larger practices only. Employers are entitled to treat an application as having been withdrawn if an employee fails to attend two meetings that have been arranged to consider the request without good cause.

Qualifying employees have a right to take their employer to the Tribunal if they feel that their employer has not considered the request as they are obliged to do and the Regulations provide for a maximum award of up to eight weeks' pay if the claim succeeds.

Beyond this, you should be sure to adapt the more practical issues covered in this section such as absences and arrangements for working from home if you allow it, being sure to include the relevant contacts within your firm.

STAFF HANDBOOK

Part 1: Personnel management systems

6.1 Job descriptions

6.1.1 It is the policy of the firm to provide all personnel with job descriptions. Job descriptions are used whenever we recruit a new member of staff and are also used in the [*annual*] performance review meetings for existing members of staff. An important element of the review process is to check that any changes in your activities in the firm are recognised in your job documentation. If, between these meetings, you feel that there is any confusion about your roles and responsibilities it is always open to you to request a review meeting with your [*head of department/supervisor*] in which case you should discuss whether your job description should be amended.

[*See templates in Appendix 17*].

6.2 Recruitment and selection

6.2.1 Recruitment decisions are made by [*insert*]. It is [*also*] the responsibility of [*insert*] to draft the necessary job description and person specification and to decide how a field of applicants will be attracted. These methods will usually be one or more of the following:

- Internal advertisement;
- Firm's own advertisement in the local or professional press; and/or
- Instructing recruitment agents.

6.2.2 Selection decisions are made by interview alone [*or, if practical or psychometric tests are used, explain here*]. The interviewer(s) will usually be [*insert*].

6.2.3 Interviews will be conducted using a list of questions prepared in advance which are directed to all candidates so as to avoid the perception of discrimination.

Interview notes are retained for a period of 12 months and then destroyed but all other application papers, including the CV provided by the jobholder, will be retained on your personal file. [*Note that the SQM requires you to provide feedback information to unsuccessful candidates if required.*]

6.2.4 Offers are always conditional on references being taken up [*if this is your practice – it is not mandatory to do so*], prior to confirming a conditional offer of employment. An appropriate check will be made of the SRA database for any relevant disciplinary findings in all cases. Where a solicitor is being appointed, a sight of their current practising certificate is required.

6.2.5 In line with SRA guidance we require proof of identity, usually by sight of a current passport and, in the case of non-EU nationals, evidence of a right to work in the UK. [*CRB checks will be taken in relation to [insert]*].

6.2.6 All staff will undergo an initial probationary period of six months with formal reviews after three and six months.

6.3 Contracts of employment

6.3.1 A written standard contract of employment as agreed between the [*partners/directors*] and an individual employee will be issued to you and will become effective from the date of issue or your first day of employment, whichever is the later. The contract of employment covers such issues as:

- The role in which the individual is employed;
- Basis of remuneration;
- Hours of work;
- Holiday entitlement;
- Maternity and paternity leave entitlement; and
- Notice periods.

6.4 Overtime

6.4.1 Overtime arrangements are limited to secretarial and administrative staff and are by prior arrangement if and when required. Payment for any such authorised additional hours will be paid at the member of staff's normal hourly rate, calculated from salary pro-rata on their contractual hours, subject to any additional rate to allow for working unsocial hours.

6.4.2   There is no standard entitlement to time off in lieu for extra hours worked for any member of staff but this may be granted in exceptional cases by [*name or title*].

6.5   Performance review meetings

6.5.1   The [*partners/directors*] are keen to encourage an 'open door' culture within the firm where problems or concerns should be raised as soon as possible with [*a partner/director/your supervisor*]. In addition, there is a more formal review structure consisting of [*specify, e.g. monthly or other review meeting/departmental or team meetings/reviews of monthly print-outs of matters, etc*].

6.6   Performance reviews (appraisals)

6.6.1   We operate a system of formal review meetings in order to discuss performance issues and set goals for the future. The process is annual and occurs [*insert – month of year or staggered according to joining dates?*].

6.6.2   The review meeting is a two-way process and is an opportunity for you to raise any concerns about your job and for you to suggest improvements that can be made. The [*partners/directors*] are particularly concerned to hear any suggestions as to how you might be more effective in your role, or if you have skills and experiences which you feel are not being properly used at present. The review meeting is also a formal opportunity for us to review the training needs of all personnel and plan an effective training programme for the firm. This is particularly important in view of the SRA's 2015-6 changes to training for solicitors, see 6.9.3 below.

[*See templates in the appendices. These are:*

- *28: Appraisal preparation form*
- *29: Appraisal record*

The appraisal preparation form is intended to help focus discussion and should not be retained after the appraisal meeting.]

6.7   Exit procedures

6.7.1   In order to ensure an orderly termination of your time with the firm and handover of work you will be invited to attend an 'exit' interview when you leave the firm. The purpose of this meeting is for the [*partners/directors*] to learn about any underlying problems which should be addressed and which might have contributed to your decision to leave the firm. Attendance at an exit interview is optional, but would be very much appreciated. A list of questions which may be asked at an exit interview can be found [*see Appendix 30*].

6.7.2   Either at this interview or at another agreed date/time all keys for the office and filing cabinets, mobile phones, other portable equipment and other property of the firm must be collected by [*your head of department/supervisor*] and arrangements will be made to cancel your access to the firm's e-mail and internet facilities.

6.7.3   It is the responsibility of [*insert*] to ensure continuity on any client work that you are responsible for, to include notifying the clients of any relevant changes in the handling of their matter(s) and the re-routing of e-mails that are addressed to you.

Part 2: Training
6.8   Induction training
New staff

6.8.1   It is important that all new staff are welcomed into the firm and become acquainted with the firm's procedures as soon as possible. Please therefore do all you can to help make new members of staff feel welcome and to provide any help needed when they first join the firm.

6.8.2   On your first day at the firm you will be provided with a copy of your job description, which will document your responsibilities, along with an explanation of the supervisory structure that applies to your job. In addition you will receive a copy of the Staff Induction Pack and undergo the initial training package to ensure that you are aware of our key policies, especially if this is your first experience of working in a law firm.

Induction process

6.8.3   There is an induction procedure and checklist that is used for all new staff and, in a shortened format, for those changing roles within the firm. The induction procedure also applies in an abbreviated format to temporary staff. The induction training process covers such issues as:

- The management structure of the firm;
- Terms and conditions of employment;
- Our main policies; and
- Any immediate training needs.

[*See Appendix 31.*]

6.9 Training and development policy
[*Lexcel firms might prefer 'Learning and development policy' in the light of the wording of section 4.3 in Lexcel*]

6.9.1 The [*partners/directors*] are committed to providing training that will ensure you are able to undertake all elements of your job and reach your true potential in your role.

6.9.2 Our training programme is conducted primarily by [*attendance at outside courses/our in-house programme/a combination of external and in-house courses*. All training must be recorded on individual training records and in-house registers must always be signed. The records are kept [*state where – by individuals or centrally*].

6.9.3 The recent changes to CPD requirements should not be taken to mean that training is no longer a professional requirement as such – outcome 7(6) of the Code of Conduct requires people to be trained to "a level of competence appropriate to their work and level of responsibility". Good training should enable you to do your job and should enhance your personal effectiveness, thus improving the standard of service that we provide to our clients. Beyond legal 'technical' training we also provide training in management and supervisory skills where relevant (including the use of our IT system) and compliance needs training, in areas such as:

- Equality and diversity;
- Client care and complaints handling;

- Money laundering and terrorist financing awareness;
- Information security and data protection; and
- Conflicts of interests.

Training needs analysis

6.9.4   The main method by which we plan our training programme or activities is by the consideration of training needs at performance review meetings, but it is open to you to request training at any other time by contacting [*name or title*]. In addition, it is open to any supervisor to suggest appropriate training at any review meeting.

Booking courses

6.9.5   The firm is a subscriber to [*name of training organisation*] and external courses should therefore generally be those provided by that organisation. In addition [*many counsels' chambers provide discounted training sessions/the local law society runs a low cost CPD scheme, etc*].

Evaluation of training

6.9.6   Training should always be planned to address a specific job performance need. For this reason it is important that you review any training provided and comment as to whether that training need has been addressed. If, for any reason, the session attended did not do so you will need to consider, with your supervisor if appropriate, whether some further steps need to be taken.

[*See template in Appendix 32*].

Professional studies and study leave

6.9.7   The [*partners/directors*] will, at their absolute discretion, consider any request for financial assistance and for time off work for anybody wishing to pursue an educational or training course leading to a recognised and relevant qualification (such as ILEX studies at a local college). Please address any such requests to [*name or title*].

Part 3: Employment policies and entitlements

6.10   Dignity at work and sexual harassment

6.10.1 The [*partners/directors*] are committed to ensuring that everyone at the firm can undertake their job responsibilities in a supportive environment where harassment and bullying is not tolerated. Harassment is defined for these purposes at s.26 of the Equality Act 2010 as subjecting a worker to unwanted conduct with either the effect or purpose of violating that person's dignity or creating an 'intimidating, hostile, degrading or offensive environment' on the basis of the prohibited grounds of discrimination under the Act.

6.10.2 Harassment and bullying will be dealt with as misconduct and therefore the disciplinary procedure at Section 6.21 will apply. If the conduct complained of is based on the grounds contained in the firm's Equality and Diversity policy see Section 2.6.

6.10.3 This policy covers, but is not limited to, sexual harassment. This is:

- Any unwanted conduct or comments of a sexual or suggestive nature, whatever their motive;
- Insulting a colleague on the grounds of their sex or sexual orientation, actual or perceived;
- Suggesting that the granting of sexual favours will in some way benefit that person.

6.10.4 For details of how such complaints will be dealt with please see the grievance procedure at Section 6.22. If, as we very much hope will not be the case, you find yourself in this position the [*partners*/directors] will take steps to protect you from any repetition of the actions complained about and will also ensure that you are not the victim of any future victimisation as a result of any complaint that has been reasonably made. Any issues brought to the attention of the [*partners/directors*] will be treated as confidential and investigated in a careful and sensitive manner.

6.10.5 The [*partners/directors*] are just as concerned to hear of any incident where the behaviour of a client or of others that you are dealing with outside the firm could be seen as a breach of this policy and are committed to challenging such behaviour and protecting you from it.

6.11 Whistle-blowing

6.11.1 If there is anything which you think the firm should know about you should use the procedure outlined to 'blow the whistle' on malpractice. The kinds of malpractice covered by the Public Interest Disclosure Act 1998 are:

- Criminal offences;
- Miscarriages of justice;
- Health and safety issues;
- Environmental damage; and
- Breach of any legal or professional obligation.

6.11.2 Within a law firm, serious breaches of the professional requirements that we are subject to – especially under the SRA Handbook – should be added to this list. In this context see the duties to report malpractice to the SRA at O(10.4).

6.11.3 If you have any concerns as to the above you should raise your concerns with [*name or title*]. You will not be expected to prove anything about the allegation you are making, but you must reasonably believe that some malpractice is occurring. If your concerns relate to a colleague or supervisor and you ask for the issue to be treated in confidence the [*partners/directors*] will respect your request to the extent that this is feasible and only make disclosures to that person with your consent.

6.11.4 Once you have raised any concerns under this policy:

- There will be an initial investigation into the circumstances in an attempt to discover whether some sort of malpractice has occurred;
- There will then be a more formal investigation if necessary, in which case you might be invited to participate; and
- A decision will then be made as to the concerns raised, their validity and any actions to be taken in consequence. The [*partners/directors*] will do their best to complete their investigations and decision making processes within a reasonable time and will keep you informed to the degree that is appropriate.

6.11.5 In the event that you are not satisfied with the outcome of this process an appeal may be made [*insert details of any appeal or review process – this is seen as best practice but is not mandatory and might be difficult in a smaller firm. In larger firms an appeal to the senior partner might be feasible, in which case elaborate here*].

6.11.6   We would prefer that concerns are brought to the attention of the [*partners/directors*] in person but if you feel unable or unwilling to do so you may prefer to address you concerns in writing and on an anonymous basis by passing in an envelope marked "private and confidential" to [*name or title*]

6.12   Holidays

6.12.1   The standard holiday entitlement for full time members of staff is [*specify – see introductory notes regarding the impact of the Working Time Regulations*].

6.12.2   As a part time member of staff you are entitled to the same allowance but subject to adjustment where, for example, one of your days worked is Monday and you are not therefore entitled to a greater proportion of holiday time as a result of the number of bank holidays falling on that day of the week.

6.12.3   The office holiday year runs from [*insert*] to [*insert*] and there is no entitlement to carry over any unused holiday allowance. The [*partners/directors*] will consider variations to the usual arrangements in exceptional cases, but any such request should be made to [*name or title*] as soon as possible.

6.12.4   Holidays of more than ten consecutive working days require the prior consent of [*name or title*]. Again, as much notice is possible is required.

6.12.5   In all cases do not book or commit yourself to a holiday until you have received clearance for the dates in question from [*name or title*].

6.12.6   The arrangements for holidays over the Christmas and New Year period are [*insert*].

6.12.7   If you leave the firm without taking all of your holiday entitlement then you will receive payment for any outstanding entitlement during the current holiday year based on the time worked in the holiday year to date. If, however, you have taken in excess of your entitlement in the year to date a deduction will be made from your final salary payment.

6.13 Absence

6.13.1 If you are unable to attend the office through sickness, then you must inform [*name or title*] as soon as possible. If you are unable to do so you must do your best to get someone else to do so on your behalf. You, or the person acting on your behalf, must notify us of the reason for your absence and your expected date of return.

6.13.2 Where the absence is more than three days you must provide [*name or title*] with regular progress reports and if you are absent from the office for more than seven consecutive calendar days you must obtain a doctor's certificate which should be given or sent to [*name or title*] as soon as possible. Please do not wait until your eventual return to work before doing so.

6.13.3 After any sickness absence you must complete a self certification form immediately upon your return, normally at the return to work interview.

6.13.4 The firm will continue to pay your salary during incapacity for a period or aggregated periods of sick leave up to [*insert*]. Under the Statutory Sick Pay (SSP) scheme the firm generally pays SSP when you have been off work for [*insert*] or more consecutive days. This is treated like wages and is subject to normal deductions. If you are entitled to any state sickness or injury benefits you should be sure to claim them. For more details see [*name or title*].

6.13.5 We reserve the right to request that you undergo a medical examination by a doctor or other qualified person at our expense to ascertain the cause of your illness. Sickness absence occurring over a period of paid annual holiday period can be treated as sickness (rather than holiday) only on production of a doctor's medical certificate.

6.13.6 On returning to work after sick leave you should contact [*name or title*] who will conduct a 'return to work' interview, normally within two days of your return. You will be asked to complete a self certification form if the absence was seven days or less or provide a doctor's note if the period of absence was any longer and we have not yet received it. Where there is or might be some continuing disability we are committed to making such adjustments as are necessary to enable you to return to normal working.

Compassionate leave

6.13.7 The firm will, in certain circumstances such as bereavement or the serious illness of a member of your immediate family, allow you to be absent from the office on paid leave (in addition to any holiday entitlement) up to a maximum of three days in any calendar year. Please make any request to [*name or title*]. Your immediate family is defined as including parents, spouses/partners, children and others living with you, other than paying lodgers, and others such as siblings in appropriate cases.

Unpaid leave

6.13.8 Any requests for unpaid leave should be made to [*name or title*]. Decisions will be made on all such requests at the sole discretion of the [*partners/directors*] taking into account the difficulties of arranging cover and the smooth running of your department.

[See introductory notes regarding the right to unpaid emergency leave at s.57A(1) of the Employment Rights Act 1996 in relation to 6.13.7-8 above.]

Homeworking

6.13.9 There may be occasions when fee earners would like the opportunity to work from home during office hours. This is permissible provided that you obtain the approval of your [*head of department/supervisor*]. Please ensure that those answering your calls in the office know how and when they can contact you or pass on your details to clients and other callers.

6.14 Maternity leave

6.14.1 If you become pregnant, please let [*name or title*] know as soon as possible in order that consideration can be given to any health and safety concerns. We will also need to know the anticipated date of the birth and the date you will be leaving (whether permanently or temporarily) so that alternative arrangements can be made to cover your work.

6.14.2 Depending on a number of factors, including your time at the firm as an employee, you will have certain rights to:

- Time off for antenatal care;
- Maternity leave; and
- Maternity benefits.

Antenatal care

6.14.3   All pregnant employees are entitled to take time off normal working hours to attend antenatal care, but you are asked to try to arrange all such appointments near the beginning or the end of the working day if possible and to notify your [*head of department/supervisor*] of any forthcoming appointments as soon as you know them.

Maternity leave

6.14.4   All expectant mothers are entitled to 26 weeks of 'ordinary maternity leave' ('OML') and an additional period of 26 weeks by way of 'additional maternity leave' ('AML'). You will have this entitlement regardless of how long you have worked for us or for how many hours per week you work. You are entitled to choose to commence your period of OML at any time after the 11th week before the expected week of the confinement ('EWC'). You are asked to let us know your plans, including the date at which you wish to start your OML and your proposed date of return to work, if you plan to do so, as soon as possible in order that we can plan cover for your position.

Maternity pay

6.14.5   If you have at least 26 weeks' continuous service by the 15th week before your EWC and you have complied with the necessary formalities you are entitled to statutory maternity pay (SMP) regardless of whether or not you intend to return to work after the birth. SMP is payable for a maximum of 39 weeks; for details of your possible entitlement see [*name or title*].

Staying in touch

6.14.6   During the period of absence please keep us informed of developments and if your plans for a return to work change at any time. Your rights on your return to work do vary according to whether you have taken OML or AML as well – please consult [name or title].

6.15   Paternity leave

6.15.1   Fathers who have been continuously employed for a period of no less than 26 weeks before the EWC are entitled to take one week's leave or two weeks' consecutive leave during the period of the 56 days following the birth or the placement of the adoption of the child. There are also rights to additional paternity leave in certain circumstances. For more details please consult [name or title].

6.16   Adoption leave

6.16.1   You will be entitled to 26 weeks' ordinary adoption leave ('OAL') provided:

- You have been matched with a child for adoption by a UK adoption agency;
- You have been continuously employed for a period of not less than 26 weeks ending with the week in which you were notified of having been matched with a child; and
- You have notified the agency that you agree that the child should be placed with you and you have agreed on a date of placement.

6.16.2   OAL is only payable where a child is 'newly matched' (e.g. it would not be available if you are already a step parent to the child when adoption occurs). In order to qualify for statutory adoption pay ('SAP') you must meet certain criteria, such as having been continuously employed for a period of at least 26 weeks at the time you are notified that you have been matched with a child for adoption. For further details see [name or title].

6.16.3   At the end of your period of OAL you are entitled to take 26 weeks additional adoption leave ('AAL'). This period of additional leave, which will be unpaid, will begin immediately after your ordinary leave and will make your total leave period a maximum of 52 weeks. The above provisions on return to work after maternity leave also apply to this section.

6.17   Shared parental leave

6.17.1   Shared parental leave ("SPL") might enable you and your partner to have greater

---

flexibility in the arrangements for how you care for your child in the year after their birth. If you qualify for it the right to SPL would mean that you could stagger your absences from work or choose to be off at the same time, and either take one period of absence or take different blocks of time.

6.17.2　The entitlement arises if you are the child's parent and share the main responsibility with the other parent, or if you are otherwise the mother's partner and share the main responsibility with the mother for the care of the child. You must also have been continuously employed by us for at least 26 weeks by the end of the "qualifying week", and must still be employed by us in the week before leave is taken. In addition, the other parent or carer must have worked in an employed or self-employed capacity for at least 26 weeks of the 66 before the expected week of childbirth ("EWC"), and have had average weekly earnings of at least £30 in at least 13 of those weeks. You and the other parent/carer must also have served the necessary notices and declarations.

6.17.3　The interaction of SPL and pay with other parental entitlements is quite complex. You will need to give us your written notice of your intention to commence SPL no later than eight weeks before you intend to start the leave and provide us with all other relevant details also. For further information please consult *name or title*.

6.18　Flexible working

6.18.1　Formerly the right to request flexible working was limited to those with responsibility for caring for others, but the Flexible Working Regulations 2014 extended the right to request a variation of working hours or other arrangements, such as working from home, to most other employees with very few exceptions. It should be noted that the right is limited to making a request for any such change and there is no legal obligation for the practice to actually grant any such request.

6.18.2　In order to be entitled to make a "statutory request" you must have been continuously employed by the practice for at least 26 weeks and it would be helpful if you could first discuss your ideas with [*name or title*.] If you wish to make a formal request you will need to do so in writing and the *partners/directors* will then consider the request fairly and promptly. In so doing the *partners/directors* will weigh up the benefits to you as against any possible impact that the changes might have on the practice. All such deliberations will be conducted in accordance with our equality and diversity policy (see 2.6).

6.18.3   If you do make a statutory request you will need to do so in writing and you will then usually be invited to a meeting to discuss your suggestions. If, once you have made a formal application, you wish to withdraw it please do so in writing. If you fail to attend two meetings that have been arranged to discuss your application without good cause your application will be deemed to have been withdrawn. The *partners/directors* will consider your request carefully in the light of the impact they might have on the practice as a whole, your team or department, or on the smooth running of the practice as a whole. We will do our best to respond to your application within the period of [*two weeks/one month/two months*].

Either

6.18.4   We do not operate an appeals process so our response to your application is final.

or

6.18.4   If we reject your application you may make an appeal to [*name or title*] who will not have been party to the original decision. If you wish to do so please write to them explaining why you disagree with the decision within [*two/three/four*] weeks of being notified of the decision. The decision will then be reviewed in the light of your further comments and you will be notified of the outcome of the appeals process within [*timescale – this should be within the maximum three months time limit taking into account earlier deliberations also*].

6.19   Adverse weather

6.19.1   In the event of adverse weather you will be expected to make every reasonable effort to get to work, assuming that the office is open, even if it means adjusting your usual travel arrangements. You should not do so, however, if this would put you at risk (e.g. you would have to walk along dangerous untreated pavements) or if any disabilities that you have would make this unreasonable.

6.19.2   Where you are unable to get to the office, arrangements might be made for you to work from home by contacting [*name or title*]. There is otherwise no entitlement to pay if you are unable to attend the office and it is open; the [*partners/directors*] will have discretion as to whether any pay deductions will have to be made.

6.20 Jury service

6.20.1 There is now no prohibition against solicitors or their staff from acting as jurors, but clearly nobody from the firm could take part in any proceedings where we as a firm are acting or where you know any of the parties involved in the trial process. If you are summoned to take part in jury service please consult [*name or title*] as soon as possible. Jurors' expenses are paid for your time in court or on call and you should claim the maximum to which the employer is entitled. The usual arrangements for trials that are likely to take longer than the period for which you are compelled to be in attendance is that potential jurors are asked to volunteer to appear in such cases: we would expect you not to do so, and also to attend work as normal for any day that you are told in advance not to be at court.

6.21 Disciplinary

6.21.1 The purpose of our disciplinary procedures is to ensure that the policies and standards that the [*partners/directors*] have established are maintained and that any failure to observe these principles is fairly dealt with. A record of all disciplinary actions under these procedures will be recorded and placed with your personnel records.

Investigation

6.21.2 Prior to any disciplinary meeting or action being taken, there will be an investigation into the allegation(s) of misconduct or behaviour which is the cause of concern. Where appropriate, an investigatory meeting may be held with you. You are entitled to be accompanied at any such meeting by a fellow employee or appropriate trade union representative.

6.21.3 Depending on the nature of the allegation(s), it may be necessary to suspend you from work for a specified period during which time an investigation will be undertaken. If you are subject to suspension you will continue to be paid your salary and the suspension will not be taken to be a disciplinary sanction. Your contract of employment will be deemed to continue but you will not be entitled to have access to the firm's premises, except with the prior consent of [*name or title*].

6.21.4   The disciplinary action might be discontinued at this stage if the allegations do not appear to have any substance, in which case we will confirm this in writing to you.

Meetings

6.21.5   If matters do proceed you will be invited to a meeting with [*name or title*] before any action is taken. This will be a formal meeting and you will be informed in writing, in advance, of the basis for the disciplinary action that is being considered and you will be provided with any relevant details or information. We will aim to provide you with this information at least two working days before any disciplinary hearing takes place.

6.21.6   You must take all reasonable steps to attend the meeting and will have an opportunity to respond to the information that is provided to you. You are entitled to be accompanied at the meeting by a work colleague or an appropriate trade union representative. After the meeting, the firm will inform you of its decision and notify you of the right to appeal against the decision if you are not satisfied with it.

Misconduct

6.21.7   The types of misconduct that might arise would include, but are not limited to:

- Poor time-keeping;
- Unreasonable or unexplained absence;
- Persistent or irregular absenteeism;
- Inattention to your duties, as by inappropriate use of social media during working hours;
- Minor non-accidental damage to the firm's property;
- Minor breaches of the firm's requirements as set out in the Office Manual; and
- Abusive or aggressive behaviour to a [*partner/director*], colleague, client or anybody else with whom we have dealings.

6.21.8 The following types of issues are likely to be treated as gross misconduct if they are substantiated:

- Bullying or harassment (see Section 6.10);
- Actions that would bring the firm into disrepute;
- Theft or unauthorised possession of the firm's property or facilities;
- Dishonesty, including criminal actions that are taken against you in your private life;
- Breach of our policy on bribery and the acceptance of gifts (see Section 2.18);
- Serious non-accidental damage to the firm's property;
- Refusal to carry out duties or reasonable instructions, or gross insubordination;
- Being under the influence of alcohol or unprescribed drugs on the firm's premises;
- Physical assault and abusive behaviour;
- Breach of duty of confidentiality; and
- Any breach of our equality and diversity policy, especially acts of discrimination.

6.21.9 Disciplinary proceedings might also be based on poor performance, or incompetence in your job role.

Penalties

6.21.10 There is a range of penalties that might be imposed depending on the nature of the disciplinary charge and any mitigating factors that you bring to our attention.

6.21.11 In cases of minor breaches you are likely to be given a formal **oral warning** which will be recorded and will remain on your file for a period of 12 months but, subject to satisfactory conduct or performance, will be removed from your record following the expiry of that period.

6.21.12 In cases of more serious breaches, or a repetition of the sort of issue that previously attracted an oral warning, you might be issued with a **written warning**. This will state the reason for the warning and will require an improvement in your conduct or performance within a stipulated time period, failing which further disciplinary action will be taken. The written warning will remain on your file for a period of 12 months but, subject to satisfactory conduct and performance, will be removed from your record following the expiry of that period.

6.21.13 In more serious cases, or where there has been any repetition of any issues that were formerly the subject of oral and/or written warnings, or if the misconduct or performance is sufficiently serious to warrant it, a **final written warning** will normally be issued to you. This will give details of the complaint, will warn that dismissal will result if there is any repetition of such conduct or other serious misconduct or, in the case of competency issues, inadequate improvement in performance. Due to the seriousness of this penalty there is a right of appeal against any final written warnings and you will be advised of this. The warning will remain on your file for a period of 12 months but, subject to satisfactory conduct and performance, will be removed from your record following the expiry of that period.

6.21.14 In other cases of serious disciplinary breaches, or of incompetence in your job, other action might be taken short of dismissal such as demotion.

6.21.15 In cases where the breach is gross misconduct, or where there has been a repetition of previous instances of misconduct within the 12 months' notice period, the [partners/directors] may take the decision to dismiss. Dismissal will usually be with notice or pay in lieu of notice, except in the case of gross misconduct when notice or pay in lieu of notice will not usually be provided.

Appeals

6.21.16 If you wish to appeal against your dismissal or against any disciplinary decision taken by the firm at any stage, you must inform [name or title] in writing within three working days of receiving the decision, setting out the grounds of appeal.

6.21.17 If you inform the firm of your wish to appeal, the firm will invite you to attend a further meeting and you must take all reasonable steps to attend this meeting. At this appeal meeting, you will be entitled to state your case and to be accompanied by a colleague or appropriate trade union representative.

6.21.18 You will receive a written decision within seven days of the appeal meeting which will be final.

6.22   Grievance

6.22.1 There will inevitably be problems within any working environment from time to time and it is in everyone's interests to raise any such problems to clear the air. You are therefore encouraged to voice any such concerns with your colleagues or your [*head of department/supervisor/other*]. If, however, it is not possible to resolve a grievance informally you should raise the matter formally with [*name or title*]. This procedure is not available to former members of staff.

6.22.2 The [*partners/directors*] will invite you to attend a meeting to discuss your grievance, normally within seven days. You should note, however, that this meeting can only take place once you have informed us of the basis of your grievance and we have had the opportunity to consider our response to that information.

6.22.3 You must take all reasonable steps to attend the grievance meeting and you are entitled to be accompanied by a fellow employee or appropriate trade union representative. Our overriding objective in any such meeting will be to come to a solution to the problem and resume normal working relationships if, and as soon as, possible.

6.22.4 The [*partner/director/manager*] who conducts the meeting will notify you of any decision that is made and of any right of appeal if you are not content with the action taken.

Appeal

6.22.5 If you are unhappy with the decision that is made at the grievance meeting you may appeal to [*name or title*] within seven working days.

6.22.6 In this case you will be invited to attend an appeal meeting which will be conducted by another [*partner/director/manager or the senior partner/managing director*]. You must take all reasonable steps to attend the appeal meeting and you are entitled to be represented at it by a colleague or appropriate trade union representative. The objective will again be to try to reach an agreement on the way forward. After the appeal meeting you will be notified of any decision, which will be final.

Concurrent disciplinary proceedings

6.22.7   In the event that a grievance is raised while a disciplinary process is in progress it may be appropriate to either temporarily suspend the disciplinary process so that the grievance can first be examined or deal with both issues together.

6.23   Staff records

6.23.1   Each member of staff has a file containing relevant documentation as mentioned in the procedures above. Staff files are generally kept for six years after someone leaves.

6.23.2   We also keep the following records for the periods as set out below:

Type of record	Retention period
Application forms/interview notes for unsuccessful candidates	One year
Documentation proving right to work in the UK	Two years after employment ceases
Parental leave	Five years from birth/adoption, or until child is 18 if disabled
Pensioners' records	12 years after benefit ceases
Disciplinary and working time	Six years after employment ceases
Redundancy details	Six years from date of redundancy
Type of record	**Statutory retention period**
Workplace accidents	Three years after date of last entry. There are specific rules on recording incidents involving hazardous substances.
Payroll	Three years after the end of the tax year they relate to

Statutory maternity, adoption and paternity pay	Three years after the end of the tax year they relate to
Statutory sick pay	Three years after the end of the tax year they relate to
National minimum wage	Three years after the end of the pay reference period following the one that the records cover
Retirement benefits schemes – notifiable events, e.g. relating to incapacity	Six years from the end of the scheme year in which the event took place

SECTION 7

LEGAL AID

Introduction

This section deals with issues where the Legal Aid Agency has particular requirements that legal aid practitioners need to observe and are too detailed to be included in the general section relating to that particular issue.

The significant changes since the last edition of the Solicitors Office Procedures Manual are:

- Changes to supervision requirements under the 2015 Crime contracts
- New KPIs in both versions of the Crime contract
- Clients in Crown Court cases should be provided with an estimate of costs if they have to pay contributions
- Importance of achieving panel membership as an indicator of quality

Firms doing significant amounts of legal aid work may wish to integrate the relevant paragraphs into the main sections of their Manuals.

It is worth noting the Contract requires that firms must be able to deal with the following activities electronically from April 2013. The Legal Aid Agency's (LAA) Client and Cost Management System (CCMS) may not be ready for mandatory electronic working soon; but the contract does give a clear signal that this is what the Agency intends and firms should start planning accordingly.

(a) Making applications for determinations and amending Certificates' details (including scope);

(b) Information about the Counsel you have instructed on a case (subject to Certificate scope or application for prior authority);

(c) Submitting prior authorities and requests for Payments on Account;

(d) Submitting Claims for Licensed Work;

(e) Appealing or reviewing decisions made by us on Claims; or

(f) Reviewing or appealing determinations about whether an individual qualifies for civil legal services.

Section 2 – Policies

2.6 Equality and diversity

The Specialist Quality Mark ('SQM') requires firms to comply with general legal requirements in particular ways, depending on the size of the firm. When the LAA specifies numbers of employees in this respect, they refer to staff covered by the SQM, i.e. staff involved in legal aid only.

LEVEL 1 (Fewer than five employees)

Organisations with fewer than five employees are required to provide a written document that demonstrates the organisation's commitment to equality and diversity legislation and that you would implement the requirements at the higher levels if you were to expand your legal aid departments.

LEVEL 2 (5 to 49 employees)

All organisations with between 5 and 49 employees must:

- Provide an equal opportunities policy in respect of race, gender, disability, sexual orientation, age and religion/belief that covers at least:
    - o Recruitment, selection, training, promotion, discipline and dismissal;
    - o Discrimination, harassment and victimisation making it clear that these are disciplinary offences within the organisation;
    - o Identification of senior position(s) with responsibility for the policy and its effective implementation; and
    - o How this policy is communicated to your staff.
- Demonstrate effective implementation of the policy in the organisation's recruitment practices, to include open recruitment methods such as the use of job centres, careers services and press advertisements;
- Regularly review the policy (at least every three years); and
- Regularly monitor the number of job applicants by gender, disability and ethnic groups (at least annually).

LEVEL 3 (50 or more employees)

All organisations with 50 or more employees must:

- Provide written instructions to managers and supervisors on equality in recruitment selections, training promotion, discipline and dismissal of staff;
- Provide all managers, and staff responsible for recruitment and selection, with equality training;
- Monitor, annually, the number of employees by gender, disability, age and ethnic groups (by grade) when appointed, applying for posts, taking up training and development opportunities, promoted, transferred, disciplined/dismissed, leaving employment;
- Have a process in place to review monitoring data which should include taking action where groups are under-represented; and
- Report and consult on equality issues.

LEVEL 4 (250 or more employees)

Organisations with 250 or more employees must achieve the above and check the effectiveness of their equality and diversity policies and take appropriate action, including seeking professional advice, on the employment issues identified.

Section 3 – Case management

3.1.2   Supervision

[When amending the template procedures, firms need to bear in mind that the LAA has incorporated supervision standards in both the civil and crime versions of the Standard Contract Specification. Therefore, failing to provide effective supervision is not only a failure to meet the SQM or Lexcel quality standard but could also amount to a breach of contract and result in a Contract Notice. Repeated breaches can result in contract termination.

Supervision is contained in section 2 (Service Standards) of both the crime and civil versions of the Contract Specification. The specification allows independent consultants to carry out work under the contract as long as the supervision conditions are met (see below for more information). However, it is important to note that you cannot use an agent to meet the service standards set out below. So, for example, you could not use an agent as a supervisor except, with LAA permission, for a temporary period. This was spelt out clearly in the Information for Applicants in the Family Licensed Work Tender 2012 (paragraph 8, p. 27): 'It is a requirement that Applicants employ a Supervisor, use of external Supervisors is not permitted.'

The following is an extract from the 2015 Own Client Standard Contract 2015 – Note that the Duty Contract has exactly the same provisions but the paragraph numbering is 2.8-2.12:

Supervision standards

2.9   All Supervisors must meet one of the following supervisory skills standards:

(a) Have supervised at least one Full Time Equivalent (FTE) Designated Fee Earner or Caseworker in the relevant Category of Law and/or Class of Work for at least one year in the previous five year period; or

(b) Have completed such training covering key supervisory skills we approve from time to time in the previous 12 month period; or

(c) Have achieved Level 3 or higher National Vocational Qualification NVQ standard (or any replacement from time to time) in supervising in the previous five year period.

The supervision standard in this Paragraph 2.9 will be measured as at the time a person becomes a Supervisor and at any point during the Contract Period when we request confirmation of the supervision standard.

2.10   A Supervisor must ensure that all persons performing Contract Work under this Contract have a professional legal qualification or, where a professional legal qualification is not required in respect of Contract Work, that such persons perform a minimum of 12 hours of Contract Work each week in the relevant Category of Law or Class of Work.

2.11   Arrangements must be in place to ensure that each Supervisor is able to conduct their role effectively including but not limited to the following:

(a) designating time to conduct supervision of each Designated Fee Earner or Caseworker;

(b) designating time to be in Offices where Contract Work is being conducted; and

---

> (c) ensuring that the level of supervision provided reflects the skills, knowledge and experience of the individual Designated Fee Earner or Caseworker.

2.12 Each Supervisor must conduct file reviews for each Designated Fee Earner or Caseworker they supervise. The number of file reviews must reflect the skills, knowledge and experience of the individual. The Supervisor must record the outcome of files reviews, together with the details of corrective action taken (if any).

2.13 Where a Designated Fee Earner or Caseworker undertakes Contract Work in a location other than where their Supervisor is based, the Supervisor must conduct, as a minimum, face-to-face supervision at least once per calendar month.

The following is an extract from the civil and family Standard Contract Specification 2013. You will note that there is a new requirement for Supervisors to be able to demonstrate experience of a case where human rights issues have arisen. This must be due to the new backstop provisions under the LASPO Act, which allow legal aid to be granted for cases where human rights issues do or may arise, even though legal aid would ordinarily no longer be available for the type of case.

'2.18 All Supervisors must have experience of at least one case where they have demonstrated their ability to recognise the possibility of a contravention of convention rights under the Human Rights Act 1998 (as amended) and meet one of the following supervisory skills standards:

(a) has supervised in the relevant Category of Law at least one full time Caseworker (or equivalent) for at least one year in the five year period prior to such person undertaking Contract Work as a Supervisor;

(b) completed training covering key supervisory skills that we approve from time to time no earlier than 12 months prior to the Contract Start Date;

(c) completed the Level 3 or higher National Vocational Qualification (NVQ) standard (or any replacement from time to time) in supervising no earlier than five years prior to the Contract Start Date.'

Numbers supervised

The LAA is not yet consistent on this point, although it is moving towards a consistent 1:4 ratio.

In Crime, under the 2010 contract, there were no formal limits. The number of people being supervised needed to justified and more so in multi office situations; but there were no formal limits.

The SQM sets formal limits for external supervisors, where authorised (1:3).

However, the Standard Contracts since 2013 have set a ratio of 1 FTE supervisor to 4 FTE caseworkers in each category per office.

In Immigration and Asylum, the 2013 Standard Contract specification (para 8.17) requires each of your offices to maintain a ratio of at least one full-time equivalent level 2 caseworker for every two level 1 caseworkers.

Crime supervision under 2015 contracts

The 1:4 ratio will apply in Crime from the date the new contracts become effective in 2016, with the exception of Prison Law where the ratio under the 2015 contract will be 1:6.

Freelancers can be used under both the new Duty and Own Client contracts

See FAQ answer 16.9

https://www.gov.uk/government/uploads/system/uploads/attach ment_data/file/390402/2015-duty-provider-crime-contracts-final-faq.pdf

See also the relevant paras in the Crime Contract Specifications (2.18 – 2.25 of the draft Duty Provider Crime Contract Specification and 2.24-2.29 in the draft Own Client Contract Specification).

These make it clear that you can use freelancers who are not employed by the Firm and are not Agents (which are firms with their own Contracts).

Firms can also 'designate' freelancers under the new contracts as under the 2010 Contract. All staff who work under any Crime Contract must be designated – which means the Firm that employs or uses them as a freelancer has to supervise them, do file reviews of their work, keep records of compliance with eg CLAS accreditation etc. So, firms with 2015 Crime Contracts may wish to add the following text to their manual at 3.1.2.

Supervisors will discuss the Probationary Police Station representative supervision plan and supervision arrangements before the representative starts the accreditation process.

Supervisors will undertake individual feedback sessions after each of the qualifying attendances and complete the supervision record for that attendance. Supervisors will review the probationer's portfolio and confirm its contents before it is submitted. The supervisor and representative are responsible for monitoring the representative's progress and ensuring that tests are completed within the time limits.

3.1.2 Supervision – Key performance indicators – Crime Standard Contract 2010

It is worth noting that under the Standard Contract 2010 Crime Specification para 2.50, failure to achieve key performance indicators may result in the application of a sanction under Clause 11 of the Standard Contract 2010. A repeated breach may result in contract termination. However, it does not appear that these have been a priority for the LAA by comparison to monitoring the accuracy of claims.

Crime key performance indicators 2015 – Duty and Own Client Contracts

KPI Number	The Key Performance Indicators that you must meet in performing Contract Work in any three month rolling period
1	To avoid a reduction of more than 15% of your costs on Assessment on any of your Claims for: • Police Station Advice and Assistance (Escape Fee Cases); • Free Standing Advice and Assistance Claims; • Advocacy Assistance Claims; • Magistrates' court non-Standard Fees; • Prison Law Escape Fee Cases; • Prison Law non-Standard Fees. If your costs are reduced by more than 15% on Assessment in any 3 month rolling period, then you have not met KPI 1.
2	To accept and deal appropriately with a minimum of 90% of communications (howsoever received) from the DSCC for Police Station Advice and Assistance.
3	To ensure that 95% or more of your Cases conclude before any change of Provider under the Contract.

Civil and family Supervisor standards in the 2013 Standard Contract

The rules are to be found in the Standard Contract 2013, Specification paras 2.10 – 2.27.

Under the LAA's contracts from 2013 onwards, you must (unless Category Specific Rules specify otherwise – which they generally they don't) have at least one full time equivalent Supervisor in that Category. This means you need at least one full time equivalent (FTE) in those categories (you may need more than one depending on how many people they will supervise – see 'Numbers Supervised' above).

For this purpose "full time equivalent" means the equivalent of one individual working 5 days a week and 7 hours on each day (excluding breaks).

The contract goes on to say that a Supervisor must at all times during their working hours (except as required for the proper performance of their role, (such as attending court and/or Clients) work from one of or any combination of your offices.

In addition, Supervisors must be a sole principal, an employee or a director of or partner in or member of your organisation if your practice is a company, partnership (other than an LLP) or an LLP.

The LAA will only authorise external supervisors at its discretion and for temporary periods, for example if your Supervisor becomes unwell and is unable to discharge their duties for 6 weeks.

3.1.2 – Standard Contract 2013 – Civil and Family: Key performance indicators

When designing your supervision and monitoring systems, you need to ensure that you will be able to meet the KPIs as shown below:

KPI 1   Controlled work (non-fixed fee) – assessment reduction 10 per cent max

When your 'escape cases' are assessed (these are the cases that used to be called exceptional cases, where the costs on a time and item basis are 3x the fixed fee), the costs claimed must not be reduced by more than 10 per cent. This includes disbursements but not VAT.

KPI 2   Licensed work – assessment reduction 10 per cent max

This sets the same target in relation to licensed work cases that are claimed on a time and item basis.

KPI 3 – Fixed fee margin – 20 per cent max

The LAA is concerned that some organisations will select clients with straightforward cases that do not require much work, in order to *retain a high surplus under each fixed fee case. This KPI can only be met if the total cost of cases under fixed fees when calculated in minutes and items is at least 80 per cent of the appropriate fixed fees.*

This KPI applies to Controlled Work cases, and Family Private and Public Law Representation Scheme cases that are paid by way of fixed fees.

KPI 4 – Rejection rates for Licensed Work – 5 per cent max in the schedule period

Rejections are when applications or claims are refused because of technical errors in form completion, or lack of enclosures etc. This applies to applications for legal aid (known as applications for determinations that an individual qualifies for legal aid in the post LASPO scheme), and claims for payment.

KPI 5 – Refusal rates for Licensed Work – 15 per cent max in the schedule period

This applies to applications for legal aid which are refused because the LAA considers that the practitioner has failed to show that they meet the applicable merits test.

KPI 6 – Immigration CLR positive outcome – 40% minimum

This KPI is taken as an indicator of quality and applies to Immigration CLR work only.

3.4.4   Crime – Linked cases

In Crime, one standard fee is payable per case. A case consists of all work for all clients in respect of one offence or more than one offence, where they are charged at the same time; or they are founded on the same facts; or they form part of a series of offences. Ideally, one fee-earner will deal with all matters for one client as they may affect bail, sentence and strategic decisions about the preparation of other cases, as well as fees. However if this is not possible, fee-earners are expected to identify linked cases [*/will be made aware of linked cases by the Accounts Department*] and liaise with each other as appropriate.

3.6.7   Outset of legal aid cases

In legal aid cases, in addition to the matters dealt with in Section 3.6, you also need to confirm the following in writing to clients:

- If there are any issues which would restrict the firm's ability to represent the client, perhaps because legal aid is not available;
- The operation of the statutory charge in cases where it could apply;
- In appropriate cases that, if they win, their opponent may not be ordered to pay the full amount of their legal costs, or may be unable to pay what has been ordered;
- The duty to pay any legal aid contributions assessed, and that the representation order or certificate may be discharged if they fail to do so;
- If their financial circumstances change, for better or worse, they must inform the Legal Aid Agency;
- If they plead or are found guilty, they may be ordered to pay a contribution to prosecution costs; and
- Where it appears likely that a recovery of defence costs order may be made, the client must be advised how much he or she may be asked to pay.

There is no need to advise on costs in the following instances in the following legal aid matters:

- Non means/non merit tested public law child care;
- Child Abduction and Custody Act 1985 cases;
- Registration of foreign orders cases;
- Legal help cases in which the statutory charge would never apply;
- Police station and magistrates' court cases; and
- Most Crown Court cases (but see above if a client has to pay contributions or it appears likely that a recovery of defence costs order may be made).

Many of these issues will be dealt with in our standard terms of business letters.

3.12   Planning and progressing matters

Those legal aid cases that are regarded as complex and so requiring a case plan, under the provisions of the LAA contract, include:

- Multi-party actions;

- Cases in the High Court (unless justification is provided that a case plan is unnecessary);
- Cases subject to a very high cost case contract:
- Crime – The representation order was granted on or after 3rd October 2011 and the trial is likely to last over 60 days.
- Civil – Where costs and disbursements are expected to exceed £25,000; also exceptional funding cases (when funding is approved outside of the general criteria because the client's human rights will or may be breached).

You can find more information about the detailed requirements for case plans on the legal aid website:

https://www.gov.uk/civil-high-cost-cases-family or
https://www.gov.uk/government/publications/high-cost-cases-non-family-civil

Crime

The LAA has provided guidance to the effect that it expects 'evidence of case planning', though not necessarily formal case plans, in relation to Crown Court cases. It accepts that evidence of case planning is not needed in the following types of case:

- Cases where a guilty plea is decided upon at a very early stage;
- Appeals against conviction or sentence from the magistrates' court;
- Committals for sentence;
- Hearings post-sentence;
- Hearings concerning breaches of Crown Court orders; and
- Contempt cases.

You can find more information about very high cost cases on the legal aid website:

https://www.gov.uk/high-cost-cases-crime

3.13.4 Civil and Family legal aid

It is important to monitor costs in relation to the financial limitation on the client's certificate and apply for a higher limitation in good time, as the LAA will not pay for costs which exceed the limitation in force. Where the client has an interest in the cost of the case, the client should be consulted before you apply for a higher financial limitation.

The SQM (F2.3) requires you to keep clients informed of the costs including:

(a) Actual costs to date;
(b) Disbursements; and
(c) VAT.

This must be done at regular intervals and not less than every six months, in writing (unless exceptional circumstances apply). Revised estimates of total likely costs must also be provided.

3.13.5   Crime

In criminal cases, if the client has to pay contributions in Crown Court cases or once it appears likely that an RDCO may be made, you must provide an estimate of costs, which must be updated at regular intervals and not less than every six months, in writing (unless exceptional circumstances apply).

3.16.2   File reviews

[The SQM (E2.1) states that file reviews must be carried out for 'each casework member of staff to whom cases have been allocated'. This means that trainees/caseworkers who are not allocated case files need not be included in your file review process. If a different fee earner is named as the person with conduct, then it is considered to be their file and would be file reviewed if it fell into a file review sample for their work. The person would be regarded as responsible for the quality of work on the file and would be expected to check the work which the trainee or caseworker had been asked to do.

The SQM guidance provides a table of the number of files to be reviewed per month or per quarter (page 62), but this is advisory only. The number of files reviewed, frequency and method of review have to be documented and justifiable. However, the SQM stipulates that, in the crime category, at least one file must be reviewed per qualified supervisor per month, and two for other staff, and that 50 per cent of reviews in any quarter must be carried out face to face. The frequency cannot be longer than quarterly. It is odd that numbers and frequencies are not stipulated in other categories of law, but crime effectively sets the benchmark of what the LAA expects.

However, under the Standard Contract, no minima are set in either crime or civil categories although numbers and frequencies must be justifiable.]

6.9   Training and development policy

When considering the training and development needs of fee earners, firms should think about encouraging those eligible to apply for membership of relevant Law Society and other accreditation schemes. These satisfy the LAA's legal competence requirements for supervisors in a particular category of law. As mentioned above, the LAA stipulates numbers of supervisors that must be employed to numbers of 'caseworkers' (whether qualified lawyers or otherwise).

In addition, it is a basic requirement of the LAA's contract that a firm must have at least one person who qualifies as a supervisor per category in which a contract is held. This means they must be able to demonstrate that they have the required legal competence and experience of working in the category of law, as well as knowledge of supervision. Supervisors are required to complete category specific supervisor declaration forms.

It is prudent for firms to encourage fee earners to become accredited to the following Law Society or SRA accreditation schemes:

- The Criminal Litigation Accreditation Scheme;
- The Immigration and Asylum Accreditation Scheme (supervisors must also pass the supervision qualification);
- The Family Law and Children Panels;
- The Mental Health Review Tribunal Panel;
- The Clinical Negligence Panel;
- The Personal Injury Panel; and
- Higher Rights of Audience (Crime) (SRA).

Note that Resolution accredited specialists and those who have passed stage one of the Resolution accreditation process also satisfy the LAA's legal competence requirements for supervisors in family law.

The LAA has used panel membership as an indictor of preferred quality in competitive tenders. In the 2007 Family tender, additional points were awarded for membership of the following panels: Law Society's Children Panel; Law Society's Family Panel (domestic abuse module); and Resolution accredited specialist (domestic abuse). However, whether it would do so again in the same way, following the Law Society's successful judicial review (R (Law Society) v Legal Services Commission; Dexter Montague and Partners a firm) v Same [2007] EWCA Civ 1264), is open to question. However, it is arguable that having higher numbers of accredited staff assisted firms to achieve better scores in relation to some of the selection criteria and award questions in the 2015 Crime tender.

Fee enhancements

In family cases, panel members may claim an automatic enhancement of 15 per cent on legal aid rates, where the work is payable at hourly rates (as opposed to standard fees), for work done personally by them as follows:

- *Members of the Resolution Accredited Specialist Panel and the Law Society Advanced Family Panel – in all cases; and*
- *Members of the Law Society Children Panel – all cases involving children; that is, 'proceedings in which the welfare of children is determined, including, without limitation, proceedings under the Children Act 1989 or under the inherent jurisdiction of the High Court in relation to children' (Standard Civil Contract 2013, Specification paragraph 7.24).*

An immigration solicitor or caseworker is entitled to an additional five per cent on the relevant controlled work legal aid rates where they are accredited to level three of the Immigration and Asylum Accreditation Scheme and where the work is payable at hourly rates (as opposed to standard fees) (Standard Civil Contract 2013, Specification paragraph 8.79).

APPENDICES

FORMS AND GUIDANCE

No.	Description	Page
A	**Plans and policies**	
1	Business plan format	213
2	Business continuity plan	217
3	Schedule of policies required by Lexcel v6	220
4	Quality review plan	223
5	Compliance plan outline	226
6	Risk review	229
7	Seller and buyer property conflicts policy	232
B	**Money laundering compliance forms**	
8	ML1: Client identity form	237
9	ML2: Passport and driving licence checklist	239
10	ML3: Source of funds (conveyancing purchase)	240
11	ML4: Report form	242
C	**Client care and case management**	
12	Complaints monitoring form	243
13	Complaints handling procedure	244
14	Client survey form	246
15	Departmental risk appendices	247
16	Risk points and key dates lists	249
17	File opening form	252
18	File review form	253
19	File review form: Family law private	255
20	File review form: Family law public	257
21	File review form: Crime	259

22	Demands and needs statement	261
23	Counsel and experts recommendation form	264
24	File closing checklist	265
D	**Staff handbook forms**	
25	Job description (partner)	266
26	Job description (assistant solicitor)	268
27	Job description (secretary)	270
28	Appraisal form: preparation	272
29	Appraisal report form	273
30	Exit interview questions	274
31	Induction training checklist	277
32	Training course evaluation sheet	279
33	Training and development plan	280
34	Information Technology policy	281

The appendices to the Manual have changed a good deal since the first edition of this book. The main changes are to:

- address the revisions to Lexcel v6, especially in relation to business planning (appendix 1) and the additional contents of the annual review of risk required by section 5.16 of the standard (appendix 6);
- partly because of the greater links between Lexcel and certain requirements of the SRA Handbook, especially those relating to the roles of COLP and COFA, we have edited in more guidance for the compliance officers at appendices 5 and 6; and
- changed materials on complaints handling to reflect the guidance on this topic now issued by the Legal Ombudsman and the Law Society.

The other change of note is that we have withdrawn the lengthy section on retainers and terms of business. We always recognised that there were risks in including these materials in a book as critical changes are bound to be (and have been, since the publication of the first edition) made at any time. As an Infolegal subscriber you can access the updated version of these materials, along with more comprehensive guidance on the suggested contents of the retainer documentation, as factsheet 7 on the Infolegal website. This also means that we can update you as and when changes of note are required, meaning that we can offer an enhanced service in this important aspect of client relationships.

APPENDIX 1

BUSINESS PLAN FORMAT
(Including marketing)

Introduction

There are obvious advantages for any business – law firm or other – in adopting some form of strategic plan for its future. The plan might well need amendment or correction as events unfold but, as John Harvey-Jones once observed, it is 'better to leave the future to change than to chance'. Despite the increased emphasis on effective management within the SRA Handbook – and the Code of Conduct in particular – the need for a business plan does not appear in its provisions. The need for a business plan therefore arises more within the context of the various quality management standards that are the main reference point for this publication.

The requirements of business plans have changed in Lexcel 6. The various requirements for business, marketing and services plans have now been combined within section 1.2 which simply requires instead a "strategic plan" which incorporates:

- objectives for the next 12 months at least;
- identification of the resources required by the plan;
- details of the planned services and how client groups will be served, also how the services will be delivered and marketed;
- a risk evaluation of the objectives; and
- procedures for reporting on performance.

The SQM requires you to have a detailed plan for the year ahead and an outline at least for the following two years (A1.1). Some feel this is a bit of a tall order, given the extent and rate of change in legal aid policy. The following issues must, however, appear in your business plan if you are a legal aid practice:

- A description of the client group(s) to be served;
- Services to be delivered;
- Details of opening hours, access arrangements and facilities to assist clients' access (e.g. hospital or home visit arrangements for people with disabilities);
- A summary of caseworkers' areas of expertise and professional/legal qualification, i.e. who covers which types of case and what their status is as a caseworker;
- A finance plan/budget, which the Legal Aid Agency describes as 'the monetary impact, in broad terms, of the planned service on income and expenditure (and any capital investment), i.e. an analysis that shows how you can afford to deliver the planned services (including steps to secure funding or to generate investment capital if necessary)';
- A SWOT analysis (see below); and
- Details about how you intend to promote your service.

Notwithstanding the preference in Lexcel for one integrated strategic plan it might still be worthwhile to examine the contents by its likely different elements.

Business plan outline

Summary of current position of firm (including positions in league tables and other professional reviews in the case of larger firms).

Either a summary of the services provided, the client groups served and to be served, and features of the service or a reference to where these details can be found (brochure or website?).

SWOT: Strengths, weaknesses, opportunities and threats – what are the main issues confronting the practice, both internal and external?

Financial analysis: position of the firm re:

- Percentage profitability (profit/turnover as %)
- Profit per partner
- Staff costs
- Premises costs
- PII profile
- Lock-up (WIP + Debts/turnover x 365 gives a figure expressed in days)
- Marketing – What are the main promotional activities that you are now planning to enable you to achieve the growth or change you have decided upon?

- IT and the need for further development or updating of the current system (see Lexcel 3.1 on what needs to be addressed in an IT plan);
- Resources, in terms of expenditure and time input;
- Risk factors that might impact on the above

Remember: the shorter and more focused your business plan the better – specific commitments are to be preferred to well drafted and lengthy narrative!

Marketing plan

Where the marketing plan is to be dealt with as one section of the strategic plan or as an adjunct to it there should be measurable objectives for at least the current or future 12 month period. By way of an example:

The Family law department has an increased fee earning target from £200,000 to £230,000.

The business plan suggests that this might be achieved by a 5 per cent growth in private client numbers.

The promotion is to be achieved by advertising a series of free factsheets on the firm's website and a 'Divorce Helpline' in the local newspaper.

A budget has been agreed for the advertising.

The measurable objective is the 5 per cent growth in private client numbers, to be measured at the end of the financial year.

By repeating the same process for each department a viable marketing plan will have been compiled.

How will these targets be achieved?

- Increase in turnover and/or increase in profitability of work;
- HR implications – Recruitment and other changes;
- Services – Will you be amending your current range of services, method of delivery or target client groups?
- Marketing – What are the main promotional activities that you are now

planning to enable you to achieve the growth or change you have decided upon? And/or

- Information technology.

Services plan

There is also a requirement in Lexcel at section 1.2.e for details of the services to be set out including details of the client groups to be served and the features of the services provided. Most firms will satisfy these requirements through their website or any brochures and little more will need to be done, though it might be an idea to refer to this in more detail now that Lexcel requires a more integrated approach to strategic planning. It is a good idea to include within this plan details of any special provisions to be made for disabled people (see 6.1.f in Lexcel 6).

APPENDIX 2

BUSINESS CONTINUITY PLAN FORMAT

Introduction

The requirement for a business continuity plan ('BCP') can be found in the Code of Conduct as, perhaps surprisingly, two of the indicative behaviours in Chapter 7 (see IB(7.3-4)) rather than outcomes: this notwithstanding the fact that the need to run the firm in accordance with risk management principles features in Principle 8 and also forms part of the 'compliance plan' recommended in the SRA Authorisation Rules.

Within Lexcel the need for a BCP can be found at section 1.3, which includes the need for a procedure to test the plan at least annually.

As with most management plans the job of developing a BCP should be seen as being more an exercise in common sense than complex drafting. The aim should be to have a short, simple and accessible plan of action of what needs to be done at – usually – short notice. As one volume conveyancing practice commented on the uncomfortable experience of having a power cable severed by contractors working in the area one lunchtime:

> "The last thing we wanted to do was to start to work through our detailed 40 page   document – we simply didn't have time to do so."

The business continuity plan

Phase 1: Advance planning

Determine responsibility. It would be advisable to make this a team effort in most firms as:

- There will be different strands in the continuity of service (IT and personnel most obviously); and
- Emergencies will not necessarily respect holiday commitments and one of the issues to be addressed is the need for back-up for those with key responsibilities.

Analyse the factors most likely to interrupt normal business operations:

- Civic events, making access to the offices impossible or imposing significant difficulties as by power cuts;
- Fire – damage or the destruction of the offices;
- IT failure or significant virus attack;
- Failure of service provision by others such as banks; and
- Significant absence levels, as through pandemic illness.

In smaller firms the possibility of the partners being killed or severely injured should also be considered. It has long been suggested or required that sole practitioners should have suitable arrangements in place for such eventualities, such as nominating a successor practice.

Ensuring readiness:

- Ensure that you have contact details for all partners and staff, insurances, banking codes, etc. off site in case your offices are destroyed or inaccessible.
- Are all such details kept up to date – when did you last check them?
- Planning for interim offices – partners' homes or business facilities?

Phase 2: Coping with the emergency

Consider the immediate aftermath of any of the above. Factors to consider would typically include:

- Rescue of people and data;
- Allocation of roles and responsibilities;
- Site security;
- Back-up arrangements – data and offices;
- Communication – e-mail alerts and website notices; and
- Contact insurers.

It is advisable to maintain a 'Disaster Recovery Log' to record what happens at this stage. Detail actions taken, injuries sustained, losses and expenses.

Phase 3: Restoring the service

It should be possible to restore the service by implementing the above. In most cases the disruption will be temporary in which case recovery should also be short term. In other cases longer term planning might be required.

Phase 4: Testing

Any such incident is an opportunity to make better plans for next time. The disaster recovery team should consider a 'lessons learnt' process.

You will obviously prefer not to test your plan for real, in which case consider what simulation is a suitable alternative. Consider:

- Testing contact details (contact all personnel one evening as though to tell them not to go to the office the following day);
- Availability of alternative office accommodation the following day, etc.

It is worth bearing in mind that an annual test is required in Lexcel at 1.3.d and is a common non-compliance at assessments.

APPENDIX 3

SCHEDULE OF POLICIES AND PLANS UNDER LEXCEL V6

Whereas Lexcel 5 had numerous references to the need for most of its policies and plans to have a nominated person responsible and an annual review version 6 instead requires at 3.6 a register of every "plan, policy and procedure" that is contained in the revised standard. It is unlikely that many firms will wish to drill down to the detail of every procedure in their manual to denote the responsibility for it: a more practical format will be to denote responsibility for the main policies and plans as in earlier versions of the standard and then to designate responsibility for the various areas of the manual. An alternative will be to designate the managing or quality partner, or the practice manager, as being responsible for the entire manual unless otherwise stated. This approach should mean that the firm can avoid having to list each and every procedure simply to put a name against it and concentrate instead on the more important and significant policies and plans.

Lexcel ref.	Description	Person responsible	Review month
1	**Structures and Strategy**		
1.1	Documentation on legal framework		
1.2	Strategic plan		
1.3	Business continuity plan		
1.4	Corporate social responsibility		
2	**Financial Management**		
2.1	Responsibility for overall financial management		
2.2	Evidence of financial management processes		

2.3	Time recording		
2.4	Billing procedure		
2.5	Financial transactions		
3	**Information Management**		
3.1	Information management policy		
3.2	E-mail policy		
3.3	Website		
3.4	Internet access policy		
3.5	Social media		
3.6	Register of each plan, policy and procedure		
4	**People Management**		
4.1	Health and safety policy		
4.2	Equality and diversity policy		
4.3	Learning and development policy		
4.4	Role profiles		
4.5	Recruitment and selection procedures		
4.6	Induction process		
4.7	Exit procedures		
4.8	Performance management policy		
4.9	Whistle-blowing		
4.10	Flexible working policy		
5	**Risk Management**		
5.1	Risk management policy		
5.2	Outsourcing policy		
5.3	Named supervisor for each area of work		
5.4	Manage instructions with higher risk profile		
5.5	Maintain lists of work undertaken and declined		
5.6	Generic risks and causes of claims		
5.7	Key dates		
5.8	Conflicts of interests		
5.9	Active supervision		
5.10	Inactivity checks		
5.11	Regular, independent file reviews		
5.12	Operational risk to be considered and recorded		

5.13	Anti-money laundering policy		
5.14	Procedures for avoiding mortgage fraud		
5.15	Bribery Act 2010		
5.16	Analysis of risk assessment data		
6	**Client Service and Care**		
6.1	Policy for client care		
6.2	Processes (for compliance with chapter 1 of Code)		
6.3	Record of standing terms of business		
6.4	Costs information		
6.5	Written complaints handling procedure		
6.6	Process to monitor client satisfaction		
6.7	Matter acceptance		
7	**File and Case Management**		
7.1	Matter strategy		
7.2	Undertakings		
7.3	File status and confidentiality		
7.4	Progress of matters		
7.5	Use of barristers and other external advisers		
7.6	End of matter		

APPENDIX 4

QUALITY REVIEW PLAN

Introduction

Section 5.16 of Lexcel requires an analysis of 'all risk assessment data' that arises and which should be kept under review. There are similar provisions in the SQM in relation to:

- File reviews (E2.6);
- Complaints (G1.3); and
- Client feedback (G2.2)

The rationale for these provisions is that the firm should learn from its experiences – and its mistakes, most importantly – so as to make sense of its commitment to improve.

Lexcel v6 adds to the sources of data that will need to be considered. In addition to the claims, complaints, file reviews and client surveys that have always formed part of this requirement firms now need to add a number of COLP and COFA issues, namely a summary or list of all breaches (as defined by the SRA Authorisation Rules) – both material and non-material. The requirement for all 'matters notified' to the compliance officers may provide to be more problematic, especially where (as is commonly the case) the concerns are considered to be ill-founded. Situations where the firm has acted where a conflicts of interests did exist are included, but there are, of course, exceptional cases where it is permitted to act despite conflicts in chapter 6 and it is again unclear whether permitted conflicts will have to be noted.

1. Introduction

This document addresses the operation of the quality system of the firm and suggests the quality objectives for the year ahead. It will be considered at [*the next partners' meeting/the annual strategy day*].

[*Any relevant methodology and dates.*]

The [*partners/directors*] view the quality management programme as being core to the future success of the practice [*elaborate on what you want from your system and the support you expect for it from others within the firm*].

2. Changes to the quality system
[*Comment on any changes to the quality system and the firm's objectives from it, for example:*

- *Switch to Lexcel from SQM;*
- *Application to CQS or WIQS;*
- *Updating from Lexcel 5 to 6.*

Comment on responsibility for the review and for the management of the firm's system.]

3. Review of last year's quality objectives
[*If you have undertaken this process before, comment here on last year's objectives and whether they were achieved. If not, why not, and do they remain valid this year?*

What other objectives are now relevant? Remember that business planning and marketing plan objectives should be 'measurable' under Lexcel and this is a good principle for all of the other issues that will arise here as well.]

4. COLP and COFA Reports
[*Summary of reports received and filed, list of breaches both non-material and material. Report on any SRA action taken in response to any reports filed with them. Include situations where the firm has acted where a conflict of interests as defined by chapter 3 of the Code of Conduct has existed nonetheless.*]

5. Client complaints
[*Numbers.*
Numbers resolved.
Dealings with Legal Ombudsman, if any.
Trends to be addressed and any action already taken.]

6. Client and staff surveys
[*Narrative on actions taken – numbers sent out and returned, and percentage analysis response, perhaps by pie chart graphics.*

Staff surveys are not a requirement but can be highly instructive to changes and improvements needed.]

---

7. Claims and circumstances reported to insurers

[Again, not a requirement as such but a schedule addressing all such issues will be a useful accompaniment to this report in most firms.]

8. Quality objectives

[This is the real point of the exercise – what improvements are you suggesting you commit yourselves to, over what time frame, and who will be responsible for them?]

9. Legal aid

Although not directly required by the SQM, an annual management review is advisable to ensure that all aspects are kept under review as they need to be. Bear in mind that at least an interim review of the business plan must occur each six months between annual main reviews.

An annual review would be good evidence that you are complying with clause 7 in the Standard Contract, which requires you to monitor your performance under the contract. The following are suggested headings:

- Relationship with LAA (etc.), contract key performance indicators (KPIs) and service standards;
- Exercise of delegated functions;
- Patterns of matter starts, matter completions and turnover time;
- Pattern of referrals; and
- Evaluation of counsel and experts.

APPENDIX 5

SRA COMPLIANCE PLAN OUTLINE

Guidance note iii to Rule 8 of the SRA Authorisation Rules suggests that firms should compile a compliance plan as evidence of its commitment to this part of the Handbook. In practice this has now become an SRA requirement with a request for a copy of this plan accompanying most notifications of inspections.

The following items are listed by the SRA as illustrations of the sorts of issues that should be covered:

- clearly defined governance arrangements providing a transparent framework for responsibilities within the firm;
- appropriate arrangements for accounting procedures and the authorisation of payments from client account;
- the control of undertakings;
- 'appropriate checks on new staff or contractors';
- compliance with regulatory deadlines;
- 'a system for monitoring, reviewing and managing risks';
- ensuring that conduct issues are given proper weight in the firm's decision-making processes;
- file reviews;
- training; and
- obtaining the approvals where needed of the COLP and COFA.

A quick glance at this list will suggest that it is just as significant for what it does *not* say as for what it does. Many would regard the business plan as the obvious starting point for any concerted attempt to address all of the major issues within the firm that relate to client service and regulatory compliance, yet business strategy and marketing do not merit a mention. In other respects the list is strangely selective: is it only checks on new staff that are worthy of a mention in relation to personnel systems, as opposed to recruitment processes in general? Likewise, training clearly merits a mention, but why not review or appraisal processes or the increasingly adopted practice of 'exit' interviews as one step in ensuring an orderly departure of personnel? Why undertakings as an obvious issue of law firm risk but not key dates reminder systems? All in all, the issues that are mentioned are better seen as a 'taster' than a checklist.

We recommend that the compliance plan is seen as a high level summary of your practice, summarising what makes it special and the key management systems and features. On this basis we suggest the following headings, referring to the Practice Manual where applicable. for a more detailed explanation of the SRA's requirements for a compliance plan for additional advice in how to compile one for your practice see Infolegal Guidance Note 3

Introduction to the firm
Summary description of the firm
Governance and management
Our status as a practice and our overall control structure Management structure Organisational chart
SRA Responsibilities
COLP and COFA (with terms of reference) SRA renewals and reporting
Monitoring
Monitoring by the COLP Monitoring by the COFA Record keeping by COLP and COFA
Business Planning
Main plan Business continuity planning
Equality and Diversity
Suitable policy adopted (refer to manual)

Supervision and risk management
Supervisory systems (summarise)
Risk management systems (summarise)
Outsourcing (refer to manual)
Financial Crime
Money laundering and terrorist financing
Mortgage fraud avoidance measures
The Bribery Act 2010
FCA Regulation
If listed on the exempt professional firms register (see Chapter 2 para 20) and if so who the FCA Compliance Officer is, or if the firm is also FCA regulated.
Client Care
Treating clients fairly
Client care systems
Handling enquiries and ceasing to act
Retainer and terms of business
Complaints handling
Distance selling and billing
Conflicts of Interests, and the duties of confidentiality and disclosure
Conflict checking systems
Confidentiality and disclosure
Property conflicts
Information security and data protection
Registration under the DPA 1998
The need for a policy
The Land Registry Portal obligations
Staff management
Health and safety
Personnel systems
Checks on new staff and contractors
Training
The SRA Accounts Rules
Refer to existence of accounts manual

APPENDIX 6

RISK REVIEW

Introduction

The risk policy required by section 5.1 of Lexcel has now moved away from the headings of strategic, operational and regulatory and reflects more the SRA's routine requirements for a compliance plan and a risk review. Many firms will find it helpful to retain these headings, however, and they still feature in the following sample risk review precedent. They also still feature in the Core Practice Management Standards as of July 2015 which will be relevant to any practices applying to WIQS if they do not have Lexcel accreditation.

The Charity Commission, amongst others, suggests that organisations should attempt to state their overall exposure to risk (the 'gross' risk) and then re-state their exposure having taken such steps as are expedient in the circumstances to define their 'net' or residual risk.

This exercise is likely to overlap with the business continuity planning exercise and might be confined to certain areas of the practice in the light of other steps taken by the management of the firm.

Having identified a risk there are four main responses to it:

- Transfer (e.g. pass the risk to an insurer);
- Avoidance (decline to undertake the activity that creates that risk);
- Management (take steps to alleviate the risk); or
- Acceptance (choose to live with that risk, usually where it is unlikely to materialise).

The scoring system should take into account the risk of an event and its impact if it does materialise. The judgment will be essentially subjective: in the form below a scale of 1-10 is envisaged with 1 being the lowest score (of no significance) to 10 (extreme risk). To take one example:

Suppose that the staff of the firm operate a lottery sweepstake. The 'risk' of their winning is negligible and the impact of staff leaving, although significant, could be managed. The partners therefore take the view that this is a risk that can be accepted and requires no management action on their part (such as the purchase of specialist insurance for this risk).

If adopting this format you will need to take into account risk and impact in assessing your gross score, and then perhaps agree a level at which net risk remains unacceptable, meaning that you must avoid that risk, insure against it further or take further risk management measures to reduce the net score.

Risk factor	Gross score	Steps taken	Net score
Strategic			
Insufficient attention to management issues	6	Mandatory attendance at partners' meetings	3
Insufficient expertise on management issues	6	Involve expert facilitator at next strategic review	4
Over-reliance on key client in commercial department	4	Target more work from regular clients in marketing plan	3
Loss of legal aid contract	5	Undertake expert review of LAA requirements	4
Too reliant on partner billings	4	Purchase 'key person' insurance?	3
Encroachment of ABSs on certain areas of practice	6	Client care review – client retention a key element of marketing plan	5
Financial – poor cash flow resulting in problems with HMRC	4	Creation of tax reserve – drawings to be reduced from month 3 of new financial year	3
Operational			
Losses through fraud by clients	4	Tighten CDD processes in money laundering manual and staff training	2
Errors by taking on unsuitable instructions	3	Adopt partner sign-off of all new matters	1
Retainer errors – failure to scope work properly	4	Review of all retainer letter formats and terms of business drafts	2

Poor supervision	5	Tighten supervision processes: • File reviews must be maintained • Post monitoring for junior staff • Review e-mail monitoring? • Partner management training?	2
Confidentiality breaches	6	Ensure proper passwording of all electronic devices – check by practice manager	3
IT failure – loss of data	5	See business continuity plan	1
Infiltration by fraudster to the firm	1	Tighten staff recruitment and checking procedures	0
Environmental			
Health and safety – risk of prosecution	3	Practice manager to attend training and conduct risk assessments Must also attend fire safety training	1
See also business continuity plan for other identified risks			

APPENDIX 7

ACTING FOR SELLER AND BUYER UNDER THE SRA CODE OF CONDUCT 2011

Introduction

Under the former Code of Conduct 2007 it was permissible to act for seller and buyer in the same transaction where:

- Both clients were established clients, or
- Different offices were acting, or
- The consideration was less than £10,000.

This was then dependent, however, on there being no conflict of interests in that particular matter (rule 3.09-3.10). The situation is now more vague and is mostly governed by two indicative behaviours, neither of which (being IBs) is mandatory.

In the current Code of Conduct IB(3.3) states that 'declining to act for clients where you may need to negotiate on matters of substance on their behalf, for example negotiating on price between a seller and buyer of property' will be evidence of having complied with the outcomes requiring that firms do not act where there is a conflict of interests; but that (IB(3.14)) 'acting for buyer (including a lessee) and a seller (including a lessor) in a transaction relating to a transfer of land for value, the grant or assignment of a lease or some other interest in land for value' is evidence of not having complied with the same requirements.

The available guidance

So, is it still possible to act for seller and buyer? There remains no definitive advice on this from either the SRA or the Law Society. The Law Society practice note on conflicts merely suggests that the decision rests with the firm.

The SRA indicated in its quick guide 'Outcomes-focused regulation at a glance' that it believes acting for buyer and seller is an area which carries a high risk of conflict of interests and that it does not expect you to act for buyer and seller routinely.

In the instances when you might decide that you can act under the Code of Conduct for both buyer and seller, it is up to you in these circumstances to show the basis for your decision and justify your actions to the SRA. In the Law Society's view it would be good practice to record your decision and reason for it if you decide to act in these circumstances.

If you decide to act in a particular circumstance then you should actively monitor this situation for a conflict arising as there could be considerable implications for each of the clients and for others involved in a conveyancing chain if you need to withdraw because of a conflict situation.

If you decide that there is no conflict of interests between a buyer and seller then you must consider whether there is any risk of not adhering to any of the principles. The key principle you should take into account is principle 4, 'act in the best interests of each client'. Other key principles are principle 2, 'act with integrity', principle 3, 'not allow your independence to be compromised' and principle 5, 'provide a proper standard of service to your clients'. Chapter 4 on confidentiality and disclosure is also important and more information on this is outlined below.

Recommended policy

Given the uncertainty over the situation, the better policy is to decline to act for both parties if possible. Where this is not realistic and you wish to assume the risk of censure by the SRA should things not go well:

- Have a clear policy for your firm on the circumstances where you will accept instructions from both sides;
- Carefully document any decision to act for both parties and record all the circumstances known to you at the time;
- Have one (neutral if possible) individual who approves all such decisions;
- Tell both clients of the risks and make clear the limitations to your service, e.g. not to be able to negotiate price reductions for the buyer; and
- Get both parties to give written consent.

If you do decide to act for seller and buyer in any given matter then you should actively monitor the progress of the matter in order to identify any conflict that might arise as it moves towards completion. Bear in mind that there may be considerable implications for your clients – and for others involved in the conveyancing chain – if you need to withdraw because of a conflict situation that is identified part way through the transaction, and that this may well be just the sort of issue that ends up being referred to the Legal Ombudsman. You and your practice should consider this factor when deciding whether to act, and then at all times during the life of the file.

Some sample precedents follow but please bear in mind that, pending better and more detailed advice from the SRA and/or the Law Society, their effectiveness in any given case cannot be guaranteed.

Additional retainer information (to be added to the usual letter or edited into a supplemental enclosure)

As you [*are/are perhaps*] aware, the [*seller/buyer*] of this property has also instructed this firm to act on their behalf. The practice of one law firm acting for both parties to a transaction is discouraged by the regulatory body for solicitors – the Solicitors Regulation Authority – and is only permitted where it is clearly in the interests of both parties for the one firm to be involved. We believe that this might be such a case, but it is important that we explain the potential disadvantages to you in proceeding in this manner, and that you only consent to our doing so if you are sure that it is in your best interests to do so.

The system operated by this firm in such cases is that each of the parties – the seller and buyer – is represented by [*different offices/different fee earners/fee earners supervised by different partners, etc*].

There is one major limitation to our proceeding in this manner. As a result of our professional obligation to act in the best interests of all clients we may not enter into any negotiations on your behalf, for example on variations to the agreed price as a result of any problems that might be highlighted in a surveyor's report, or information that emerges from the various searches of information on the property. You would have to understand that such negotiations would have to be conducted without our assistance, perhaps through the agents acting in this transaction. We would be able to provide legal advice to you on any such issue, but not act for you in any ensuing discussions.

Please also bear in mind that if a conflict of interests should arise during the transaction (which would be unusual if we are not participating in any form of negotiations, but is still possible) then we might have to withdraw from acting for you. This possible inconvenience would not be the case if the other side were represented by another firm. In these circumstances our policy would be to [*explain your attitude to costs, etc*].

If you have any concerns about the level of service we would be able to offer to you by acting in this way please contact [...]. Other than this, and only if you feel entirely satisfied to do so, please sign the form below and return it to us so that we can be sure that you understand the implications of this firm acting for both seller and buyer in this transaction.

I have read the letter of the .... and understand the basis on which [*firm name*] may act for both seller and buyer in this transaction, and agree to their doing so. I acknowledge that I have been invited to discuss any concerns that I have in this regard with the firm.

Signed .... date ....

Signed .... date ....

Seller and buyer checklist and consent form

1	Property details and price Profile of transaction	
2	Fee earner acting for seller	
3	Fee earner acting for buyer	
4	Office and partner responsible for seller	
5	Office and partner responsible for buyer	
6	If established client, when did we last act for seller and to do what?	
7	If established client, when did we last act for buyer and to do what?	
8	Are there any unusual risks with this property that are likely to give rise to a conflict of interests at a future stage? If so, please specify.	
9	Please confirm that seller/buyer has had the policy of the firm explained to them. Has your client replied to you or discussed the matter with you? If so, please send attendance note to	
10	Do you believe that your client/all of your co-clients are of sufficient sophistication to understand the consent that they are required to provide and to be able to make their own arrangements to deal with negotiations on price, etc. without your involvement?	
11	Do you believe that this is a suitable matter where we might fairly act for seller and buyer? Please state here any concerns that you might have on this issue.	

On the basis of the above I confirm that we can act for both parties in this matter.

Signed .... date ....

APPENDIX 8

FORM ML1: CLIENT IDENTITY FORM

Identity check not needed:

☐   Client is a business within the regulated sector ....

☐   Existing client – previous search still valid ....

☐   Partner sign-in: client well known to partner (sign) ....

Private individuals

☐ Full passport or ☐ Full driving licence. If neither of these is available tick here ☐

Electronic ID check required? ☐ Comment ....

plus one of: ☐ Utility bill (three months old maximum) ....

☐ Recent bank statement ....

☐ Other evidence of identity (specify) ....

☐ Other evidence of address (specify) ....

1.   Trustees and executors: perform as individuals, preferably on two persons.
2.   Non-professional partnerships (other than LLPs) and other unincorporated associations, deal with as individuals: professional partnerships and LLPs deal with as companies.

Private companies

☐   Names and addresses of 2 officers/directors

☐   Company search, copy certificate of incorporation or directory entry on professional firm

☐   Evidence of authority of representatives

Other risk factors	Yes / No
1. Is there a chance that this client is a politically exposed person?	....
2. Could this client be acting as the agent of an undisclosed principal?	....
3. Are you confident that the source of funds (or wealth) does not need further enquiry?	....
4. Are any further checks required (e.g. electronic ID check)?	....
5. Please supply details with this form of any beneficial owners	....

Lawyer certification

I believe that there is no undue risk to the firm in acting in this matter and I am confident that I understand the nature and purpose of the instructions.

Signed   **Date of signature**

APPENDIX 9:

FORM ML2: PASSPORT AND PHOTO DRIVING LICENCE FORM

The client and matter

Full name of client	
Former name(s) if any	
Address	
Description of matter	

Passport check

Does the photograph match the appearance of the holder?	Expiry Date
Does the colour and quality of the passport look as if it is a genuine document?	
Does the passport number at the front match the number on the identification page?	
Is there a watermark on the identification page that also includes the photograph?	

Photo driving licence check

Does the photograph match the appearance of the holder?	
Does this appear to be a valid driving licence?	
What is the expiry date of the licence?	

Check completed by .... (signature) .... (date)

Please sign or initial a photocopy of the passport identification page or licence.

This form is to be retained on file or placed in central records. This form must **not** be returned to the client if they request return of their papers at any time.

APPENDIX 10

FORM ML3: SOURCE OF FUNDS

CLIENT	Mr	Mrs	Ms		Surname	
Forenames				Previous name (or alias)		
Address						
Postcode						
Capacity [when acting on behalf of a business]: Director / Secretary / Partner / Other						

Source	Details required	Please tick	£ approximately and comment
1 Sale of existing property	Address Approximate amount		Net proceeds after agents' fees
2 Building Society or Bank mortgage	Copy mortgage offer or loan to be applied for		Name of institution and amount
3 Inheritance	Copy Estate Accounts or Copy solicitors letter with cheque or Other evidence		
4 Savings	Building Society passbook or Building Society account or Bank statement Provide explanation of how acquired		Evidence of source of wealth needed and on file?

5 Gift	Donor(s) name Donor(s) address Over £5,000 source of wealth? Over £10,000 ID check also required?		Relationship to client?
6 Private loan	Lender(s) name Lender(s) address Over £5,000 source of wealth? Over £10,000 ID check also required		Relationship to client?
7 Proceeds of sale of investments or securities	Broker's/adviser's letter with cheque or Contract notes or other evidence		
8 Other source(s):			Give details

The importance of advising my solicitors of any changes to the above has been explained to me. I understand that completion of the purchase might be delayed if there are late changes to the above that have not been explained by me/us to my/our adviser in advance.

Signed (client 1) .... Date ....

Signed (client 2) .... Date ....

APPENDIX 11

REPORT FORM ML4: STRICTLY CONFIDENTIAL

Before completing this form speak first to [*name or status*]. Great care must be taken to ensure that this form is not seen by the client at any time.

Client

(Mr) (Mrs) (Miss) (Ms) ( ) Forenames ....
Surname .... Any alias or previous name? ....
Phone (day) .... Evening .... Mobile ....
Address ....
....
Postcode .... E-mail (if any) ....
Date and place of birth, if known ....
NI no if known ....

Circumstances

Source of client? ....
Nature of Instructions
Reason For Report (attach confidential memo if necessary)

Signed .... (fee earner)   Date ....

Money Laundering Reporting Officer

MLRO Date Received .... Date of report to NCA ....

Or, reasons for not reporting and/or any further action taken

APPENDIX 12

COMPLAINTS MONITORING FORM

Client's name: Case ref: Fee earner: Supervisor:	Funding type: Private paying/Company commercial/ CFA/Legal aid/Third party (state)

Complaint received by: Date:
Passed to complaints partner – Date:

Complaint concerned – please tick one									
Conduct		Costs info deficient		Costs excessive		Criminal activity		Data protection	
Delay		Discrimination		Failure to advise		Failure to comply with remedy		Failure to follow instructions	
Failure to investigate complaint		Failure to keep informed		Failure to keep papers safe		Failure to progress		Other – please explain	

Brief outline of complaint:

Brief outline of action taken in investigating the complaint:

Outcome: Complaint upheld – Reason   Complaint not upheld – Reason

Insurers notified? Yes / No If yes, date:

Offer of redress? State what:

Issues to be taken into consideration for future risk management: Notified to risk manager – Date: Signed:

APPENDIX 13

SAMPLE COMPLAINTS HANDLING POLICY/PROCEDURE
To be sent to someone on request or making a complaint

You may have asked for our complaints procedure or you may be receiving this because you have experienced a problem with our service.

If you have experienced a problem, thank you for bringing your concerns to our attention. We will do our best to address any dissatisfaction that you have experienced in using the services of this firm. Our primary objective is to put things right.

Our complaints policy

We are committed to providing a high-quality service to our clients. This includes a commitment to putting things right when they go wrong. This policy explains how we will deal with any complaint.

Our complaints procedure

Our complaints partner is [*name or title*]. You can contact him/her by post at [*set out address or include wording such as 'at this office'*], or by e-mail at [*specify*]. It is helpful if you put your concerns into writing, but if you would prefer not to, or if you would find it difficult to do so, he/she can be contacted by phone at [*specify*].

If you have special needs which we should take into account due to language or disability, please let us know.

To explain to you how long our process might take we have included our target times for each stage of the process. Where, for any reason, it is not possible to observe any of these limits we will let you know and explain why.

Action	Timescale
Acknowledge the complaint in writing and send a copy of the complaints procedure	Within two working days
Invite you to a meeting or to discuss the issues by telephone	Within two working days
Confirm the outcome of the meeting or telephone conversation in writing	Within three working days of the meeting/telephone conversation
Investigate the issues	Within 14 days of receiving the complaint
If a meeting/telephone discussion is not possible or required: Investigate the issues and write to you with the outcome	Within 21 days
Review and close the complaint	Within 8 weeks of receiving the complaint

Legal Ombudsman

If you do not agree with the outcome of our complaints process, or we fail to investigate it within 8 weeks, you can then complain to the Legal Ombudsman. Complaints to the Legal Ombudsman must usually be made within six months of our final response to your complaint.

The Legal Ombudsman can investigate complaints for up to six years from the date a problem occurred or within three years from when you found out about the problem.

The address is PO Box 6806, Wolverhampton WV1 9WJ, telephone 0300 555 0333 or email *enquiries@legalombudsman.org.uk*

APPENDIX 14

CLIENT SURVEY FORM

Your name   Department   Fee earner
(optional)

Please assess us by ticking one of the following columns:

	1	2	3	4
1. How would you assess our reception area and the welcome you have received if and when you visited our offices? Comment				
2. How would you rate the adviser(s) who handled your instructions? Comment				
3. How well did we communicate with you? Did we do so in a timely, helpful and intelligible manner? Comment				
4. Did you get the impression that we were determined to do our best for you? Comment				
5. In general terms, how would you assess our service for you? Comment				

Would you be likely to recommend this firm to others? Yes ... No ... Undecided ...

Thank you for your time and trouble in completing this form. Please return it in the stamped addressed envelope provided.

APPENDIX 15

DEPARTMENTAL RISK APPENDICES
(see Introduction to chapter 3)

[*This form to be completed by the Head of Department or other representative in order to compile the Departmental Instructions – see Introduction to the Case Management section*]

The aim of the current compliance review is that, so far as possible, there should be one manual dealing with supervision, risk, client care and file management issues for the whole firm. The different patterns of work in each department do, however, also need to be addressed. The departmental appendix is your opportunity to do so. You should record here all of the special systems and processes that are particular to your area of work.

1	Please list here the range of instructions undertaken in your area of the firm
2	Please state here any types of instructions that might be associated with your area of work that you do not undertake (e.g. intellectual property disputes in a commercial litigation group)
3	The most significant risks of error in your area of work (e.g. late registration, failure to update searches so that they are current, etc.)

4	Particular concerns, if any, arising from conflicts of interests
5	Key dates. Please list here all the dates that you would regard as key dates that should be noted in a back-up system (see sample list at Appendix 11b)
6	If you already have a key dates reminder system in place, please describe here how it works
7	Please comment here on how undertakings impact on your area of work. This section is of more obvious relevance to domestic conveyancing work, but there might be considerations elsewhere
8	Please state here how you expect files to be maintained (e.g. colour coding of files, separate bundles, etc). Please also deal with larger items (e.g. X rays or deeds) that might not go on the file. How and where are these filed, and referred to on the matter file?
9	What are your arrangements for departmental meetings?
10	If there is already a system for regular independent file reviews please explain here how it operates

APPENDIX 16

SOME COMMON RISK POINTS AND KEY DATES

Civil litigation

- Identify and act within the applicable limitation periods.
- Follow appropriate protocols.
- Deal with commercial property notices re leases in time.
- Obtain sufficiently reliable expert advice.
- Check the accuracy of documents and pleadings with the client prior to issue.
- Advise the client of adverse costs orders.
- Limitation periods, including latent damage when relevant.
- Hearing dates.
- Dates for filing of evidence.
- Lease notices in landlord and tenant work.

Conveyancing

- Identify clearly the property being sold and bought.
- Detect mortgage fraud or money laundering (including terrorist financing).
- Check search results carefully enough.
- Identify and advise upon intended use and planning restrictions.
- Check restrictive covenants.
- Pay SDLT in time.
- Submit registration within permissible timescales.
- Register charges at Companies House within timescales.

Commercial

- Poor drafting and failing to address all eventualities.
- Stamping dates for share transfers.
- Filing dates for statutory notifications.
- Warranty expiry dates.
- Detect mortgage fraud or money laundering (including terrorist financing).

Crime

- Conflicts of interests between co-defendants/witnesses.
- Ethical approach to victims, especially in relation to retraction in domestic abuse cases.
- Ethical approach regarding gifts to clients/providing funds to clients in custody.
- Awareness of POCA in relevant cases.
- Hearing dates.
- Compliance with court orders.
- Advice on appeal.

Employment

- Identify and act within the applicable limitation periods.
- Comply with Tribunal orders.

Family

- Undertake a costs-risk analysis and advise the client accordingly.
- Obtain sufficiently reliable expert advice, including valuation of assets.
- Check the accuracy of documents and pleadings with the client prior to issue, especially the disclosure of assets.
- Applying for decree absolute without consent, or failing to do so in accordance with the client's instructions.

Landlord and tenant

- The property description and compare with any plan.
- Car parking rights or inclusion of garages in the demise.
- Exceptions and reservations.
- Ground rent arrangements.
- Unusual clauses.
- Repairing covenants.
- Service charges.
- Credentials of any management company.
- Forfeiture provisions.
- Insurance provisions.

Wills and probate

- Understanding the client's objectives and then meeting them.
- The pace of change with statutory and case law developments (especially when back-dated).
- Obtain sufficiently reliable expert advice.
- Observe limitation periods in possible inheritance claims.
- Not noting tax payment dates (income tax and IHT).
- Dates for filing of tax returns.
- Noting 21 year accumulation period.

APPENDIX 17

FILE OPENING FORM

Client details	
Name Former name (if any) Address	E-mail How should we contact this client? Source of client
Telephone (landline day) (evening) (mobile)	Client partner Fee earner acting
Finance	**General risk assessment**
Credit risk required? Money on account requested? Likely fees for this matter Comment	I consider the risk profile of this matter to be High Ordinary High risk factors, if any
Conflicts of interests	**Matter closing checklist**
Names checked .... Database check completed By .... Date	Final report to client...................................... Nil balances on accounts............................ Advised on storage....................................... Destroy date... Future notes, if any

APPENDIX 18

FILE REVIEW FORM

File name:		Matter number:			
Department:		Fee earner handling:			
File opening File summary form completed and up to date Instructions noted and filed Retainer letter sent – if no, why not? Terms of business sent	Yes	No	N/A	Comments	
File management Tidy and organised Filing up to date File complete – gaps?					
Matter progress Is it clear what is being done for the client and why? Hs the client been kept informed of progress and any changes to the case plan? Costs information kept up to date Are we still within costs estimate?					

Other issues				
Counsel or experts on approved list and client consulted				
Undertakings properly authorised and noted				
Other non-compliances				

Corrective action required	Observations
By when?............................ Confirmed............................	

Corrective action taken	Corrective action verified
(matter handler) (date)	(reviewer) (date)

APPENDIX 19

FILE REVIEW FORM – FAMILY (PRIVATE LAW)

File ref		Client		Matter type	
Fee earner		Reviewer			
Legal Aid	Yes / No	Legal Help / FHL	Yes / No	Date	

Procedural issues	*There is no need to tick each one – identify any issue requiring corrective action*
File opening form Evidence of identity Risk assessment LH / FHL form & evidence of means Terms of business & client care letter Key dates Counsel / experts Undertakings Costs information and updates File management End of case	
Legal quality and peer review	*Comment on issues handled well or any issue requiring corrective action*
Instructions and action confirmed? Advice tailored to the client's case? Linked issues dealt with? Mediation considered? Advised on law and procedures? Advised on merits? Advised on correspondence and docs received? Advised on terms and effect of orders? Delay?	

Divorce – Advice on how children will be dealt with? Effects of Decree Absolute and re-marriage? Finances – Severance of joint tenancy? Joint assets & liabilities? Disclosure? Pensions? Clean break? Children – Parental responsibility? CAFCASS? Abduction? Court's approach re DV? Weight given to older children's feelings and wishes? DV – Advice on remedies? Personal service? Power of arrest? Undertakings? Enforcement?	
Action required by (date)	
Action checked by (reviewer) date)	

APPENDIX 20

FILE REVIEW FORM – FAMILY (PUBLIC LAW)

File ref		Client		Matter type	
Fee earner		Reviewer			
Legal Aid	Yes / No	Legal Help / FHL	Yes / No	Date	

Procedural issues	*There is no need to tick each one – identify any issue requiring corrective action*
File opening form Evidence of identity Risk assessment LH / FHL form & evidence of means Terms of business & client care letter Key dates Counsel / experts Undertakings Costs information and updates File management End of case	
Legal quality and peer review	*Comment on issues handled well or any issue requiring corrective action*
Instructions and action confirmed? Advice tailored to the client's case? Linked issues dealt with? Advised on law and procedures? Advised on merits? Advised on correspondence and docs received? Advised on terms and effect of orders? Delay?	

Advice on LA's responsibilities when proceedings have not been issued? Role of the Children's Guardian? Confidentiality and experts? Advice on contact with child in care at interim stage? If acting for children – has the f/e met them? If an older child differs from the Guardian's view, is this dealt with?	
Action required by (date)	
Action checked by (reviewer) date)	

APPENDIX 21

CRIME FILE REVIEW FORM

Client name		Fee earner	
Client ref.		Reviewer	
Date		Face to face	Paper

SQM and LAA requirements – *Enter tick, x or NA as appropriate*

File orderly		Report on outcome of case	
Key dates on file		Money accounted for to cl. at end	
Key dates in diary		Original documents returned to cl.	
Undertakings shown		Advised of storage period	
Conflict check carried out by fee earner?		Counsel/experts on approved list?	
1 Instructions noted		*If no – assessment of performance?*	
2 Advice noted			
3 Action noted		Disbursements recorded?	
4 Name & status with conduct;			
5 Name of overall supervisor;		File free from complaints?	
6 Complaints procedure info sent		*If no – complaints procedure OK?*	

1 – 6 confirmed to client in writing		Money accounted for to cl. at end	
If Duty PS case – contact with client within 45 min?		If closed case – claim submitted to LAA in time?	
If Duty PS case – arrival at PS within 45 min of decision to attend?		Bill accurate?	
Written costs estimate provided to client (if client pays contributions in Crown Court)			
If above applies – Costs estimates updated six monthly			

Comments on legal or procedural issues

Corrective action

Signed (reviewer) .... Date ....

Signed (reviewer) .... Date ....

APPENDIX 22

DEMANDS AND NEEDS STATEMENT

Where a firm undertakes insurance mediation activities for a client, it must communicate certain information to the client in a way that is 'clear, fair and not misleading'. In practice this is done by adopting the wording required by the Conduct of Business Rules.

Furthermore, where a policy is obtained for or recommended to the client they must be served with a 'demands and needs statement'. This requires the fee earner to:

- Consider what they already know about the client and the matter;
- Obtain any details of relevant existing insurance;
- Consider the client's requirements from any policy and the appropriate level of cover; and
- Consider the suitability of the policy given any exclusions, excesses, limitations or conditions.

This needs to be confirmed to the client in writing, perhaps through the use of a demands and needs pro forma. The statement must be provided in advance of the recommendation being made and at the time that the issue arises.

It should also be noted that there is a need to advise the client whether the recommendation of a particular policy (other than life cover) has been made with or without 'fair market analysis', i.e. a sufficiently large number of similar polices have been considered before any one is recommended. In most cases firms will not conduct this type of analysis in which case:

- They must advise the client of any contractual commitments they have with any providers;
- The client must be informed that they may request details of any such connections; and
- The details of any such links must be provided if requested.

A template form follows.

DEMANDS AND NEEDS STATEMENT

We are issuing you with this statement because we have made a recommendation to you that you obtain insurance. When we do so we are required to advise you of certain information in order to comply with the regulation we are subject to. The notice we are required to provide you with is in our terms of business and is set out at the end of this note.

1	The insurance that we are recommending that you purchase and the level of cover
2	The reason we are making this recommendation, including the risks if you do not obtain this insurance
3	Any relevant existing insurance that you might have in place
4	Relevant details of the proposed policy, including exclusions, excesses, limitations or conditions
5	The affordability of the insurance to you

PLEASE NOTE

1. All recommendations of policies by this firm are made without fair market analysis. You may wish to compare the quote provided with one that you might obtain from an insurance broker.

2. *We are/I am* not authorised by the Financial Conduct Authority. However, *We are/I am* included on the register maintained by the Financial Conduct Authority so that *I/we* may carry on insurance mediation activity, which is broadly the advising on, selling and administration of insurance contracts. This part of *my/our* business, including arrangements for complaints or redress if something goes wrong, is regulated by the Solicitors Regulation Authority. The register can be accessed via the Financial Services website at *www.fca.gov.uk/register*.

3. If you are unhappy with any insurance advice you receive from this practice, you should raise your concerns through *my/our* complaints procedure or, if you remain unhappy once this process has been completed, with either the Solicitors Regulation Authority or the Legal Ombudsman. The address details of the Legal Ombudsman are:

   - Telephone: 0300 555 0333
   - Minicom: 0300 555 1777
   - E-mail: enquiries@legalombudsman.org.uk
   - Website: www.legalombudsman.org.uk
   - Address: Legal Ombudsman, PO Box 6806, Wolverhampton WV1 9WJ

4. You should bring your complaint to the Legal Ombudsman within six months of the end of our complaints handling process. In addition, you should note that the Legal Ombudsman will not be able to accept your complaint if:

   - more than six years have elapsed from the date of the alleged act or omission giving rise to your complaint;
   - more than three years have elapsed since the time that you should have known about your entitlement to make a complaint; has elapsed (if later than above) or
   - the date of the alleged act or omission giving rise to the complaint was before the 6th October 2010.

APPENDIX 23

COUNSEL AND EXPERTS EVALUATION

Name of Counsel/expert/other contractor:

Used on (Matter/Case ref):

Date: ....

Reason: ....

Selection criteria	Acceptable
Appropriate expertise	Yes / No
Speed of response	Yes / No
Value for money	Yes / No
Flexibility	Yes / No
Written report	Yes / No / NA
Performance in person	Yes / No / NA
Good with clients	Yes / No / NA

Recommendation:

We should add this person to the approved list	Yes / No
We should continue to monitor this person's performance	Yes / No
We should remove this person from the approved list	Yes / No

Comments:

Signed:

Date:

APPENDIX 24

FILE CLOSING CHECKLIST
(if preferred to box in file opening form at Appendix 17)

Action	Yes/no/date
Were the client's objectives met?	
Are there circumstances which could give rise to a claim or a complaint? If so – report to partner.	
Future review needed – e.g. of Will contents?	
Client advised on storage?	
Nil balances on accounts? (attach print-out)	
File thinned?	
Documents or items to be returned to client?	
Destroy date	

Signed .... Date ....

APPENDIX 25

JOB DESCRIPTION (PARTNER)

Partner

Responsible to: The partnership

Directly responsible for (staff): [*Insert job titles as appropriate*]

Person specification – Skills, knowledge and experience required:

Management:

- Experience of management in a solicitor's practice
- Experience of supervising staff

Practice experience:

- Post qualification in-depth experience as a solicitor in at least one of the main areas of law in which the firm offers services
- Experience of dealing with complex, difficult and serious cases
- Experience of attending clients
- Experience of advocacy
- Experience of briefing Counsel
- Experience of attending conferences with Counsel
- Experience of liaising with third parties such as expert witnesses
- Experience of billing practices and procedures

Practical skills:

- Interviewing
- Telephone
- Time management
- Supervisory
- Ability to prioritise own workload
- Ability to work as part of a team

Must have a good working knowledge of the SRA Code of Conduct and Accounts Rules

Job purpose:

Jointly with the other partners, to manage the firm of XXXX effectively and profitably

To run own caseload

To guide and assist other members of staff with their work as appropriate

Personal responsibilities:

[*Insert as appropriate, e.g. Money Laundering Reporting Officer, Client Care Partner, Legal Aid Supervisor, etc.*]

Joint management responsibilities:

- The strategic management of the firm
- Finance and accounts
- To ensure compliance with the SRA Code of Conduct and SRA Accounts Rules
- Personnel, recruitment and training
- Quality assurance, client care & complaints

Legal:

- To manage own caseload
- To supervise the work of other fee earners and support staff

Tasks:

- Liaising with outside bodies on behalf of the firm
- Marketing activity
- General tasks in relation to individual file management
- Advocacy
- Monitoring the financial position of the department
- Supervising billing for the departmentEnsuring compliance with quality assurance procedures in the department, especially file reviews

APPENDIX 26

JOB DESCRIPTION (ASSISTANT SOLICITOR)

Assistant Solicitor – Civil litigation

Responsible to: [*Insert as appropriate*]
Responsible for: [*Insert as appropriate*]

Person specification – Skills, knowledge and experience required
- Two years post qualification experience as a solicitor in civil law
- Experience as an advocate
- Experience of attending clients
- Experience of briefing Counsel
- Experience of attending conferences with Counsel
- Experience of liaising with third parties such as expert witnesses
- Experience of drawing up bills

Practical skills:
- Interviewing skills
- Telephone skills
- Time management skills
- Ability to communicate clearly and effectively in English
- Ability to prioritise own workload
- Ability to work as part of a team

Job purpose:
To run own caseload
To assist other fee earners with their cases
To contribute to the effective operation of the firm

General responsibilities:

- Manage own caseload
- Maintain a watching brief over the other fee earners' files when they are on holiday, sick, etc.
- Ensure that diary dates are observed
- Meet relevant quality and professional standards

Tasks:

- General administrative tasks in relation to individual file management
- Visiting clients, taking instructions
- Writing letters
- Briefing Counsel
- Giving instructions to experts
- Advocacy in civil cases
- Billing
- Other tasks as requested

APPENDIX 27

JOB DESCRIPTION (SECRETARY)

Secretary

Responsible to: [*fee earner(s)/partner(s)*]

Person specification – Skills, knowledge and experience required:
- Audio typing – 60+ words per minute
- Good working knowledge of Word software
- High standard of English grammar and spelling
- General administration/office skills
- Telephone skills
- Time management skills

Practical skills:
- Ability to communicate clearly/effectively in English
- Ability to deal sensitively with clients
- Ability to prioritise own workload
- Ability to work as part of a team
- Experience of using e-mail/the internet
- Experience of using office equipment, e.g. photocopiers, scanners, fax machines
- Filing experience
- Dealing effectively with clients
- Diary management
- Experience of dealing with clients
- Knowledge of forms/layouts used in legal documentation
- General knowledge of the legal and court systems
- Knowledge of the administrative systems used in legal case management

Job purposes:
- To provide typing and administrative support, primarily to a named fee earner/fee earners but also to others if requested
- To contribute to the effective operation of the firm

General responsibilities:
- To provide word processing and administrative support
- To take messages/deal with enquiries from clients/progress cases as appropriate

Tasks:
- Answering the telephone/taking messages
- Dealing with clients and other people calling at the office
- Progressing cases as requested by the fee earner
- Making appointments

General administrative tasks in relation to individual file management:
- Word processing
- Sending and receiving e-mails
- Filing
- Photocopying
- Making up bundles for hearings
- Linking incoming post to appropriate case files
- Ensuring outgoing post/DX is taken to reception for dispatch
- Sending and receiving faxes
- Liaising with court staff and other third parties as required
- Other tasks as required

APPENDIX 28

PERFORMANCE REVIEW (APPRAISAL) FORMS

Appraisal Preparation Form

Name

Date

This form is to help you prepare for your appraisal interview. Please fill it in, it will provide a focus for discussion at your appraisal.

What have been your most important achievements since your last appraisal?

What aspects of your work have given you the most satisfaction?

What aspects of your work have given you the least satisfaction?

For which aspects of your work do you feel more experience or training would be useful?

What progress did you achieve against the objectives agreed at your last appraisal?

What goals would you like to achieve in the next year?

Is there anything else you would like to discuss?

APPENDIX 29

APPRAISAL RECORD FORM

Name:

Date:

To be completed at the end of the review period with reference to the 'Appraisal Record Form' completed at the previous appraisal and the post holder's job description.

Is the job description accurate? If it needs to be changed, in what way?

How did the appraisee succeed in meeting the objectives agreed at the last appraisal? What were the major successes?

Were there problems which prevented him/her from meeting the objectives agreed *(if applicable)*?

What training or development activities would be useful in the next 12 months? Please record these on a Personal Training and Development Plan and attach to this form.

Appraiser's assessment of current performance, recommendations and agreed objectives for the next 12 months:

Signed: *(Appraiser)*

Date:

Signed: *(Appraisee)*

Date:

APPENDIX 30

EXIT INTERVIEW QUESTIONS

Introduction

This is a selection of questions that may be asked at exit interviews. They are not mandatory and the person carrying out the interview may decide to use a selection of them.

You should put the person at ease by introducing the interview in a positive way, and explaining that the aim of the interview is to give the person the opportunity to feed back on their experience of working at the firm. It is also important to make it clear that whatever they want to say is valuable and will remain confidential, although it will be used to help improve the way you do things in future.

Sample questions

- Could you tell me about how you decided to leave?
- What is your main reason for leaving?
- Are there any other reasons for leaving?
- What could have been done early on to prevent the situation developing/provide a basis for you to stay with us?
- How would you have preferred the situation(s) to have been handled?
- What opportunities can you see might have existed for the situation/problems to have been averted/dealt with satisfactorily?
- What specific suggestions would you have for how the organisation could manage this situation/these issues better in future?
- How do you feel about the firm?
- What has been good/enjoyable/satisfying for you in your time with us?
- What has been frustrating/difficult/upsetting to you in your time with us?
- What could you have done better or more for us had we given you the opportunity?

- What extra responsibility would you have welcomed that you were not given?
- How could the firm have enabled you to make fuller use of your capabilities and potential?
- What training would you have liked or needed that you did not get, and what effect would this have had?
- How well do you think your training and development needs were assessed and met?
- What training and development did you find most helpful and enjoyable?
- What can you say about communications within the Firm/your department?
- What improvements do you think can be made to client care?
- How would you describe the culture or 'feel' of the Firm?
- What could you say about communications and relationships between departments, and how could these be improved?
- Were you developed/inducted adequately for your role(s)?
- What improvement could be made to the way that you were inducted/prepared for your role(s)?

For recent recruits of less than a year or so:

- What did you think about the way we recruited you?
- How did the reality compare to your expectations when you first joined us?
- How could we have improved your own recruitment?
- How could your induction training have been improved?
- How could you have been helped to better know/understand/work with other departments for the firm to perform more effectively?
- What can you say about the way your performance was measured, and the feedback to you of your performance results?
- How well do you think the appraisal system worked for you?
- What would you say about how you were motivated, and how that could have been improved?
- What suggestion would you make to improve working conditions, hours, amenities, etc?
- What would you say about equipment and IT that needs replacing or upgrading, or which isn't fully/properly used for any reason?
- What can you say about the way you were managed: on a day to day basis; and on a month to month basis?
- Can you give any examples of policy, rules, instructions, etc. that seemed counter-productive or silly?

- Can you give any examples of waste (material or effort), pointless reports, meetings, bureaucracy, etc?
- How could the firm reduce stress levels among employees where stress is an issue?
- How could the firm have enabled you to have made better use of your time?
- What things did the firm or management do to make your job more difficult/frustrating/non-productive?
- How can the firm gather and make better use of the views and experience of its people?
- Aside from the reason(s) you are leaving, how strongly were you attracted to committing to a long and developing career with us?
- What can the firm do to retain its best people (and not lose any more like you)?
- Have you anything to say about your treatment from a discrimination or harassment perspective?
- Would you consider working for us again if the situation were right?
- Are you happy to say where you are going (if you have decided)?
- What particularly is it about them that makes you want to join them?
- What, importantly, are they offering that we are not?
- [If appropriate:] Could you be persuaded to renegotiate/stay/discuss the possibility of staying?
- Can we be of any particular help to you in this move/deciding what to do next (although we can't promise anything)?

APPENDIX 31

INDUCTION TRAINING CHECKLIST

Name: …………………………………………….. Date induction started: ………………………..

Responsibilities of the practice and the individual	Completed or N/A?
1. Firm's objectives 2. Department's objectives 3. Individual's role and objectives, job description 4. Risk management 5. Client care and complaints 6. Equality and diversity	
Meetings with key staff and partners 7. Cashiers/accounts office 8. Secretarial arrangements 9. Reception/telephonist 10. Partners	
Office procedures 11. Office Manual 12. Office intranet 13. Security arrangements 14. Health and safety 15. IT/Office equipment 16. Time recording 17. Stationery 18. Archive system for storage and retrieval of old files 19. Library 20. Filing systems 21. Legal Aid Agency forms and delegated functions	

Personnel	
22. Contract of employment 23. Holidays 24. Sickness 25. Salary payment 26. Training	

I confirm that my induction covered the above issues.

Signed: …………………………………………………. *Date:* …………………………….

APPENDIX 32

TRAINING COURSE EVALUATION FORM

Course title ....

Course provider ....or in-house...

Venue (if external course)... Date of course ....

1. Did you find the content relevant?

    not very   1   2   3   4   very

2. Did you find the method of presentation appropriate?

    not very   1   2   3   4   very

3. Do you feel that you have a better understanding of the subject area?

    not very   1   2   3   4   very

4. Do you feel that you gained ideas you can usefully implement in your job?

    not very   1   2   3   4   very

5. Did you find the course tutor qualified / experienced in the subject area?

    not very   1   2   3   4   very

6. How would you rate the quality of the venue and facilities?

    poor   1   2   3   4   high

Comments

Signed .... Date ....

APPENDIX 33

LEARNING AND DEVELOPMENT PLAN (See Lexcel 4.3)

Name		Period covered 2015-2016
Aim of learning *State what is to be achieved,* *e.g. improve drafting skills*	**Training or development** **method** *e.g. in house, webinar,* *external course, etc.*	**Timescale** *e.g. by when the learning and* *development should be* *completed*

APPENDIX 34

INFORMATION MANAGEMENT POLICY

For many firms one of the most difficult elements in addressing Lexcel 6 is the revised section 3.1 requiring an information management and security policy. Quite apart from the fact that law firms are becoming increasingly reliant on IT facilities in all of their everyday activities, the difficulties of safeguarding the security of data is also causing increasing alarm for all involved in the profession – clients and insurers included. One particular concern of late has been the growing practice of email intercepts and the significant losses that have ensued through fraudsters acquiring sensitive financial data and transaction details. Law firms – especially those with exposure to transactional work such as conveyancing – are often small businesses lacking in sophisticated IT departments but handling substantial amounts of money, whether in transit during the course of the transaction or placed in client account. Fraudsters, on the other hand, are becoming increasingly sophisticated in their operations and have access to software programmes that enable them to scan thousands of communications for the details they require.

The scale of the threat facing law firms is only now coming to light. It has been claimed that fraud units based in the far east target business concerns worldwide for commercial and financial details, some allegedly using kidnapped operators working in slave conditions. Nor is it simply the smaller firm without complex IT backup and security systems that is at risk – it has also been claimed that large City and international practices may have been targeted by governments wanting to know about corporate developments that might have a bearing on state security or essential resources. At a more mundane, but equally costly, level a number of firms have been targeted through "Friday morning frauds" where someone in a busy Accounts department is contacted by someone purporting to be from the firm's bank who persuades the individual to hand over confidential banking details with substantial withdrawals swiftly following on.

There is useful reading for anyone setting about the task of revising their IT policy on the Information Commissioner's website. The Commissioner was highly critical of the legal profession in a report of the 5th August 2014, written mostly from the perspective of the harm done to clients through failure to manage data securely. The main thrust of this report is that encryption should be used on a much greater scale than at present, and that data should not be regarded as being sufficiently protected if a device is merely passworded given the availability of software programmes that will unscramble such codes. We seem to have forgotten what was said in the earlier days of email usage, that sending an unprotected email was rather akin to sending a postcard through the postal system. We have resorted instead to gaining the client's consent to the use of email in our terms of business documentation and a confidentiality notice in our footers: the first will probably prove to be ineffective in the eyes of the Information Commissioner and the second is hardly likely to deter fraudsters.

On a more general level it will be useful to consult the Government's "Cyber Essentials Scheme" containing guidance on the basic controls expected from the adoption of "strong" passwords, and changing them at regular intervals, to the safe configuration of firewalls and network devices for detecting malware and spam messages. Whether on economic grounds or other, the firm that chooses to outsource these functions must be responsible for vetting any such agency, a requirement of the Code of Conduct at O(7.10) in any event.

The elements of the policy required by Lexcel consist of certain registers and then a number of procedures setting out details of the IT protections that are in place. Templates for the registers of "relevant information assets of the both the practice and the client" (3.1.a) and "all software used by the practice" (3.1.h) follow. The headings are illustrative only and in the case of the software register it is the main programmes that are relevant rather than the many thousands of individual operating systems that even the most basic of home computers will need in order to function. It should also be borne in mind that section 3.1 is not limited to electronic data (nor is the remit of the Information Commissioner) and that the integrity of hard copy files should also be considered. On these more basic confidentiality controls see sections 2.7 (Manual format) 2.6 (Intranet format) and 3.11.

3.1 (a) a register of relevant information assets of both the practice and clients

An Information Asset Register at its most basic is a list of all of the information held by the firm about its clients, former clients, prospective clients, partners/members, staff, suppliers and other third parties. It will also include any information which is owned or gathered by clients and to which the firm has access.

Because information of this kind is by its very nature potentially sensitive and likely in many cases to be confidential, it is vital that a law firm is able to keep that information secure. To achieve that, however, the firm needs to know what information it holds, the format in which that information is held, who has access to it, who is responsible for it, how it is protected from unauthorised use and how and when it is updated. This is where the information assets register comes in.

For a small practice, possibly with only one office and holding a minimal amount of information about clients and staff, the creation and format of the register should be fairly straightforward. For a more complex firm acting for a wide range of clients and possibly with data held at numerous physical locations the compilation of the register will be more complex and may involve additional steps.

Whatever the size of firm there are essentially three steps to the creation of register:

1. An audit of the relevant information held
2. An analysis of the potential risks each unit of information presents
3. The creation of a register detailing the information gained from 1 & 2 above.

The details for this process at anything other than the most basic level lie outside of the scope of this Appendix and will be dealt with in a separate guide to information assets registers which can be accessed via the Infolegal Compliance Hub. We will however, go through the basics as they apply to the smaller practice.

1. Audit
The audit process involves the firm going through all of the information which it holds and recording:

a) the nature of the information – in other words it is about listing all of the different types of information that the firm holds including client records, financial records, staff records, staff disciplinary processes, files, wills registers/banks, deeds/document store, lists of suppliers, data about counsel or experts and so forth.
b) How the information is held – that is to say is it electronic or hard copy?
c) Where the information is held – in a secure store, in filing cabinets in offices, on individual laptops, on hard drives, on a server
d) Who is responsible for that information
e) Who has access to that information

2. Analysis
Having ascertained what the information is and how it is held an analysis of the risk to that

---

information must be undertaken. This might be as simple as ascertaining who has access to a physical file, whether it is kept in a locked cabinet and the steps that can be taken generally to keep it secure, through to looking into the electronic security of data stored on a hard drive, server or even the cloud. The risk needs to be ascertained for each type of data.

3. Creation

Having worked out what data is held and the risks associated with it, the information needs to be aggregated into an assets register.

At its simplest this will be a table with a number of columns which may include:

- Item
- Description
- Location
- Responsibility
- Access
- Risk

through to a comprehensive database which includes reference to the various security measures taken in respect of each data type.

A sample table version is set out on the following page.

3.1 (b) procedures for the protection and security of the information assets

The firm will, based upon the types of data held and the risk analysis, need to put in place a procedure for the protection and security of the information which it holds.

The basis for that procedure will be found in the body of this manual in Chapter 5 at 5.13 – Information management policy and processes. This will need to be amended and/or augmented in line with the types of data and risk ascertained above.

3.1 (c) procedures for the retention and disposal of information

All information which is held must be stored and will ultimately need to be disposed of. The basis for that procedure will also be found in the body of this manual in Chapter 5 at 5.13 - Information management policy and processes and also amended and/or augmented in line with the types of data and risk ascertained above.

3.1 (d) the use of firewalls

In order to protect data held on the firm's server steps need to be taken to ensure

Register of Information Assets

Item	Description	Location	Responsibility	Access	Risk
Matter files	Confidential client information Privileged information and advice	Fee earner's offices	Fee earner handling	Fee earner, partners, secretarial staff	Theft by third party. Risk to confidentiality, integrity and availability if file lost, stolen or mislaid. Risk of information being incorrectly filed. Risk of unauthorised access to data.
Deeds and documents	Deeds and documents held on behalf of clients	Fireproof cabinet in strong room	Archivist / office manager	Fee earner, partners, secretarial staff	
Emails	Confidential client information Privileged information and advice	Mail server, within outlook on individual fee earner's hard drive, within document management system	Fee earner handling	Fee earner, partners, secretarial staff	Theft by third party. Risk to confidentiality, integrity and availability if file lost, stolen or mislaid. Risk of information being incorrectly filed. Risk of unauthorised access to data.
Personnel records	Confidential details of all personnel. Includes sensitive personal details		HR Partner or Manager		
Client records					
Client account details					
Approved supplier list					

that unauthorised access to that server does not occur. That is the function of the firewall.

The firm must ensure that if it uses a network which is capable of being accessed from outside of the firm (i.e. not usually a network that links only terminals together and has no connection to the internet) that it puts in place an effective firewall to prevent unauthorised users from gaining access to confidential client or other data.

A short form of policy wording based upon the following can be inserted into the appropriate place in the firm's security policy:

Use of Firewalls

Where data used by this firm is captured, processed or stored electronically on computers, hard disks, servers or other electronic devices within the firm, and that data is capable of being accessed via a direct or indirect Internet connection, then a Network Firewall appropriately installed, configured and maintained must be installed.

All installations and implementations of and modifications to the firewall and its configuration are the responsibility of name (the Firewall Administrator) who will ensure that the firewall is adequately maintained and fully operational at all times.

3.1 (e) procedures for the secure configuration of network devices

It is not entirely clear quite what Lexcel has in mind here as it seems to overlap with 3.1 (d).

However, it is likely that this item relates to the use generally of network related products (i.e. not limited to firewalls) and could include routers, modems and similar devices. The following should therefore be borne in mind and may be incorporated, along with the procedure in the third paragraph, into the general information management policy.

New equipment

When manufacturers and resellers supply devices, the default configurations tend to be geared towards ease-of-deployment and ease-of-use – as opposed to security. This can include the use of open services and ports, default passwords (typically "admin" or "password"), support for older (and often vulnerable) protocols and pre-installed and often useless software. Many hackers are aware of the standard settings and software which these devices employ and can use them to exploit weaknesses in the infrastructure.

Unmaintained systems

Those wishing to gain access to your confidential information may be able to take advantage of devices on your network not being correctly installed or not being adequately maintained, or updated over time as users demand exceptions for specific business needs, or as devices are added to or removed from the system. Those wishing to attack your system will search for vulnerable default settings, electronic holes in firewalls, routers, and switches and use those to penetrate your firm's defences. Through such actions, they will be able to access confidential information, pose as another trusted system on the network or alter data in such a way that they are able to perpetrate a fraud.

Procedure

Where any network device is attached to or used in connection with the firm's network, that device will need to be correctly installed, configured and maintained at all times. Where any device is supplied with a default setting or password that setting or password will be changed where possible so that it cannot be accessed by any person without the appropriate authority.

3.1(f) procedures to manage user accounts

Again it is not entirely clear quite what Lexcel has in mind here. It is believed that this is a reference to access to accounts on the firm's network, IT system, email functionality or external services such as Lexis or Lawtel.

The firm must have in place a procedure for issuing user accounts and passwords to new users, ensuring that existing users have a strong password and that the password is changed regularly, and for ensuring that users understand the importance of not divulging their user account details to any person other than an appropriately authorised person within the firm. The firm must also take such steps as are appropriate to ensure that if a user ceases to be a user on the system that his or her user account is deactivated and passwords to which they had access are changed.

It is suggested that wording designed to cover this be inserted in the general information management policy.

3.1 (g) procedures to detect and remove malicious software

The intention here is to ensure that the firm's system does not become infected with malware, spyware, viruses or Trojans which could result in others having access to confidential or sensitive data stored upon the system or give others the opportunity to add or amend data on the system allowing them to commit a fraud against the firm or its clients.

The firm must, therefore, ensure that it has in place a procedure for installing, maintaining and updating virus, spyware and malware protection software and a procedure for dealing with any such malicious software in the event that it should be discovered upon the system. Such procedure should include what the firm should do in the event that confidentiality or data security is breached, how it will protect clients' information and assets and prevent the firm being subject to, or used as a vehicle for, fraud.

It is suggested that wording designed to cover this be inserted in the general information management policy.

3.1 (h) a register of all software used by the practice

All firms will inevitably use a range of different software products including accounts packages, case management programmes, word processing software, email, spreadsheets, databases, presentation software and web site maintenance software. It is essential that the firm ensures that it has a valid licence for all such software, that it is using a version of the software that is both secure and capable of being supported and maintained, and that individuals within the firm are not installing their own software without appropriate authorisation.

The most effective way in which the firm can ensure that software is being used and maintained adequately, safely and legitimately is by means of a software audit and register. The extent of the information stored will depend upon the complexity of the firm, the software it uses and the number of staff who have access.

At its simplest, a register which records the name of the software, the version number, licence number, the number of licences held and the purpose for which it is used may suffice (see below):

Register of Software Applications

Programme	Version	Licence Number	Number of licences	Purpose for which used
Word	2013	Xxxx-yyyy-1234	5	Word processing

In more complicated cases, more data may need to be recorded with each individual item of software having its own record which may then be summarised onto a separate index list:

Software Register Item

Software Name		Version Number	
Software Type			
Manufacturer		Licence Number	
Number of Licences Held		To Whom Licences Assigned	
Department Used In		Person responsible	
Location		Phone	
Purchase Date		Expiry Date	
Price Paid		Additional Licence Costs	
Supplier			
Name		Address	
Contact		Telephone	
Warranty Information			
Maintenance Information			
Name		Address	
Contact		Telephone	

3.1(i) training for personnel on information security

All personnel should receive training on what is expected of them in relation to information security and in relation to the specific policies and procedures operated by the firm. Firms should keep a record of the training given.

This training is available where needed through Infolegal.

3.1 (j) a plan for updating and monitoring software

The firm should monitor the use and effectiveness of all software used by the firm and where it is appropriate to do so should replace, upgrade and maintain that software.

The firm should be aware that out of date versions of software and operating systems can in themselves cause defects and allow those without authorisation to access the firm's system and confidential data.

The firm must therefore monitor the software and, possibly through the software provider, ensure that updates, patches and maintenance fixes are applied as and where necessary.

The firm should also monitor whether the software is capable of continuing to serve the needs of the firm and the fee earners and where it is necessary to upgrade or replace then this should be done where possible.

Procedures

The other procedures required by 3.1 of Lexcel will probably take the format of a description of the arrangements that are in place. These are procedures for:

- the protection and security of the listed information assets;
- data retention and disposal;
- managing user accounts;
- the configuration of network devices;
- firewalls and systems to prevent malicious software; and
- updating and monitoring software.

Property Transaction Intercepts

It is worth adding a final note on the risk of mortgage or property transaction intercepts, this being a particular form of risk of the cyber-attacks described above. All conveyancers should be aware of the growing practice of mortgage, or transaction, intercepts (see section 2: Policies and Standards: 2.19 manual section and 2.17 Intranet version). This can take various forms:

- fraudsters purporting to be solicitors acting on the sale of a property, dealing with bona fide purchasers who are represented by conveyancers unaware of the scam, who cannot be traced once they have received the purchase proceeds (see *Davisons v Nationwide Building Society* [2012]EWCA 1626 and *Santander UK PLC v R A Legal Solicitors* [2014] EWCA Civ 183);

- acting in conjunction with dishonest estate agents who are able to tip the fraudsters off as to completion details intervening at a late stage of a transaction and claiming now to be acting for vendor or purchaser through a bogus firm operation with a view to intercepting the mortgage advance or the sale proceeds; and

- having successfully hacked into emails shortly before completion between the vendor and their representatives sending amended banking details to the advisers, thereby diverting the funds with the withdrawals on from there being undetectable.

The losses to those involved in some of these cases have been substantial and as they become more commonplace so law firms can no longer claim to have acted reasonably in not having prevented them. Indemnity insurers are also likely to expect more robust systems to be in place to counter this growing risk. It is important that the IT policy addresses these risks directly.

This appendix kindly contributed by Duncan Finlyson, Director, Infolegal.

COMPLIANCE CHECKLISTS

Lexcel 6

The SRA Code of Conduce 2011

Conveyancing Quality Scheme (policies and procedures)

Core Practice Management Standards

Specialist Quality Mark

Legal Aid Standard Contract

LEXCEL 6 REFERENCES
Where do we comply with the Lexcel 6 requirements?

1	Structures and Strategy	Manual ref.	Comments
1.1 a b	 Documentation on legal framework Management Structure	1.3.1-4	A partnership deed or member's agreement might be referred to in the manual but would remain private to those concerned
1.2 a b c d f g	Strategic plan 12 months objectives Resource plan Client groups Service delivery Risk evaluation of objectives Regular reporting on performance	1.3.3 Appendix 1	Sections b, f and g are new to Lexcel 6 To be reviewed at inspection
1.3 a b c d	Business continuity plan Evaluation of potential risks Methods of dealing: reduce, avoid, transfer Key people Procedure to test annually	1.3.4 Appendix 2	To be reviewed at inspection. Note that failure to test the plan is a common noncompliance
1.4	Corporate social responsibility		Remains optional in Lexcel 6
2	**Financial Management**		
2.1	Responsibility for overall financial management	4.2.1	Usually COFA but not necessarily
2.2 a b c d	Evidence of financial management procedures Annual budget Annual profit and loss/income and expenditure accounts Annual balance sheet Annual income and expenditure forecast reviewed quarterly	4.2.4	

e	Quarterly variance analysis income and expenditure	4.2.4	
f	Quarterly variance analysis of cash flow and cash flow forecast		Review of cash flow forecast a new requirement
2.3	Time recording	4.13	Time recording made optional in v6 but will be expected to be in place when billing depends on it
2.4	Billing procedure	4.14	Issues such as billing and terms would more commonly be dealt with in terms of business and retainers
a	Frequency and terms	4.12	
b	Credit limits	4.12	
c	Manage debts – credit control	4.18	
2.5	Financial transactions	Section 4	Authorisations a new requirement in Lexcel but were covered in the first edition of this manual
a	Transfer of funds	4.6; 4.9;	
b	Management of funds received by the practice	4.4; 4.6; 4.7;	
c	Authorisations	4.6.5	
3	**Information Management**		
3.1	Information management policy	5.12	The greater detail now required in this policy is one of the most challenging aspects of Lexcel v6
a	Register of information assets of practice and clients	5.13.7	
b	Procedures for protection/security of information	5.13.5	
c	Retention/disposal of assets	3.22.5	
d	Firewalls	5.12.1	Sections d-h and j all new to Lexcel v6
e	Network configuration	5.12.1	
f	Manage user accounts	5.14.2;	
g	Malicious software controls	5.12.1	See Appendix 34 for guidance
h	Software register	5.12.1	
i	Training on info security	5.13.2	
j	Software updating plan	5.12.1	Note the need for training in information security at 3.1i
3.2	E-mail policy	5.15	
a	Scope of permitted and prohibited use	5.15.2	
b	Procedures for monitoring use	5.15.2–3	
c	Procedures for storage and destruction	5.15.5	
3.3	Website	5.17	
a	Document approval and publishing and removal	5.17.2	

b	Scope of permitted and prohibited content	5.17.2	
c	Security procedure	5.17.2	
d	Disability access considerations	5.17.2	
3.4	Internet access policy	5.14	
a	Scope of permitted and prohibited use	5.14.2	
b	Monitoring access	5.14.7	
3.5	Social media	5.16	
a	Participating in media on behalf of practice	5.16.2	
b	Scope of permitted and prohibited content	5.16.3	
3.6		1.6.3 –	
a	Register of each plan, policy and procedure	1.6.5 and Appendix 3	No longer multiple references to this requirement throughout the standard, as in v5, but
b	Named person responsible for each policy, plan and procedure		
c	Procedure for review of each policy, plan and procedure	1.6.3–4	does extend to every procedure as well in V6
4	**People Management**		
4.1	Health and safety policy	2.14 2.16	Intranet Procedures are in section 5 (IT and facilities)
4.2	Equality and diversity policy	2.6	Note the need for training
a	Recruitment, selection and progression	2.6.2	at 4.2d
b	Complaints and disciplinary issues from policy	2.6.4	
c	Monitor diversity and collate equality data	2.6.8	
d	Training of all personnel	2.6.5	
e	Procedures for reasonable adjustments for staff	2.6.3	The explicit requirement to make reasonable adjustments for staff is new in v6
4.3	Learning and development policy	6.9	Lexcel v6 uses the term
a	Provision of appropriate training	6.9.1	'learning and
b	Supervisors and managers receive appropriate training	6.9.3	development' rather than 'training and
c	Procedure to evaluate training	6.9.6	development' in v5
d	Learning and development plan for all personnel	6.9.2	Forms at appendices 32–33
4.4	Role profiles	6.1	Formerly 'person specifications' but more usually job descriptions

4.5	Recruitment and selection procedures	6.2	
a	Identification of vacancies	6.2.1	
b	Drafting of job documentation	6.2.1	
c	Methods of attracting candidates	6.2.1	
d	Clear and transparent selection methods	6.2.3	
e	Storage, retention and destruction of records	6.2.3	
f	References and ID checking	6.2.4	
g	Checking disciplinary records where appropriate	6.2.4	
4.6	Induction process	6.8	See appendix 31 for sample induction training checklist
a	Management structure and job responsibilities	6.8.3	
b	Terms and conditions of employment	6.8.3	
c	Immediate training requirements	6.8.3	
d	Key policies	6.8.3	
4.7	Exit procedures	6.7	See appendix 30 for sample questions at exit interview
a	Handover of work	6.7.3	
b	Exit interviews	6.7.1	
c	Return of company property	6.7.2	
4.8	Performance management policy	6.6	See appendices 28–29 for sample forms
a	Practice's approach to performance management	6.6.1	
b	Performance review periods and timescales	6.6.1	
4.9	Whistle-blowing	6.11	New to v6: see IB(10.10)
4.10	Flexible working policy	6.18	New to v6. Note important changes made to this policy in 2014
5	**Risk Management**		
5.1	Risk management policy	2.10	2.8 in Intranet format Requirements for compliance plan, risk register new to v6, and are based on SRA Authorisation Rules (8.6)
a	Compliance plan	2.10.3	
b	Risk register	2.10.3	
c	Risk management roles and responsibilities	2.11.4	
d	Arrangements for communicating risk information	2.10.1 3.1.6	
5.2	Outsourcing policy	5.11	Refers to business functions rather than counsel and experts (3.21)
a	Details of outsourced activities and providers	5.11.2	
b	Checking quality of outsourced work	5.11.2	
c	Confidentiality procedures	5.11.2	
5.3	Named supervisor for each area of work	1.4	
5.4	Manage instructions with higher risk profile	3.8.2	

5.5	Maintain lists of work that are undertaken and declined Communication on this to all relevant staff	3.1.6	It is envisaged that this list, along with other risk details at 5.6, will be dealt with in departmental appendices (Appendix 15)
5.6	Generic risks and causes of claims Communication on this to relevant staff	3.1.6	See above
5.7 a b	Key dates Definition by work type Recorded on file and in back-up system	3.18 3.18.1 3.18.2	See Appendix 16 for suggestions
5.8 a b c	Conflicts of interests Definition of conflicts Training for all relevant personnel to identify conflicts Steps to be followed	3.5 2.8.1 2.8.10 3.5.2–3	See appendix 7 re seller and buyer conflicts 2.8 in manual format and 2.6 in Intranet
5.9 a b c d e f	Active supervision Checks on incoming and outgoing correspondence Departmental/team/office meetings and communication Reviews of matter details Devolved powers (sic) in public funding matters Availability of supervisor Allocation and re-allocation of work	3.1 3.1.2–3 3.1.2 3.1.2 3.1.2 3.1.1 3.1.1	a is now stated to be "where appropriate" Devolved powers through the Legal Aid Agency are now "delegated functions"
5.10	Inactivity checks	3.15	
5.11 a b c d e f	Regular, independent file reviews Define and explain selection criteria Define and explain number and frequency of reviews Records of review Corrective action within 28 days Designated supervisor to monitor data File review data review	3.16 3.16.2 3.16.2 3.16.3 3.16.3 3.16.4 3.16.4	
5.12 a b	Operational risk to be considered and recorded Client /matter acceptance Risk profile of all new instructions	3.8 3.8	

c	Change to risk profile	3.14	
d	Clients to be advised of adverse costs order	3.14	
e	Concluding risk assessment	3.22.2	
f	Notify risk manager of circumstances	3.22.2	
5.13	AML policy	2.17	2.15 in Intranet format and see
a	Appointment of MLRO	2.17.21	appended policy in that section
b	Internal disclosures policy	2.17.17–20	
c	ID checking of client:	2.17.4–5	
d	Training	2.17.21–22	
e	Records	2.17.13	
5.14	Procedures for avoiding mortgage fraud	2.19	Now optional – 17 in Intranet
a	Checking other conveyancers	2.19.7	section
5.15	Bribery Act 2010	2.18	2.16 in Intranet section
5.16	Analysis of risk assessment data	1.7	Note new elements in Lexcel v
a	Indemnity claims		6 – d, e, f and g
b	Client complaints trends		
c	File review data		See Appendix 4
d	Matters notified by COLP/COFA		
e	Material breaches notified to the SRA		
f	Non material breaches recorded		
g	Where the practice acted when conflict existed		
h	Identification of remedial action		
6	**Client Service and Care**		
6.1	Policy for client care	2.4	In intranet version see 2.2
a	Handling enquiries	3.2	
b	Ensure sufficient resources	3.3	
c	Client confidentiality	3.11	
d	Timely responses to phone calls/ correspondence	3.12.3	
e	Referral to third parties	3.20–3.21	
f	Reasonable adjustment for disabled clients	2.6.4	
6.2	Communicate the following in writing:	3.6	In Lexcel 6 a and h are now
a	Establish requirements and objectives	3.6.2	"where appropriate"
b	Explanation of issues and options	3.6.2	Most of these issues will be
c	What fee earner will and will not do	3.6.2	inspected in retainer letters at
d	Agree next steps	3.6.2	assessment
e	Keep client informed on progress, as agreed	3.6.2	
f	Establish timescale	3.6.2	
g	Establish method of funding	3.6.4	

h	Cost benefit analysis where appropriate	3.6.5	
i	Agree level of service	3.6.2	
j	Explain responsibilities of firm and client	3.6.2	
k	Name and status of adviser	3.6.2	
l	Name and status of person responsible for overall supervision	3.6.2 3.6.2	
6.3	Record of standing terms of business	3.6.6	
6.4	Best information on likely overall costs at outset and subsequently	3.6.4	These requirements would usually be assessed from
a	Advise client basis of charging	3.6.2	retainer letters and terms of
b	Advising on receipt of commissions and other benefits	3.20.2	business documents on files at assessments
c	Increase in charging rates	3.6.2	
d	Payments to others	3.6.2	
e	How client will pay	3.6.5	
f	Lien for unpaid costs	3.6.2	
g	Potential liability for other party's costs	3.6.2	
6.5	Written complaints handling procedure	2.21	In Intranet format of section 2
a	Defines complaint	2.21.3	see 2.19 and the accompanying
b	Client's right to complain	2.21.1	policy in this section
c	Name of person responsible	2.21.1	
d	Provision of complaints policy on request	2.21.1	In relation to "a" note that the
e	Response when complaint received: how handled and response times	2.21.4	Glossary to the SRA Handbook contains a definition of
f	Records and reports centrally all complaints from clients	2.21.7	complaint
g	Identifies cause and offers redress, correcting unsatisfactory procedures	2.21.9	
6.6	Process to monitor client satisfaction	2.22	In Intranet 2.19
6.7	Matter acceptance	3.3.1	
a	How decisions made to accept instructions	3.3.1	
b	Cease acting	3.12.6	
c	Decisions to decline instructions	3.3.3	
7	**File and Case Management**		
7.1	Matter strategy	3.12	
7.2	Undertakings	3.17	
7.3 a	List all files for client and funder including linked files	3.4.3	

b	Trace all documents, files, deeds, wills etc	3.10.1	Wills and deeds see 5.9
c	Confidentiality	3.11	
d	Status of matter and action taken checked	3.9.1	
e	Documents stored in an orderly way	3.9.1	
7.4	Matters progressed	3.12	
a	Key information on the file	3.9.1 & 3.10.1	
b	Timely response	3.12.3	
c	Continuing costs information	3.13	
d	Advice to clients on change of fee earner handling or point of contact for complaints	3.12.5	
7.5	Use of barristers and other external advisers	3.21	
a	Use of clear selection criteria	3.21.2	
b	Consultation with client and advice to client	3.21.2	
c	Details to client of name and status of adviser, time to respond and cost if paid by client	3.21.4	
d	Records of barristers and experts used	3.21.2	
e	Evaluation of performance	3.21.6	
f	Clear instructions	3.21.5	
g	Checking of opinions and reports (and court orders)	3.21.6	
h	Payment of fees	3.21.7	
7.6	End of matter	3.22	
a	Reports to client on outcome if required	3.22.1	
b	Accounts for outstanding money	3.22.2	
c	Return to client of documents and property	3.22.2	
d	Advice on storage and retrieval	3.22.1	
e	Future review	3.22.2	
f	Archiving and destruction	3.22.3	

THE SRA CODE OF CONDUCT 2011

It has been stressed by the SRA that it does not wish to see the Code of Conduct being used in a 'tick-box' manner, with firms thinking that they are obliged to address in writing all of the outcomes and indicative behaviours that are contained within it. On the other hand, the Law Society could be seen to have encouraged this way of thinking with some of the questions in the current Conveyancing Quality Scheme questionnaire, in particular question 58, asking if there are processes for compliance with chapters 1 (client care) and 3 (conflicts of interests).

This chart is therefore intended to show you where the manual you have adopted has points of relevance to your obligations to comply with the SRA Handbook, and the Code of Conduct in particular. Any gaps will not necessarily mean a non-compliance and, throughout the Code of Conduct, what a practice is actually doing is more important than what it says in its manual.

In this table CC = client care information (retainer letter or terms of business) which is how many of the client care requirements will be addressed.

	Summary	Reference	Comment
	The Principles		
1	Uphold law and admin of justice		All of the principles are general considerations
2	Act with integrity		
3	Independence		
4	Best interests of client		
5	Proper standard of service		
6	Maintain public trust		

7	Comply with regulatory obligations		
8	Run business or carry out role effectively		
9	Encourage equality and diversity		
10	Protect client money and assets		
	The Code of Conduct		
1.1	Treat clients fairly		General provision
1.2	Protect client interests		General provision
1.3	Deciding whether to act or cease to do so	3.2.1 & 3.12.6	3.2.1 to act and 3.12.6 to cease
1.4	Resources and skills to carry out that work	3.2.2	
1.5	Competent service, timely delivery		General provision
1.6	Fee agreements that are legal	3.6.8	
1.7	Inform clients of regulation and protection		CC (Terms of Business)
1.8	Limitation of liability and minimum cover		CC (Terms of Business)
1.9	Inform clients of right to complain and how		CC (Terms of Business)
1.10	Details of Legal Ombudsman		CC (Terms of Business)
1.11	Dealing with complaints	2.21	In intranet format of section 2 see 2.19 and document 5
1.12	Retainer information required	3.6.2	
1.13	Best information on likely costs	3.6.4	
1.14	Info on client's right to challenge bills		CC (Terms of Business)
1.15	Account for financial benefits received	3.20.2	
1.16	Inform clients of potential claims	2.12.1	In intranet format see 2.10

IBs	Dealing with the client's matters		
1.1	Agreeing appropriate level of service		
1.2	Explaining responsibilities		
1.3	Name and status of adviser and supervisor		
1.4	Explain referral/fee sharing arrangements		
1.5	Explaining limitations or conditions		
1.6	Mental capacity or other, such as duress		
1.7	Decline to act as not in client's interests		
1.8	Explaining limitation of liability to client		
1.9	Accepting gifts only if client is advised	2.18.10-11	In intranet format see 2.16 and document 3
1.10	If cease to act explaining options to client	3.12.6	
1.11	Compensation fund		
1.12	Position where possible claim arises	2.12.1	In intranet format see 2.10
	Fee arrangements		
1.13	Cost-effectiveness of action to be taken	3.6.5	
1.14	Advising possible changes to fees		CC (Terms of Business)
1.15	Warning about payments (disbursements)		CC (Terms of Business)
1.16	Methods of payment		CC (Terms of Business)
1.17	All relevant information on CFAs		CC (Terms of Business)
1.18	Explaining implications of legal aid		CC (Terms of Business)
1.19	Information is clear and accessible		
1.20	Treatment of financial benefits	3.20	
1.21	Disbursements limited to actual amounts		
	Complaints		
1.22	Need for written complaints procedure	2.21	Appendices 12 and 13
1.23	Providing copy of above on request	2.21	Complaints section in intranet format is 2.19

1.24	Information on handling of complaint	2.21	CC
	Negative indicators		
1.25	Joint clients or agents		
1.26	Ceasing to act		
1.27	Unlawful fee agreements		
1.28	Duress and undue influence		
2	**Equality and diversity**		
2.1	Do not discriminate	2.6.2	In intranet format of s.2 see 2.4 and document 1
2.2	Client service to respect diversity	2.6.2	
2.3	Reasonable adjustments for disabled people	2.6.3	
2.4	Equality recruitment/employment	2.6.2	
2.5	Deal with discrimination complaints	2.6.4	
IBs	**Indicative behaviours**		
2.1	Have a suitable equality/diversity policy	2.6	
2.2	Providing equality/diversity training		
2.3	Monitoring and updating	2.6.8	
	Negative indicators		
2.4	Finding of court or tribunal against you		
2.5	Discriminating in client instructions		
3	**Conflicts of interests**		
3.1	Identify and assess client conflicts	2.8 & 3.5	In intranet format of s.2 see 2.6 and document 1
3.2	Systems to monitor for own conflicts	2.8.2	
3.3	Systems for client conflicts appropriate	2.8.4; 3.5.2	
3.4	Do not act if own client conflict	2.8.1–2	
3.5	Do not act if client conflict	2.8.1	

3.6	Substantial common interest exception	2.8.3	
3.7	Competing for same objective exception	2.8.3	
IBs	**Indicative behaviours**		
3.1	Training employees and managers	2.8.10	
3.2	Declining to act where conflict	2.8 & 3.6	
3.3	Avoiding negotiations on price, etc		
3.4	Unequal bargaining power		
3.5	Limits to O3.6 and O3.7 above	2.8.3	
3.6	Under O3.7 must be sophisticated client	2.8.3	
3.7	Lender and borrower restrictions	2.19.9	See also 2.8.6
	Negative indicators		
3.8	Personal dealings with client		
3.9	Client investing in your business		
3.10	Power of attorney restrictions		
3.11	Limits to substantial common interest		
3.12	Limits to O3.6		
3.13	Limits to O3.7		
3.14	Acting for buyer and seller of land		
4	**Confidentiality and disclosure**		
4.1	Duty of confidentiality	2.8.7 & 3.11	
4.2	Duty of disclosure	2.8.7	
4.3	Confidentiality prevails over disclosure	2.8.7	
4.4	Information barriers	2.8.8	
4.5	Systems and controls on confidentiality	2.7	In intranet format see 2.5
IBs	**Indicative behaviours**		
4.1	Appropriate controls for confidentiality		
4.2	Comply with legal and fiduciary duties		
4.3	Safeguarding confidentiality if outsourcing	5.11.3	

4.4	Disclosure exceptions		
4.5	Information barrier example		
	Negative indicators		
4.6	Will contents w/o personal reps' consent		
4.7	Bills with client details and factoring		
5	**Your client and the court**		This section not covered
5.1	Do not deceive or mislead the court		
5.2	Not complicit in above		
5.3	Comply with court orders		
5.4	Not in contempt of court		
5.5	Inform clients of duties to court		
5.6	Comply with duties to court		
5.7	Evidence of sensitive issues not misused		
5.8	Witness offers subject to outcome		
IBs	**Indicative behaviours**		
5.1	Advise clients to comply with court orders		
5.2	Drawing court's attention to cases, etc		
5.3	Security of child witness evidence		
5.4	Advising court if you have misled it		
5.5	Refusing to act if client perjury		
5.6	Personal or firm involvement as witness		
	Negative indicators		
5.7	Examples of breaches		
5.8	Avoiding suggestions of guilt, fraud, etc		
5.9	Calling untrue witness evidence		
5.10	Influencing witness		
5.11	Tampering with evidence		

5.12	Avoiding naming third parties in court		
5.13	Avoiding questioning witness character		
6	**Introductions to third parties**	3.20	
6.1	All recommendations in client's interests	3.20.1	
6.2	Clients informed of financial interests	3.20.1	
6.3	Intermediaries	3.20.1	
6.4	Prohibited fees	3.20.1	See LASPO
IBs	**Indicative behaviours**		
6.1	Arrangements re mortgage and insurance		
6.2	Advising limitations		
6.3	Limiting freedom to recommend as above		
6.4	Being an appointed representative		
7	**Management of the business**		
7.1	Governance structure and reporting lines	1.3	
7.2	Systems/controls comply with Handbook		Part of function of manual
7.3	Identify/monitor/manage Handbook risks	1.3.7	
7.4	Monitoring financial stability of firm	4.2.4	
7.5	Money laundering, data protection, etc	2.17 / 5.13.4	In Intranet Version – 2.15
7.6	Train people appropriately	6.9	
7.7	Supervision of reserved legal activity (RLA)	3.2	
7.8	Checking of work by suitable people	3.2 & 3.16	
7.9	Do not outsource RLA to unauthorised	5.11.4	
7.10	Controls over other outsourcing	5.11.1	
IBs	**Indicative behaviours**		
7.1	Safekeeping of documents and assets		
7.2	Controlling budgets and expenditure		
7.3	Business continuity		
7.4	Continuation of firm absence/emergency		

8	**Publicity**		
8.1	Publicity accurate and not misleading	1.3.3	
8.2	Info on charges, VAT and disbursements	cc	
8.3	Unsolicited approaches to private clients	1.3.3	
8.4	Appropriate info on firm and regulation	cc	
8.5	Wording/details required on regulation	cc	
IBs	**Indicative behaviours**		
8.1	Regulation of other activities		
8.2	If MDP, which services are regulated		
8.3	Compliance with local jurisdiction		
8.4	Joint marketing		
	Negative indicators		
8.5	Approaching people in street, etc		
8.6	Agents breaching code on firm's behalf		
8.7	Advertising unrealistically low fees		
8.8	Overheads described as disbursements		
8.9	Not disclosing additional charges		
8.10	Use of word 'solicitors'		
8.11	Outsourced services		
8.12	Misleading status of partner/employee		
9	**Fee sharing and referrals**		
9.1	Maintaining independence/judgement	3.7.2	
9.2	Advising client on best interests	3.7.2	
9.3	Clients can make informed decisions	3.7.2	
9.4	Clients told of financial/other interests	3.7.2	
9.5	Clients informed of arrangements	3.7.1	
9.6	No paid introductions crime/legal aid	3.7.2	
9.7	Financial agreements in writing	3.7.2	
9.8	Prohibited fees	3.7.1	See LASPO

IBs	Indicative behaviours		
9.1	Only dealing with reputable persons		
9.2	Advising client on best interests		
9.3	Duty to terminate arrangement if needed		
9.4	Satisfying yourself no breach of Code		
9.5	Client attention to payments made		
9.6	Information to be clear and in writing		
	Negative indicators		
9.7	Entering prohibited arrangements		
9.8	Introducer influencing your advice		
9.9	Clients pressurised or misled		
10	You and your regulator	Appendix 5	Compliance plan
10.1	Comply with all reporting requirements		
10.2	Provision of information to SRA		
10.3	Inform SRA of financial difficulties		
10.4	Notify SRA of serious misconduct		
10.5	Proper information on prior approval		
10.6	Co-operation with SRA and Ombudsman		
10.7	Do not deter complaints		
10.8	Comply promptly with notices from SRA		
10.9	Production of documents for SRA		
10.10	Provide permissions to SRA		
10.11	Duties where matters referred to SRA		
10.12	Duty not to abrogate responsibilities		
10.13	Orderly wind-down of firm if closure		
IBs	Indicative behaviours		
10.1	Monitoring achievement of outcomes		
10.2	Monitoring financial stability		
10.3	Notifying SRA of serious financial difficulty		

10.4	Notifying SRA of viability concerns		
10.5	Notify serious issues from IBs (10.1 10.2)		
10.6	Response to serious concerns re staff, etc		
10.7	Report other disciplinary action		
10.8	Notifying significant changes to firm		
10.9	Transfer of client property if closing		
10.10	Have whistle-blowing policy	6.11	
	Negative indicators		
10.11	Precluding SRA/Ombudsman		
10.12	Issue defamation v client unless malice		
11	**Relations with third parties**		
11.1	Duty not to take unfair advantage	2.5.2	Intranet see 2.3
11.2	Perform undertakings	3.17	
11.3	Information needed in contract races		
11.4	Proper administration of oaths		
IBs	**Indicative behaviours**		
11.1	Providing sufficient time to agree costs		
11.2	Returning money or documents		
11.3	Returning money or documents		
11.4	Not contacting other party if represented		
11.5	Monitoring undertakings and discharge		
11.6	Notifying recipient re future event		
	Negative indicators		
11.7	Unfair advantage of unrepresented party		
11.8	Demanding what is not recoverable		
11.9	Unfair advantage for personal gain		
11.10	Unfair advantage of public office		

12	**Separate businesses**		Not covered in manual
12.1	No prohibited separate business activities		
12.2	Not owned/connected to such a concern		
12.3	Ensure no client confusion if permitted		
12.4	Avoid confusion re SRA regulation		
12.5	Only connected with reputable concerns		
12.6	Must be independent financial adviser		
IBs	**Indicative behaviours**		
12.1	Client information and records		
12.2	Complying with SRA Accounts Rules		
12.3	Informing client of interest if referring		
12.4	Terminating if necessary		

CONVEYANCING QUALITY SCHEME

The Conveyancing Quality Scheme ('CQS') has rapidly gained in importance for firms providing property services, not least because of the support shown for the initiative by most of the lending institutions. For the most part the application form (which will be found on the Law Society's website) requires detailed information on the firm and its personnel, but section G covers issues of the firm's core practice management standards. If you are using this publication as the basis for your application the references to the text are as shown (as based on the application form in use as at the 1st July 2015).

This section of the CQS is based heavily on Lexcel and firms have been exempted from answering this section if they accredited to this standard to date. If you are not Lexcel accredited and have recently developed a manual in conjunction with this publication you will have to decide whether you can claim to have adopted the process in question, or if it would be more accurate to say that it will be in the future. Much might depend on whether you have yet formally adopted your revised manual within your practice.

If applying for accreditation to the CQS and you do not currently hold the Lexcel standard you will also need to consider the Core Management Standards in the table that follows this one.

CQS	Requirement	Manual ref.
46	**Financial management** Responsibility for financial management	4.1
47	Financial management processes	4.2.4
48	**Supervision and operational risk management** Governance procedures and reporting	1.3
49	Supervision of all relevant persons	3.1
50	Checking for inactivity	3.15

51	Monitoring and review	3.1.2
52	Written risk management procedures Reporting processes on risk issues Lists of work that is undertaken and declined and generic risk lists	2.10 (Intranet 2.18) 3.8 See 3.1 and Appendices 15 and 16
53	Assessment of risk data	1.7
54	Does the practice have a business continuity plan?	1.3.4
55	**Client care** Client care policy	2.4 (Intranet 2.2)
56	Resources and skills assessed on work screening	3.2.2
57	Monitoring client satisfaction	2.22 (Intranet 19)
58	Chapters 1 (client care) and 3 (conflicts) compliance This is a wide-ranging question. Most firms will meet the various requirements through a combination of the procedures highlighted here and also their retainer letters and terms of business.	On client care see 2.4 (Intranet 2.2); on complaints see 2.21 (intranet 2.19) ; and on conflicts see 3.5
59	**File and case management** Handling of client enquiries	3.3
60	Deciding whether to accept new instructions	3.2
61	Conflicts screening arrangements	2.8 (Intranet 2.6) & 3.5
62	Taking instructions: Understanding the client's requirements and objectives Explanation as to the issues raised and advice given Timescale Action on merited action (cost-effectiveness) All of these issues are addressed in this procedure though it would be unusual to review cost effectiveness in most conveyancing matters and now "where appropriate" in Lexcel	3.6.2 3.6.2 3.6.2 3.6.5
63	Strategy for the matter Mostly contained in the engagement letter in conveyancing matters	3.12.1
64	Progressing matters	3.12
65	Giving, receiving, monitoring and discharge of undertakings	3.17
66	File identification processes Tracing documents and ensuring confidentiality File status File maintenance orderly and in accordance with DPA 1998	 3.10.1 3.9.1 3.9.1

67	Case management system A yes/no question depending on your systems	n/a
68	Reporting to lenders This forms part of the mortgage fraud policy	2.19.9
69	Mortgage fraud procedures	2.19 (Intranet 2.17)
70	Anti-money laundering policy and procedures	2.17 (Intranet 2.15)

CORE PRACTICE MANAGEMENT STANDARDS

References to section 2 of the compliance materials (policies and standards) are to the manual version first and the intranet version in italics. If using the intranet version the details will often be found in the documents on the issue concerned at the end of that section.

Section	Requirement	Ref	Comment
1	**Risk Management**		
1.1	Risk management policy	2.10 (*2.8*)	The headings of statutory,
a	Strategic risk	2.10.1	operational and regulatory
b	Operational risk	2.10.1	appeared in earlier versions of
c	Regulatory risk	2.10.1	Lexcel but are not used in Lexcel
d	Person responsible	1.3.8	v6. For person responsible see
e	Annual review	1.3.8	also Appendix 3.
1.2	Business continuity plan	1.3.4	1.3.4 records the fact that there
a	Risk evaluation		is BCP in place. The various
b	Reduce avoid and transfer risks		details required and listed here
c	Key people		at a-c (and testing at e) will need
d	Person responsible	1.3.8	to be found in the plan itself. See
e	Testing at least annually		Appendix 2 for guidance.
1.3	One overall risk manager	2.11.2 (*2.9*)	It is generally assumed that the COLP will be the Head of Risk, but this is not necessarily the case, in which case amend 2.11.2
1.4	Named supervisor for each area of work	1.4.1	It may be necessary to add to the list of specialisations provided.
1.5	High risk profile work control processes	3.8.2-4	These references address initial risk assessments
1.6	Lists of work undertaken and declined	3.1.6	See also Appendix 15
1.7	Details of generic risks	3.1.6	See also Appendix 15

1.8 a b	Key dates Definition of key dates Recorded on file and centrally	3.18 3.18.1 3.18.2	
1.9	Monitor key dates	3.18.4	
1.10 a b c d e	Conflicts Definition by work type Training Steps to follow Person responsible Annual review of policy	2.8 Appendix 16 2.8.10 3.5.2-3 1.3.8 1.3.8	The issue of conflicts is dealt with as a policy issue in section 2 and in terms of the steps to take at 3.5. As a policy issue it may often be combined with confidentiality so as to merge chapters 3 and 4 of the Code of Conduct
1.11 a b c d e	Active supervision Checks on post incoming and outgoing Team meetings and communication Matter print-out reviews Availability of supervisor Allocation and re-allocation of work	3.1 3.1.2 3.1.2 3.1.2 3.1.2 3.1.1	
1.12	Checking for inactivity	3.15	
1.13 a b c d e f	Independent file reviews Define file review criteria Number and frequency of reviews Record of review on file and centrally Corrective action within 28 days Review by designated supervisor Review at least annually	3.16 3.16.2 3.16.2 3.16.3 3.16.3 3.16.4 3.16.4	
1.14 a b c d e	Risk considerations Monitor new instructions Assess risk profile of new instructions Consider any changes to risk profile Concluding risk assessment Notify risk manager	3.8 3.8.1-2 3.8.1-2 3.8.4 3.22.2 3.22.2	The different sections reflect the need to monitor risk 'before, during and after' the matter is dealt with.
1.15 a b c d	Risk assessment data review Indemnity insurance claims Client complaints trends File review data Remedial action	1.7	See also Appendix 4 and note the additional headings in Lexcel v6 which are likely to added to this section in due course: PII claims, COLP and COFA notifications, material breaches reported to the SRA,

			non-material breaches recorded, where the firm has acted in a conflict situation and remedial action (Lexcel 5.16)
2	**Financial Management**		
2.1	Responsibility for overall control	4.2.1	
2.2 a b c d e f	Financial management procedures Annual budget Income and expenditure accounts Annual balance sheet Income and expenditure forecast Variance analysis Quarterly cash flow variance analysis	4.2.4	
2.3 a b	Time recording procedure Measurement for billing Monitoring of work in progress	4.13	
2.4 a b c d e	Procedure for billing clients Frequency and terms Credit limits Procedure to manage debts Person responsible Documented review	4.14 4.12 4.12 4.18 1.3.8 1.3.8	Usually COFA Under Financial Management
2.5 a b	Prevention of financial crime Person responsible Documented review	2.17-2.19 (2.15–2.17)	2.17 Money laundering 2.18: Bribery 2.19: Mortgage fraud
3	**Information Management**		
3.1 a b c d e f	Information security List of relevant information assets Risk to those assets and possible impact Protection and security of assets Training Person responsible Documented review	5.13 5.13.7 5.13.7 5.13.10 5.13.2 1.3.8 1.3.8	As person responsible for ICT: see also Appendix 3
3.2 a b c	Email policy Scope of permitted use Monitoring personnel Management and security of emails	5.15 5.15.2-4 5.15.3 5.15.6 5.15.6-10	

d	Storage and destruction	1.3.8	
e	Person responsible	1.3.8	As person responsible for ICT:
f	Annual review	1.3.8	see also Appendix 3

3.3	Website management policy	5.17	
a	Content management	5.17.2	
b	Scope of permitted content	5.17.2	
c	Security management	5.15.2	
d	Person responsible	1.3.8	As person responsible for ICT:
e	Annual review	1.3.8	see also Appendix 3

3.4	Social media policy	5.16	
a	Participation	5.16.2	
b	Permitted content	5.16.2-3	
c	Person responsible	5.16.1	
d	Annual review	5.16.1	

4	**Client Care**		

4.1	Client care policy	2.4	
a	Handling enquiries	3.2	
b	Checking resources and competence	3.3	
c	Protecting client confidentiality	3.11	
d	Person responsible	1.3.8	See also Appendix 3
e	Annual review	1.3.8	

4.2	Taking instructions	3.6.2	3.6.2 addresses all of these issues
a	Requirements and objectives	3.6.2	other than (e) which is addressed
b	Issues involved and client options	3.6.2	not so much in the retainer
c	What the fee earner will do	3.6.2	information as set out for the
d	Agree next steps	3.6.2	most part here but once the
e	Inform client of progress	3.12.4	matter is under way. This section
f	Timescale	3.6.2	is likely to be assessed through
g	Funding	3.6.2	the retainer correspondence on
h	Cost/benefit	3.6.5	file as much as in the practice
i	Level of service	3.6.2	manual.
j	Adviser's and client's responsibilities	3.6.2	
k	Name and status of adviser	3.6.2	
l	Name and status of supervisor	3.6.2	

4.3	Record of standing terms of business	3.6.6	

4.4	Cost information	3.6	
a	Basis of charging	3.6.4	
b	Introductory commission	3.20	
c	Increases to charging rates	TOB	TOB is 'terms of business'. These

d	Likely disbursements	TOB	issues would not usually be the
e	Client payment arrangements	TOB	subject of documented
f	Lien for unpaid costs	TOB	procedures unless indirectly (by
g	Potential liability to others	TOB	requiring use of the approved
			precedent TOB documents)
4.5	Complaints handling	2.21 *(2.19)*	It is better now to use the SRA
a	Define complaint	2.21.3	definition of a complaint as in
b	Informing client of rights to complain	TOB	the Glossary to the Handbook. The TOB information here
c	To whom complaints to be addressed	TOB	would need to be in the retainer letter at least in part even if the
d	Provide copy of procedure if required	2.21.1	details of the complaints process and contact details for
e	Client information on progress	2.21.8-9	the Legal Ombudsman might be
f	Recording and reporting centrally	2.21.7	in the TOB document instead
g	Indentify cause of complaints	2.21.9	(see IB (1.22.a) and the need to
h	Person responsible	1.3.8	bring the complaints procedure
i	Review	1.3.8 (and Appdx 3)	to the client's attention at the outset.
4.6	Client satisfaction	2.22 *(2.19)*	
5	**File and Case Management**		
5.1	Acceptance of instructions	3.2.1	
a	Decisions on new instructions	3.2.1	
b	Cease acting	3.12.6	
c	Decline instructions	3.2.1	
d	Person responsible	1.3.8	As person responsible for client
e	Documented review	1.3.8	care: see also Appendix 3
5.2	Case strategy	3.12	
5.3	Progressing matters	3.12	
a	Key information on file	3.10.1	
b	Timely response	3.12.3	
c	Change of adviser or supervisor	3.12.5	
5.4	Undertakings	3.17	
5.5	File information		
a	List open and closed files	3.4	
b	Traceability of files and documents	3.10.1	
c	Safeguard confidentiality	3.11	
d	Checking status of matter	3.9.1	
e	Stored in orderly way	3.9.1	

5.6	End of matter	3.22	
a	Final report to client	3.22.1	
b	Account for outstanding monies	3.22.2	
c	Return of client documents	3.22.3	
d	Storage and retrieval	3.22.3	
e	Future review	3.22.1	
f	Archiving and destruction	3.22.3-4	

SPECIALIST QUALITY MARK COMPLIANCE TABLE

This chart summarises all the requirements of the Specialist Quality Mark version 2.1 December 2014 (SQM).

You can use the table to review your existing Office Manual. When you are confident that your Manual meets the SQM requirements, you can use this as a self-assessment checklist.

Standard	Requirement	Manual reference
A1	**Business planning** A1.1 The Business Plan must cover 12 months in detail and give an outline for years two and three. It must have: • A finance plan/budget; and • SWOT analysis. A1.2 You must review the plan at least every six months and keep a record of reviews.	1.3.3 and Appendix 1 Note 6 months review still required by SQM but dropped as such by Lexcel
A2	**Promoting your service** A2.1 Make details available to clients/members of the public about the type(s) of work done and update details if there are changes.	1.3.3
	• Must provide information to LAA when requested.	2.23.4
A3	**Equality of access** A3.1 Non discrimination policy in the provision of services. A3.2 If you target a client group you must have signposting arrangements for others, understood by all members of staff.	2.6.2

B1	Signposting and referral	
	B1.1 Staff know when to use signposting and referral.	2.23.2
	B1.2 Procedure for signposting and referral.	2.23.2
	B1.3 Records of referral.	2.23.8
	B1.4 Legal Access to Legal Advisor and & Family Mediator Finder, details of alternative services are kept up to date.	2.23.4
C1	**Running the organisation**	
	C1.1 Document identifying members of staff, their jobs and lines of responsibility.	1.3.2, 1.3.7
	C1.2 Document identifying key roles and decision-making responsibilities.	1.3
	C1.3 Organisation confirms and demonstrates provision of independent advice.	SRA
C2	**Financial control**	
	C2.1 Named person with overall financial control; any delegated responsibilities are documented.	1.3.8 Section 4
	C2.2 Process to produce: profit and loss account; balance sheet; and income and expenditure budget including capital expenditure.	4.2.4
	C2.3 You can confirm that independent financial reviews have taken place (i.e. certified or audited accounts), accounting period no more than 18 months.	N/A
	C2.4 Evidence of internal financial reviews, i.e. quarterly variance analysis of income and expenditure against budget.	4.2.4
D1	**People management**	
	D1.1 Job description for every member of staff (and partners); job description and person specification for every post covered by the SQM.	6.1
	D1.2 People know their key responsibilities and objectives, which are documented.	6.1
	D1.3 Non discrimination in the provision of services – equality and diversity policy in effective operation. It must:	2.6.2
	• Be tailored to the size of organisation; • Have a named person with responsibility; and • Outline the action to be taken if breaches occur.	
	D1.4 Operating an open recruitment process – you must:	
	• Be able to demonstrate the job is offered to the most suitable individual; • Provide feedback to applicants if they request it; and • Keep all assessment records for at least 12 months	6.2.3

D2	Induction, appraisal and training	
	D2.1 Induction process for people joining the organisation.	6.8.1
	D2.2 Performance appraisal, at least annually (including partners/managers/external supervisors).	6.6
	• Records must be signed by both parties.	Appendix 29
	D2.3 Training and development plans, reviewed at least annually.	Appendix 21
	D2.4 Training records.	6.9.2/6.9.6
D3	Supervisors	
	D3.1 A named supervisor in each specialist category.	1.4
	D3.2 Appropriate experience in supervisory skills and competence.	3.1
	D3.3 Supervisors must have six hours CPD training (or equivalent) per year relating directly to the category supervised.	Checked at audit
	D3.4 Arrangements to ensure supervisors can conduct their role effectively.	3.1.2
D4	Operation of the supervisory role	
	D4.1 Case allocation.	3.1.2
	D4.2 Effective supervision systems.	3.1.2
	D4.3 Staff know limits and tell supervisor if case is beyond them.	3.1.2
	D4.4 Access to legal reference materials.	5.10
	D4.5 Information on changes in law, practice and procedure.	6.9.4
D5	Individual competence	
	D5.1 Training records show minimum six hours for caseworkers in each 12 month period.	Checked at audit
	D5.2 Minimum 12 hours per week casework for all casework staff if not legally qualified.	Checked at audit
E1	Running the service	
	E1.1 File management system shows lists of open and closed cases.	3.4.1
	E1.2 File management procedures:	
	a) Conflict checks.	a) 3.5
	b) Locating files, etc.	b) 3.10
	c) Key dates backup.	c) 3.18
	d) Undertakings.	d) 3.17
	e) Inactivity monitoring.	e) 3.15
	f) Identifying relevant matters.	f) 3.4.4

	E1.3 Case files are orderly and logical, key information readily apparent to someone other than the person with conduct.	3.9.1
E2	**File review**	
	E2.1(a) Reviews determined by experience, expertise and quality of work, sample includes cases in each category.	3.16.2
	E2.1(b) Representative sample.	3.16.2
	E2.1(c) Procedure must cover how review findings are communicated to staff.	3.16.3
	E2.1(d) Procedure must cover how you ensure corrective action is completed within timescale to the reviewer's satisfaction.	3.16.3
	E2.2 Review process managed by supervisor.	3.16.4
	E2.3 Reviews must be carried out by a qualified individual.	Will be checked at audit
	E2.4 Conduct of review and corrective action must be evident on file.	3.16.3
	E2.5 Comprehensive record of review findings must be produced.	3.16.3
	E2.6 Records must be reviewed annually.	1.7
F1	**Meeting clients' needs** **Individual cases – outset**	This section 3.6.2
	F1.1(a) Record/confirm clients' requirements/instructions. F1.1(b) Advice/action. F1.1(c) Client informed of the name/status of person with conduct/with whom to raise concerns. F1.1(d) Information on payment/funding.	
	F1.2(a) Name of complaints contact.	3.6.2
	F1.2(b) Client informed of key dates.	5.7/3.6.2
	F1.2(c) Advance costs information.	3.6.4
	F1.2(d) Further costs information, updating information in (c).	3.6.4
F2	**Progress of case**	
	F2.1 Case plan prepared and made available to clients in complex cases.	3.12
	F2.2 Updates on progress at least every six months.	3.13
	F2.3(a) Updates on actual costs at least six monthly.	3.13
	F2.3(b) Update on cost and risk.	3.13; 3.14
	F2.3(c) Confirm/revise estimate at least six monthly.	3.12
	F2.3(d) Reminding potential cost liability.	3.13
	F2.4 Client informed in writing if the person with conduct, or the person with whom they should raise any problem, is changed.	3.12.4

F3	**End of the case**	This
		section
	F3.1(a) Confirm outcome.	3.22.1
	F3.1(b) Arrangements for storage of papers.	
	F3.1(c) Account for money.	
	F3.1(d) Return documents.	
	F3.1(e) Advise if there is need for review in future.	
F4	**Client confidentiality**	
	F4.1 Confidentiality policy covering information given to the organisation.	2.7
	F4.3 Arrangements to afford privacy at meetings with clients.	
F5	**Use of approved suppliers**	
	F5.1 Non discrimination policy for instructing suppliers.	2.6.2
	F5.2 Selected by objective assessment.	3.21.2
	F5.3 Evaluation of opinions/reports and performance in court/conference and adverse findings recorded.	3.21.2
	F5.4 Consult client and inform of cost.	3.21.5
	F5.5 Instructions clear and comprehensive.	3.21.5
G1	**Commitment to quality**	
	G1.1 Clients provided with information about what to do if they have a complaint.	2.21
	G1.2 Procedure for identifying and dealing with complaints:	2.21
	• Definition;	
	• Who has responsibility;	
	• How complaints are identified;	
	• How complaints are recorded;	
	• How to identify the cause of a complaint and respond to it; and	
	• Process for reviewing complaints.	
	G1.3 Central record of every complaint and annual review to identify trends.	2.21.6
G2	**Client satisfaction feedback**	
	G2.1 Client satisfaction feedback procedure covering:	2.22
	• A comprehensive mechanism;	
	• How and when clients give feedback; and	
	• Frequency and methodology.	
	G2.2 Annual review of data.	1.7

G3	**Quality management** G3.1 Named individual responsible for quality procedures.	1.3.8
	G3.2 Procedures up to date and reviewed annually.	1.7
	G3.3 Quality Representative aware of instances where Quality Mark standards are not met and can show a response has been made.	Checked at audit
G4	**Quality Manual** G4.1 Office Manual must exist, be available to staff and must have dated amendments.	1.6
	G4.2 Office Manual available to all staff. Staff able to explain why they might need to refer to it.	Checked at audit

LAA STANDARD CONTRACT COMPLIANCE TABLE

This chart lists the requirements of the Legal Aid Agency's Standard Contracts from 2013 onwards and shows the section of the Manual kit which corresponds with them.

It also sets out key issues in the main civil and crime Contract Specifications where monitoring systems are required to show that you meet a requirement. It does not provide a comprehensive guide to complying with the contract in all respects as that would go beyond the remit of this book which deals with management systems.

However, we do provide a guide to those elements of the contract that require management and monitoring systems that need to be reflected in your Office Manual. This includes instances where the LAA's contract requires you to do things in a particular way. For example, there are professional duties in respect of equality and diversity, and requirements in Lexcel and the SQM. However, the requirements in the contract are slightly different from – and, it has to be said, less specific than – the SQM.

This can mean that if you are accredited to Lexcel you have more freedom in how to interpret the LAA's requirements, e.g. in respect of equality and diversity. If you follow this checklist, and the one for your applicable quality standard (Lexcel or the SQM), you will comply with all applicable requirements.

You will note that some clauses are marked 'N/A', either because they are not applicable in terms of management systems or because they are things you have to do and do not require additional documentation.

Clause	Heading/summary Clause reference	Comment Reference in this Manual
1	*Interpretation*	N/A
2	*Relationship and communication* You must appoint a 'Contract Liaison Manager'. (2.3)	1.3.8

3	Working with third parties	
	Requirements for third parties (e.g. experts to time record and allow LAA access to their time records and premises. (3.7 – 3.9)	You should cover this in your standard letter of instruction.
	Requirement to supervise the work of sub contractors and agents in all respects as though you employed them. (3.3)	This suggests that freelance consultants for example should be subject to file review. 3.16.
4	Financial disclosure and risk	
	You must have:	
	(a) Profit and loss account; (b) A balance sheet; (c) A cash flow statement for the accounting period; d)Full notes to the accounts which must include a complete statement of all the accounting policies adopted; and (e) Where specified, details of Standard Monthly Payments. (4.1)	Section 4
5	Equality and diversity	
	You must have:	2.6
	• Regard to the Equality and Diversity Guidance; • A written equality and diversity policy; • An equality and diversity training plan; and • Implement a communications plan.	
	Review the policies and plans at least once during the Contract Period. (5.2)	
6	Logos and marketing	
	You cannot market by means of unsolicited visits/calls, advertising 'free' welfare benefits checks/housing disrepair surveys. (6.5)	Check your marketing strategy/materials.

	You cannot pay or receive referral fees in respect of legal aid work. (6.8, 6.9)	Check your policy regarding paying/receiving referral fees.

7	*Your obligations, looking after Clients, compliance and self-monitoring*
	
	You must:
	
	• Ensure that Clients are provided with appropriate information (including costs where relevant);
	• Monitor your performance under, and compliance with, this Contract;
	• Take prompt and effective corrective action if your monitoring identifies any failure of or deficiency in relation to:
	  o Quality of advice and legal work
	  o Client service
	  o Clients' perceptions of the service
	• Undertake periodic Client satisfaction surveys; and
	• Have and comply with a procedure for dealing with Client complaints. (7.7, 7.8)
		3.6.2
		
		Appendix 4: Quality Review Plan
		
		2.22
		2.21

	Your IT system must: • Be able to identify all your Contract Work files as such; • Enable you to identify Client conflicts; • Be able to identify all relevant matters and cases for a Client; • Be able to list all open and closed matters; • Be able to identify key dates in respect of any matter/case; • Have a time recording system for all matters/cases; and • Be able to identify an up to date record of the value of your work in progress (disbursements shown separately) on all matters and cases. (7.16)	3.4.1 3.5 3.4.1 3.4.1 3.18 4.13 4.13
	You must have a Business Continuity Plan. (7.20)	Appendix 2: Business Continuity Plan
	You must make up to date daily back-ups of Contract work information that is in electronic format and store back-ups off site. (7.21)	
	You must improve the environmental efficiency of the way you deliver contract work. (7.23)	

8	*Keeping records and completing and returning forms*	
	You must keep the following records:	
	• Performance monitoring and compliance with the Contract;	Appendix 4: Quality Review Plan
	• Client complaints;	1.7
	• Client satisfaction surveys;	2.22
	• Reports of any internal/external audits, including SQM or Lexcel;	N/A
	• Records of all identified non-compliances with the Contract/corrective action;	2.22
	• Details of the operation of your Equality and Diversity Policy, communications and assessment of effectiveness;	2.6
	• Records of file reviews;	3.16.3
	• The identity of, and work performed by, any Agents, Counsel, Approved Third Parties and sub-contractors;	Approved suppliers list, time recording system.
	• Files for each matter/case; and	3.4.1
	• Accurate values of current work in progress in respect of all contract work. (8.3)	4.13
9	*Provision of information and access to your premises*	N/A
10	*Standard of Contract Work (including Independent Peer Review Process)*	
	You must ensure that: • Suitable personnel perform contract work according to their skills, experience and capacity; and	3.1.2
	• You obtain a peer review score of at least 'threshold competence'.	N/A
11	*Key Performance Indicators*	
	These vary by category of law and are shown in the applicable contract specification.	It is advisable to have an internal system for supervisors/heads of department to monitor compliance with KPIs.
12	*Contract Documents and precedence, Schedules and the Specification*	N/A
13	*Amendments to the Contract Documents*	N/A

14	*Your account with us, Claims, Payments and Assessments*	
	You must submit a claim for payment on matters/cases in accordance with the provisions of the contract. (14.2)	4.16
15	*Confidentiality*	3.11
16	*Data Protection*	
	You must obtain and maintain all consents, licences and registrations required to enable you to provide Personal Data to LAA as required for you to comply with Data Protection Legislation. (16.6)	5.13
	You must not transfer LAA Data or Shared Data outside of the EEA without the LAA's prior written approval. (16.7)	Consider your outsourcing policy in this respect.
17	*The Freedom of Information Act*	N/A
18	*Warranties*	N/A
19	*Indemnity*	N/A
20	*Giving notices*	N/A
21	*Things you must tell us about*	N/A
	You must notify the LAA of: • Any anticipated material constitutional change (21.1); • Intervention by the SRA, etc. (21.5); • Voluntary arrangements, insolvency (21.7); • Any significant changes in personnel deployed on Contract Work (21.8); • Other changes affecting performance of Contract Work (21.8); and/or • If any of your personnel is charged with an offence punishable by imprisonment. (21.12)	
22	*Novations*	N/A for most practitioners but important if you are considering a merger.
23	*Bribery, fraud and unethical behaviour*	
	You must have procedures to identify, address and counter them.	2.18

24	*Sanctions*	N/A
25	*How this Contract can be ended*	N/A
26	*Consequences of termination*	N/A
27	*Reconsidering decisions and the review procedure*	N/A
28	*Dispute Resolution*	N/A
29	*Governing law and jurisdiction*	N/A
30	*General*	N/A

Standard Contract Specifications

There are numerous versions of the Standard Contract Specification, but the main ones are for crime and civil. They contain detailed rules concerning the operation of the various legal aid schemes, which we do not go into here as they are beyond the scope of this book. We do highlight those requirements which you will or may need to reflect in systems such as monitoring of data or supervision.

Standard Crime Contract 2015 Specification

This was still in draft at the time of writing. We have covered the 'Own Client' version of the contract as the LAA intends that all crime practices will have an 'Own Client' contract. Note that the draft Duty Contract contains the same provisions as shown below and some additional ones in relation to the Duty scheme (in section 6), so the numbering of the Duty Specification is different.

Sections 1-7 of the Own Client Specification deal with general requirements and systems.

Sections 8-12 of the Own Client Specification give detailed guidance and requirements for the operation of the classes and units of work under the contract and the fee schemes. We do not address these sections here, but supervisors need to be aware of the provisions and monitor compliance with them through supervision and file reviews.

Standard Crime Contract Specification		
Section	Heading and paragraph reference	Comment **Reference in the Manual**
1	*Introduction to Contract Work*	N/A
2	*Service standards*	
	You must have or employ as appropriate:	1.4
	• A Crime Category Supervisor (excluding Prison Law); • An Appeals and Reviews Supervisor; and/or • A Prison Law Supervisor. (2.1)	
	The supervisor must conduct file reviews for each designated fee earner or case-worker they supervise.	3.16.1
	The number of file reviews must reflect the skills, knowledge and experience of the individual. (2.14)	3.16.2
	Where a Designated Fee Earner or case-worker is based other than where their supervisor is based, the supervisor must conduct, as a minimum, face-to-face supervision at least once per calendar month. (2.15)	3.1.2
	If your Supervisor may be unable to supervise for more than six weeks you must immediately inform the LAA. (2.23)	Note this requirement.
	The general ratio is 1 supervisor full-time equivalent Supervisor for every four full-time equivalent designated fee earners/case-workers. (2.21)	Section 7: Legal Aid
	In Prison Law work, the ratio is at least one full-time equivalent Supervisor for every six full-time equivalent designated fee earners/case-workers. (2.22)	
	You must have a document that identifies all staff, their current jobs and lines of responsibility. (2.24)	1.3.2; 1.3.7
	This must cover all Designated Fee Earners and must show:	Note this requirement.
	• Whether the fee earner is a Duty Solicitor, a	

		Solicitor, an Accredited Representative, a Probationary Representative or other non-Solicitor staff; and • Any fee earner codings/PIN numbers. (2.24)	Note this requirement.
		You must designate all fee earners doing more than three hours Crime work a month. (2.27)	Note this requirement.
		(a) 75 per cent of the value of Police Station Advice and Assistance must be conducted by Designated Fee Earners; and (b) 75 per cent of the value of Advocacy Assistance or Representation at the magistrates' court to be conducted by Designated Fee Earners. (2.30)	Note this requirement.
		You are authorised to perform Contract Work from the Office(s) specified in your Schedule. They need to meet specified requirements for access in person and by telephone (2.32)	Note this requirement.
		You must have appropriate signposting and referral arrangements (2.36)	2.23.2
		You must signpost to the civil Legal Aid pages www.gov.uk if it appears the problem falls within scope. (2.41)	2.23.2
		You must comply with the key performance indicators (KPIs) set out in the table in paragraph 2.48.	Note this requirement.
3	*Qualifying criteria*		You need to ensure that supervisors are familiar with these provisions.
4	*Carrying out Contract Work*		You need to ensure that supervisors are familiar with these provisions.
5	*Remuneration for Contract Work*		You need to ensure that whoever is responsible for billing crime matters/cases is familiar with these provisions.
6	*Very High Cost Cases*		VHCC work is outside the scope of the Standard Contract. (7.1)

7	*Claims, Costs Assessments and Reviews*	You need to ensure that whoever is responsible for billing crime matters/cases is familiar with these provisions.

Advisory

It is recommended that supervisors have a system for monitoring of rejects and refusals of applications and bills.

2013 Standard Civil Contract

The Standard Terms are as in the Crime Contract table above.

Sections 1 – 6 of the Standard Civil Contract deal with general requirements and systems. Sections 7 – 10 are category specific and give detailed guidance and set specific requirements. We do not address the category specific sections here, but supervisors need to be aware of the provisions and monitor compliance with them through supervision and file reviews.

Standard Civil Contract Specification – Sections 1-6		
Section	**Heading and paragraph reference**	**Comment** **Reference in the Manual**
1	*General provisions*	N/A
2	*Service standards*	
	You must have or employ a Supervisor in each category of law who meets the supervisor standards (generally this is a full time equivalent but this varies by category of law, so check the relevant Specification). (2.10)	1.4
	The Supervisor must conduct file reviews for each designated fee earner or case-worker they supervise. (2.21)	3.16.1
	The number of file reviews must reflect the skills, knowledge and experience of the individual. (2.21)	3.16.2
	Where a designated fee earner or case-worker is based	3.1.2

	other than where their Supervisor is based, the supervisor must conduct, as a minimum, face-to-face supervision at least once per calendar month. (2.22)	
	If your Supervisor may be unable to supervise for more than six weeks you must immediately inform the LAA. (2.24)	Note this requirement.
	In all civil categories, you must have or employ at least one full-time equivalent supervisor per office for every six full-time case-workers. (2.25)	Note this requirement.
	You must maintain a presence (permanent/part time or local arrangement) as set out in your schedule. (2.30-31)	Note this requirement.
	You must have appropriate signposting and referral arrangements. (2.44)	2.23.2
	You must comply with the key performance indicators (KPIs) set out in paragraphs 2.56-2.66.	2.23.2
3	*Carrying out Controlled Work*	You need to ensure that supervisors are familiar with these provisions.
4	*Payment for Controlled Work*	You need to ensure that whoever is responsible for billing civil matters/cases is familiar with these provisions.
5	*Carrying out Licensed Work*	You need to ensure that supervisors are familiar with these provisions.
6	*Remuneration for Licensed Work*	You need to ensure that whoever is responsible for billing civil matters/cases is familiar with these provisions.

Advisory

It is recommended that supervisors have a system for monitoring of rejects and refusals of applications and bills.

INDEX